The Old and the New

MARTHE ROBERT

The Old and the New

From Don Quixote to Kafka

Translated by
CAROL COSMAN

Foreword by
ROBERT ALTER

University of California Press
Berkeley · Los Angeles · London

University of California Press
Berkeley and Los Angeles, California

University of California Press, Ltd.
London, England

ISBN 0-520-02509-1
Library of Congress Catalog Card Number: 73-80831
Printed in the United States of America

Contents

Note on Editions Used in This Translation

Miguel de Cervantes, *Don Quixote,* translated by Samuel Putnam. New York: Modern Library, 1949.

Franz Kafka, *The Castle,* translated by Willa and Edwin Muir. New York: Alfred A. Knopf, 1969.

C.C.

Foreword

THE LATE Lionel Trilling once aptly observed that the whole history of the novel could justifiably be thought of as "a variation on the theme of *Don Quixote*." It is a perception many critics have shared but one which, especially outside the Hispanic sphere, few have pursued at length with analytic rigor. In this country, the one influential critic who has in effect based a conception of the novel on the Spanish Renaissance masterpiece that began the genre is Harry Levin. *The Gates of Horn*, Levin's classic study of the major French realists, persuasively shows how "the literary technique of systematic disillusionment," more or less consciously learned from Cervantes, informs the work of writers as different as Balzac, Stendhal, Flaubert, and Proust.

In France, where since the early 1960's considerations of literary history have tended to recede in the face of new preoccupations with structure, linguistics, semiotics, and the metaphysical implications of literary art, only two notable works of criticism have tried to explore the novel in its historical development as the quintessentially quixotic genre. One, René Girard's *Deceit, Desire, and the Novel* (1961), argues that *Don Quixote* establishes the terms for a problematic of desire and imitation which, with variations, will underlie most of the major achievements of the genre. Though many of Girard's ideas are suggestive, one begins to suspect that he may be imposing too simple and symmetric a scheme of moral psychology on the novel, that the scheme itself may look considerably less interesting by its second or third application than it did at first.

By contrast, Marthe Robert's *The Old and the New,* which originally appeared two years after the Girard study, beautifully demonstrates how the model of Cervantes can illuminate the nature of the novel in most of its changing manifestations. Mme Robert does this chiefly through her keen sense of the genre from *Don Quixote* onward as a sustained, daring, and often anguished confrontation with a basic cultural crisis of the modern period: the erosion of literature's authority as a source of value, of language itself as a vehicle of truth. One might think of Marthe Robert's work as an imaginative unfolding of all the multiple implications—both for fictional form and for cultural history—packed into Harry Levin's wonderfully succinct phrase: "the literary technique of systematic disillusionment."

To this end, Mme Robert's decision to juxtapose *The Castle* with *Don Quixote* turns out to be a bold and brilliant move. At first thought, no two novels could be more dissimilar: the one, a sprawling comic panorama, anchored in the earthy realism of the Renaissance, drawing on the relaxed improvisations of the picaresque form, its vision defined by the bright sunlight and the sudden shifts in perspective of its Iberian setting; the other, a fantasy-world of radical alienation spun out by a modern Central-European Jew preoccupied with metaphysical issues, its vertical vistas occluded with swirls of snow and mist, the claustrophobic terrors of entrapment lurking behind whatever may pass in it for comedy. Marthe Robert, by arguing so persuasively for direct continuities of thematic concern and fictional strategy between these two novels that stand, as it were, at the two ends of the genre's development, demonstrates, perhaps more fully than any other critic has done, how powerfully *Don Quixote* figures as the paradigmatic novel of novels.

The key concept in her analysis is, I think, what she describes as "an identity of function" between author and fictional hero. This insight cuts through the tangle of confusions of most biographical criticism—is K. the Land-Surveyor ultimately Franz Kafka, is Don Quixote Cervantes?—and probes beneath questions of mood, ambience, and fictional mode to an underlying project of the modern imagination. In an era when all aspects of experience are covered over by layer upon layer of literary accretions (it is, among other things, the Gutenberg Era) at the very moment when literature has been cut off from its ground in traditional wisdom or divine revelation, how is the would-be hero to arrive through the suspect implements of literature, for which alas he can conceive no alternative, at some usable truth, some possible authenticity? What the quixotic hero attempts through imagined actions within the frame of the fiction is what the quixotic author is attempting through the creation of the whole fictional world in which the hero moves. In Cervantes, the identity of function between the two is more explicit because the ingenious hidalgo of the novel is so clearly the author of the derivative chivalric romances he tries to live out. In Kafka, the quixotic enterprise has reached an ultimate stage of devolution, the hero attempting to invent himself not by consciously following one or more explicit models but through a kind of helpless recapitulation of the Western literary tradition, here in particular as it clusters through epic, myth, fairy tale, adventure story, social novel, and much else, around the central notion, "castle."

Writing in a country where schools of criticism proliferate with a fierce sectarian intensity, Marthe Robert belongs to no school or coterie, espouses no method or system. She has been an important expositor of German literature and thought in France, commenting on a series of German writers from Kleist to Kafka, acting as one of Kafka's French translators, chronicling the life of Freud and the development of his theory. In her most recent book, *Roman des origines et origine du roman* (1972), she attempts to define the novel generically as a historically conditioned working-out of the Freudian Family Romance, but in *The Old and the New* there is little evidence of her involvement with psychoanalytic concepts. Here her perspective is broadly historical, and pre-eminently Continental (as befits someone who has been a mediator between French and German culture), informed by a large sense of shared European cultural predicament over the past three and a half centuries. Her categories of old and new are based on a perception of the radically —perhaps disastrously—different rates of change of historical process and literary tradition. History seems to shift with disorienting rapidity, especially in an age of technology, sometimes through changes of geological massiveness, while literary tradition evolves with minute slowness, by its nature constantly turned round toward its own antecedents all the way back to the world of the Homeric epics which continues to exert an incongruous pressure, both intermediately and directly, on modern imaginations.

Such a perception, as I have said, provides a perspective but not a fixed critical method. *The Old and the New* is a long meditation on the ramified implications of this perception as they are borne out in two strategic masterworks of European fiction. The only real "key" to the rewarding nature of the meditation is the fineness and the persistent resourcefulness of Marthe Robert's intelligence. The argument, by its

nature, moves forward slowly, patiently, at times almost
with a kind of incremental repetition, tracing the many varied ways in which a yawning gap between literary continuity and historical change has been the supreme subject
and the impelling quandary of the novel. Mme Robert's
critical idiom is itself an unusual instrument—certainly by
Anglo-American standards—for the conduct of such an argument, combining as it does an intellectually subtle vocabulary of concepts with a lyric evocativeness, representing the fictional heroes both from the outside as figures in a
large cultural continuum and from the inside as virtually
"real" persons with whose existential plight the reader, by
virtue of the critic's imaginative prose, is led to identify.

Here, for example, is her comment on that peculiar quality of puritanical fanaticism in Cervantes' would-be
knight-errant: "Don Quixote introduces into literature the
asceticism unbound to any obedience and purged of magic
that characterizes the quest for a norm, in which the individual follows his own self-imposed laws, generating a kind
of spiritual anarchy." French critics in general seem to have
a special gift for capturing the violent paradoxicality that
often characterizes literary phenomena, and Marthe Robert
firmly fixes in this observation the extreme contradictions
of Don Quixote's enterprise, which preserves all the rigid
singlemindedness of certain traditional stances, but in a
post-traditional world ("unbound to any obedience and
purged of magic") where a norm is sought rather than followed, so that the mental habits of uncompromising devotion must produce not order but chaos. Mme Robert continues: "Alone, uprooted, with no family, condemned to
suffer strictly for his own gratification and intellectual pleasure, Don Quixote is the negation of all the Ithacas he wants
to revive." Here, in this swift evocation of the aspirant

hero's existential solitude, the critic draws us into the felt anguish of his inner world, while that fine phrase about the negation of all the Ithacas is more than a rhetorical flourish in context because it resonates against a general discussion of the relevance of the Homeric background to Cervantes' novel. Then, with a sure sense of transition from the concrete fictional instance to its large historical setting, the writer proceeds to generalize on how the contradiction in Don Quixote between a rage for order and the sowing of disorder reflects the historical chasm between the old and the new: "He marks the end of an age—the old order—that feeds his hunger for the absolute, and he heralds something which is not a new order but an unbridled individualism that by its very nature slips to the extremes of anarchy." This sort of writing has a way of making the emotional weight of general ideas palpable to the imagination, and through it we come to understand better not only Don Quixote but all his varied fictional progeny, from Julien Sorel, Ahab, and Raskolnikov to K., Stephen Dedalus, and Humbert Humbert.

I have alluded to the fineness of Marthe Robert's intelligence. What this means in critical practice, working as she does here with two of the most often-discussed texts in the modern literary corpus, is that she is repeatedly able to give familiar judgments a slight but crucially important shift from approximation to satisfying precision. It is common, for example, to speak of an "absurd world" bodied forth in Kafka's novels. Marthe Robert aptly notes that Kafka's world is not really absurd but rather *disoriented*. Both literally and figuratively, geographically and spiritually, the hapless protagonist who, ironically, wants to be accepted as a land-surveyor does not know in which direction to move, what is really forward and what is up. The difference between this radical disorientation and an absurdist vision may at first not seem immense, but the more one pursues its ramifications—and it is in such pursuit that Marthe Robert particularly excels—the greater the distinction looms. Or again, critics often speak of the "uncanny" nature of the reality of the Castle that confronts K. Marthe Robert instead emphasizes its *unprecedented* nature and thus shifts our attention to that addiction to precedents in K. which repeatedly deflects him from whatever reality might be. "He continually relates the unknown to the known, the new to the old, his own present to the ethical and religious ideas of an accomplished past. This proof of K.'s radical estrangement is Kafka's way of expressing, through quixotic exaggeration, the basic human need for precedents and models."

There are constant little discoveries of this sort in *The Old and the New*, all of them linking back to a large understanding of how the novel as a genre addresses itself to the most fundamental confusions of the modern spiritual condition. The manner in which all this is exposed and the intelligence conducting the exposition make *The Old and the New* an intellectual adventure, and that is a rare and precious experience to encounter in any work of literary criticism. Its deft to-and-fro movement between two great novels three centuries apart puts us more closely in touch both with the books discussed and with a whole problematic drift of Western culture with which we are still struggling to come to terms.

ROBERT ALTER
Berkeley
January, 1976

Preface

ONE FINE DAY a middle-aged man, close to fifty, decides to leave everything and take to the road. He seems to go off quite haphazardly, but in fact he has a definite goal in mind. In the course of his adventures no suffering, disappointment, or even mockery can deter him from his plan to live strictly like a character in a book in order to discover what literature is all about. Is it true or false, useful or superfluous, credible or not? Indeed, does it have any inherent justification? For the sake of this supreme task Don Quixote renounces his possessions and prepares to sacrifice his personal identity and his life. He is stubborn, dogmatic, deaf to the lessons of experience; and he is destined to continual defeat. Still, he is not discouraged, committed as he is to an enterprise he knows to be futile but nonetheless necessary. So he proceeds toward his inevitable end. He will not be lucky enough to die in one of those imaginary crises whose occurrence might prove conclusively the power and truth of books; all he can do is die quietly, from sadness and, perhaps even more, from exhaustion.

Clearly, however, Don Quixote's adventures are left unfinished because all of literature is implicated in his initial demand that books become life. His radical act ends once and for all the Golden Age of Belles-Lettres and inaugurates the troubled "modern" era—the era, simply, of literature.

1

During the last three centuries, frequent attempts have been made to carry out the audacious, potentially revolutionary enterprise that would test life and literature against each other, a test that is reenacted each time a modern writer, remembering his origins, agrees to obey his quixotic calling. Don Quixote, therefore, has enjoyed a celebrated immortality and has succeeded even where his own respected models necessarily failed. For those who have taken up his enterprise, at least, he has escaped from Cervantes' book and become so real that his life, his acts, his failures, are not a novel or a legend, but rather a compelling example. Few, indeed, have followed him to the end. But those few have done more than continue his work for the delight of the reader: they have given modern literature the definition of its task.

Modern fiction, though comprised of such a confusing variety of works, possesses an essentially quixotic unity that is evident in many otherwise disparate books which need not trace their origins to Cervantes to be identified with his vision. The work I have chosen to accompany *Don Quixote* does not of course represent all of Cervantes' progeny, but it holds an exemplary place. Beyond the more or less evident parallels with *Don Quixote*, *The Castle* unquestionably belongs to the same literary mode, employs the same rigor and humor, skepticism and credulity, and asks the same dangerous questions Cervantes had the audacity to raise three centuries earlier—questions that have troubled literature ever since. What place do books have in reality? Are they absolutely true or true only relatively; and if they are true, how do they prove it? These and related questions form the point of departure and the purpose of the quixotic novel, where they are dramatically enacted. For if books express truth, this truth must somehow triumph by changing life. If they are false, their very fascination makes them useless or harmful and they must be rendered null and void, or better still, *burned*. This is the meaning of the *auto-da-fé* with which *Don Quixote* begins, and which Kafka intended to be the actual fate of his own work. But however logical it may be, the *auto-da-fé* is at best an ambiguous solution, leaving the whole question of truth unsettled. Besides, the *auto-da-fé* is neither complete nor definitive; it cannot burn books as quickly as they are produced, thanks to writers who are as stubbornly persistent as Don Quixote himself. After symbolically burning the chivalric romances he struggled to renounce, Cervantes began again and died writing a last chivalric work. As for Kafka—who surely destroyed as many pages as he left—he ordered all his writings burned after his death, but gave this order to his best friend, perhaps the one man who could not follow it.[1] Although the destruction of literature continues to be the most heroic, and in a sense the most significant, consequence of the quixotic enterprise, it neither resolves nor proves anything: the quixotic novel must always challenge its own assumptions and be the locus of its own decisive test.

Of course the question of truth is not treated in the same tone, or with the same emphasis, or as explicitly in the two cases considered here. Cervantes poses it clearly at the outset: truth is Don Quixote's abiding preoccupation. After him, the question of truth takes on more complex meanings that drive it underground along an allusive and hidden course.

Whereas Don Quixote talks incessantly about literature, Kafka's Land-Surveyor apparently has other concerns; their common purpose, however, is to demonstrate that strange things happen when the fictional truth of books is applied brutally to reality. There are certainly differences in epoch,

[1]Max Brod, who has explained at length why he did not carry out Kafka's instructions.

atmosphere, and even more, temperament, between Don Quixote imitating Amadis or Orlando or any knight-errant whose story he has read, and K. the Land-Surveyor, who takes his cue from all the fictional heroes of adventurous quests. Yet whatever their differences (and these are significant), the two heroes share a language of similar referents that lead them to look at real things with the same eyes —at once dreamy and piercing, lucid and distracted. These points of resemblance are rarely noticed[2] and might be otherwise rather baffling, since we cannot posit a common source or influence in the narrow sense of the word. Although their actions unfold in different directions, the two novels actually share the same subject: a quest of a precise nature, though apparently absurd, which must be carried through at any cost. In both books the hero of this quest is entirely determined by his self-appointed task and sacrifices everything to its necessity. He is a middle-aged man, alone, without a past or definite obligations, who appears quite suddenly, his fate already formulated and fixed. There is nothing obviously heroic about him, but he pursues his goal with a seriousness and persistence that no obstacle, no warning or failure, can diminish. It is indeed his most striking quality. He is, and remains, impervious to facts and takes no account of experience, however painful or disappointing. In a sense, his story is a continual repetition of the same events, a succession of discrete episodes that seems endless. In fact, Cervantes never succeeded in finishing *Don Quixote* (he only resolved to finish it after discovering the shameful plagiarism of the first part of the book). Kafka left *The Castle* uncompleted as well. The quixotic quest, then, imposes its

[2]In all the literature devoted to Kafka, I have found only one work that deals with this subject: Santiago Monserrat's *Franz Kafka y el oscuro presente* (Interpretacion historica del Quijote, Cordoba, 1956).

necessity and its open-endedness on its own impossible story, which is always being written anew.

This common paradigm of a long, arduous quest, whose ending seems quite natural to the protagonist but is as baffling from the inside for the other characters as from the outside for the reader—all this is at once too simple and too vast to allow a detailed comparison of novelistic elements in the two books. But clearly this structure generates a way of considering people and things and placing them in a narrative that makes the method of the two novels singularly comparable. They share an extreme descriptive realism joined with an element of fantasy difficult to define. In both there is a constant play between the natural and the supernatural, the rational and the irrational, seriousness and humor. And finally, they have in common the ambiguous attitude of the narrator, who remains outside the story but lets us understand by certain hints that he is one with his hero. All of these shared elements result in a similar puzzling condensation of literary material. With all their apparent simplicity, clarity of language, and classical narrative structure, the two books strike us as indecipherable because they suggest a multiplicity of possible meanings among which the reader himself is forced to choose.

Such a choice invites exegesis, and in fact few books have been written about so often, so diversely, and with such passion. After more than three centuries of critical and scholarly effort to establish the definitive meaning of *Don Quixote,* we are still uncertain how to approach the work. Is it a satire of an impotent and irresponsible idealism inimical to life, a reading that suggests an opposition between Don Quixote's vague notions and the honest materialism of Sancho Panza? Or is it a heroic defense of all lost causes, of the absolute virtues of faith, magnanimity, and the passion for

justice, embodied in the chivalric spirit, which is always
cruelly defeated by history and reality but is eternally reborn
in the heart of some generous Don Quixote and, indeed, in
the soul of eternal Spain? As such extreme opinions tolerate
no compromise, it is difficult to see how the question might
be resolved, especially since all of these opinions appear to
be equally well-founded on details from the text.

The same critical problem occurs in reading Kafka,
whose works contain nearly all the dominant ideas and
preoccupations of our era. Complicated by everything that
since Don Quixote's time has confused and falsified the
already obscure relations between literature and life, Kafka's
narratives propose not two or three clearly defined theses,
but a swarm of learned and ingenious ideas that impinge on
all the possible domains of knowledge. The result is a profound and fruitful exploration, but also a confusion so extravagant that literary history offers few examples like it.
Whenever the quixotic novel appears, it seems marked in
differing degrees by confusion, misunderstanding, and disorder, characteristics for which it is not responsible but
which nevertheless deeply affect it. This shouldn't surprise
us. This kind of novel is necessarily deceptive because it is
erected upon an underlying confusion of its historical era—
the confusion between seeming *facts,* rendered in the objects of representation, and literary *fictions,* constantly
mediating what we think of as reality.

Books—or rather, the Book, in the abstract, the traditional symbol of literature and its mystery—give its incomparable originality to what I call literary quixotism. We
recognize the genuinely quixotic adventure by this obsession with the book that is its *raison d'être* and its law, its joy
and its torment; indeed, the enterprise is intelligible only in
relation to the book that constitutes its underlying motive.

Don Quixote's adventures, therefore, like the Land-Surveyor's, can only be understood, with all their contradictions and deep coherence, in relation to analogous adventures drawn from a familiar and respected model. Reference to this exemplary book may be explicit, as when Don Quixote openly refers to Amadis, or it may be hidden and purely allusive. Although the word "castle" in Kafka is unmodified, it reverberates with all its missing adjectives, so that we associate it automatically with the "dangerous," "enchanted," or "interior" castles everyone knows from books. In both cases such references or allusions form the hidden core of the novel, determining its shape and meaning as well as its apparent anomalies. Doubly literary, and by definition inherently double, the reference to books introduces an essential duality that explains the constant dramatic movement of the quixotic novel, confronting the real hero with the fictional hero who serves as his model, the real book with the ideal Book, whose pages every reader and every writer has perused at some time.

In this way a conflict is generated that is both tragic and comic: tragic because the stakes of the struggle are high, comic because it offers a comparison of absolutely heterogeneous elements without even suspecting their disparity. Who is right, the flesh-and-blood hero or the model he must expend every effort to emulate? Which is the truth, the new book whose existence is still uncertain and whose authority is more than doubtful, or the old book that has always passed for truth? The quixotic work has too much modesty—and too much humor—to offer any revelations. Its inexhaustible novelty derives precisely from the fact that it takes shape before our eyes, striving all the while to comprehend how it invents itself.

SOVEREIGN IMITATION

. . . and the luster of the older
books would be dimmed by the
light of these newer ones . . .
Don Quixote

Doubles

THE subject of the quixotic novel embodies the multiple aspects of an underlying conflict between the fictional and the real, the flesh-and-blood hero and the paper hero, the new and the old; and the highly traditional method of imitation seems admirably suited to develop these oppositions on every possible level of the narrative. Imitation, and even its clichés, serves the special purpose of the quixotic novel by establishing the connections between the *current* imitator and his *past* model, and by furnishing a crude but immediately intelligible summary of the complex relations between the living and the dead, the real and the imaginary, the past and the present, the true and the false. As a simple method of invention, imitation can be considered as a language without words, a dumb-show expressing directly many more ideas, feelings, beliefs, and judgments than one could include in a long treatise. Morality, aesthetics, literary conceptions, are all displayed simultaneously in a kind of seriocomic theater, where literature, and finally language itself, fatefully grapples with the centuries.

Shrewd as he is, Don Quixote recognizes the immense advantage to be gained from a technique offering so many new resources for his own hidden designs. He understands that indeed nothing is better suited to his enterprise than the extreme posture of imitation, which corresponds precisely to the demands of his literary passion and provides him with a practical, as well as a strict, rule of conduct. So he decides to "sally forth," not, as we are too often inclined to believe, to battle windmills, but to obey in full consciousness the self-appointed vocation of imitator.

The most radical quixotic act, then, is never the accomplishment of some personal ambition, but on the contrary, the imitation of an ideal fixed by tradition, indeed by literary convention, and consequently stripped of all originality. Don Quixote is not inspired to invent his faith or his own actions; he is rather guided by an imitation whose rule is clearly dictated to him by his favorite author. He is therefore profoundly irritated each time his companions, for whom literature means nothing, treat him like an eccentric, a vulgar redresser of wrongs moved only by the derangement of his fantastical mind. "'Have I not told you,'" he explains to Sancho at the critical moment of his madness, "'that I mean to imitate Amadis by playing the part of a desperate and raving madman, thus imitating Orlando at the same time . . .? . . . So, Sancho my friend, do not waste time in advising me to forego so rare, so felicitous, and so unheard of an imitation as this. Mad I am and mad I must be. . .'" (I,25). With a precision, a clarity, and in spite of his anger, a patience characteristic of the authority of a master, Don Quixote explains his madness in a way that, to be sure, will never convince priests and barbers, but that the reader, and particularly the serious critic, must acknowledge. Thus, despite appearances that arbitrarily obscure his simplest features, Don Quixote is not in the least at odds with Cervantes, who decreed that the novelist must employ "only imitation in what he writes; the more perfect the imitation, the better the writing will be." Surely Cervantes could not disavow a hero whose conduct conforms so perfectly to the very principle of his own technique. Whatever differences the commentators imagine they can prove, Don Quixote's rare, felicitous, and unheard of imitation makes such differences largely unimportant and convinces us that essentially author and hero are in absolute agreement.

When imitation imposes a way of writing on the novelist and a way of living on the hero, it creates a functional identity between these two similar and disparate figures that tells us more than any external circumstance about the true extent of their relation. Indeed, the usual assumptions of biographical and psychological criticism are not very helpful in distinguishing the precise affinities between Don Quixote and Cervantes, the Land-Surveyor and Kafka. Although these conventional critical methods can reveal certain common features—Cervantes' passion for chivalric novels, Kafka's exile—they are unable to explain the kind of astonishing mutation by which the author transforms himself, making his own features entirely unrecognizable. From this point of view, the quixotic work can be distinguished from the romantic novel in which the hero takes shape from an image of the author touched up for the requirements of poetic transposition but still recognizable; and it can be distinguished as well from the naturalistic or realistic novel in which the author, supposedly separate from his creatures, is content to describe them and judge them without being personally implicated in their actions. The critics of quixotism clash principally over this problematic nature of the hero who, produced by a radical metamorphosis, both *is* and *is not* the author in a way that continually disguises his real origin.

Unable to measure a fixed distance between the author and his novelistic surrogate, most interpretations propose either a simple identification or a clear opposition. In Kaf-

ka's case, either the author is automatically taken for his
hero, or inversely, there is no consideration of the
metamorphosis that from the very outset transforms Kafka
irreversibly into K. Don Quixote, on the other hand, is
most often taken for a caricature, not of Cervantes himself,
which would still be conceivable, but of character types seen
objectively from the outside by the penetrating but finally
banal vision of a moralist. On the basis of such interpretations, the hero is soon deprived of a good part of his own
existence. If K. is entirely identified with Kafka, he is no
longer treated as a fictional character but rather is lifted out
of the novel, the only place where his acts have any importance, and granted an absolutely autonomous life of his own
for which the author is scarcely considered responsible.
Similarly, Don Quixote becomes a perfectly independent
person whose greatness, intelligence, and genius far surpass
the assumed intentions of Cervantes, who is accused of un-
consciousness and even stupidity by his most passionate
admirers. It is only another step (one that celebrated critics
do not hesitate to take) to the suggestion that the quixotic
author does not know what he is doing, that he is unworthy
of his own genius and crushed by it. Although a similar
suggestion might be justified in other cases (however dubious it might be to anyone who would not confuse uncon-
sciousness with stupidity), certainly in the case of *Don
Quixote* such a notion is not very clear or economical. It
uselessly creates a new paradox by which the partisans of
Don Quixote forever confront the partisans of Cervantes![1]

[1]As a last resort, many authors seek the explanation of these contradictions in Cervantes' unconscious. Certainly, from this point of view, no one
has gone to such lengths as Miguel de Unamuno, who, in *The Life of Don
Quixote and Sancho Panza,* squarely accuses Cervantes of being mean-
spirited and constitutionally incapable of understanding the saintliness of

We are asked to choose sides on the basis of the few details of biographical information and of psychological analysis presented in the text. But the adventurous life of Cervantes does not correspond to Don Quixote's, and Kafka, whatever he might have suffered, was not a vagabond. Clearly, nothing in the text itself suffices to span the enormous gulf separating the novelist's real personality from his fictional mask. The narrative tells us rather that the hero, a born imitator, defines himself by a function clearly analogous to literature, which, whatever its subject, pretends only to reproduce, represent, and imitate some real or supposedly real aspect of life. Mimesis, which is the point of departure for all literary creation, and even for all art, here offers proof of the creator's solidarity with his creature, otherwise rather difficult to establish, since the same texts can equally serve to exaggerate or entirely ignore this solidarity. Within the narrative itself, imitation represents an equivalent to the very act of writing and clarifies the extent to which author and hero are separate and yet absolutely united in their common cause.

Therefore, since Cervantes has no intention of confusing his fictional character with himself, it is useless to ask him either to repudiate or to accept responsibility for all of Don Quixote's notions. Cervantes only intends to delegate his *literary* functions to his protagonist, to give him the right to represent the writer's condition, which he urgently needs to understand for himself. Cervantes splits himself off from

---

Don Quixote. This accusation is made in all sincerity, and it is logical besides if we look only for the moral and spiritual reflection of the author in his character. This, however, amounts to demanding that Cervantes choose between the two extremes of saintliness and absurdity, when precisely what he demonstrates is that a formal choice between extremes is only a trap or last resort.

Don Quixote and thereby mirrors the split he perceives inside himself between the ordinary man and the bizarre being who, instead of living, stops right in the middle of things to describe them. From this separation, which is a conjuration, or perhaps an exorcism, the secret novel is born whose thread is woven into the fabric of the visible text. In this half-hidden novel, Don Quixote shoulders the responsibility for his author's condition: he becomes the writer incarnate, absolute and alienated, freed from any compromise with life and therefore from the latent conflict between the writer's vocation and reality. Abstracted from everything that is not purely literary, Don Quixote is a monstrosity: at best a buffoon, at worst a madman. He is both the caricature and the idealization of Cervantes, his fear and his hope, proof of his simplicity and perhaps, too, the deepest cause of his sadness.

We can see then that the "modernity" justly credited to Cervantes is not primarily a matter of realism, if realism is understood narrowly as the crude description of the customs of an epoch. Rather this "modernity" lies in the camouflaged presence of the author in his own work, which, for the first time, affirms and develops a meaningful doubling, an image of precisely the same conflict that art engenders in the modern consciousness. The real concern is *art,* not a particular artist presented in the guise of a writer-protagonist who speaks as a professional, an obvious mouthpiece for the author, simply revealing his inner debates or his theories. Nothing is more truly alien to the quixotic hero than that image of a particular novelist or fictional artist, familiar since Balzac and Zola, who, having missed his calling for strictly personal reasons, sees literature or art as a form of his fate. Don Quixote is not interested in these crises. He is moved, worried, and perpetually amazed by the literary phenomenon itself: the banal and marvelous fact that books have always existed, in some fashion, with people who write them and others who read them. He is fascinated by the existence of an unlimited legacy that belongs to all men, whether they recognize it or not. And he is struck by the surprising role of language, which is always both excessive and inadequate. These considerations create the special situation from which all writers, by definition, profit and suffer, a situation whose anomalies can be perceived only by an extraordinarily discerning or a childishly naïve intelligence.

In order to put into novelistic play such a sum of ruthless questions and naïve confusions, Cervantes has recourse to a characteristically modern method. He splits the artist in two, depriving him of the prestige that makes him too attractive and at the same time continually preventing him from fulfilling his vocation. As the child of this schism, Don Quixote carries literature inside himself like an incurable wound. If he writes poems on occasion, and if, by way of compensation, he indiscriminately *christens* beings and things, appropriating the most personal privilege of the poet, he does not write the work he dreams of. In this he is very like the modern writer whose mysteriously baffling vocation remains unfulfilled: "Many a time he was tempted to take up his pen and literally finish the tale as had been promised, and he undoubtedly would have done so, and would have succeeded at it very well, if his thoughts had not been constantly occupied with other things of greater moment" (I,1). From the second page of the book, we understand why Don Quixote cannot appear in his own adventures adorned with the name and prestige of the writer: his postponed vocation obliges him to show a certain discretion on this point. Later, when the final consequences of the "other things of greater moment" that keep him from writing have developed, his descendants, bound by quixotic honesty, will lose even this literary dilettantism by which Cervantes permits Don Quixote to betray himself.

In his style of life and speech, his habits, and his appearance, the Land-Surveyor no longer has anything to remind him of literature, not even remotely. He is left—and this is enough to justify his role—with only the dubious social condition of the writer and the immoderate ambitions that make him, depending on the case, either dangerous or absurd. Whereas Don Quixote lives his ungratified passion for literature to the full, the Land-Surveyor is no more than an allusion to a supposedly exact art (land-surveying), which he hasn't the means to practice and which is not, in any case, in much demand. As a failed writer, the last quixotic hero is an imposter, a shrewd adventurer who demands a following but does not offer the slightest justification for his exorbitant pretensions. True, his madness has not changed, but unfortunately it makes him dangerous, or at the very least, suspect.

Thanks to the doubling that reveals a certain functional correspondence between the novelist and the hero, the novel can develop without the aid of rhetoric: "pro" and "con" are not discussed but made manifest and translated into action. At issue here are not exactly ideas, but contradictory tendencies, deep-rooted and equally active, which can neither suppress nor mutually accept each other, and therefore ask us to respect them together and, if possible, to set them free. Just as the multiple oppositions embodied in the pair "hero-author" cannot always be superimposed, the play of antitheses repeats itself through all the characters in the narrative, which is literally populated with *doubles*. The inseparable quixotic pair, Don Quixote and Sancho, the two assistants and the Land-Surveyor, issue from a secondary doubling of the author, who has in mind not the kind of academic quarrel where purely allegorical figures are assigned stereotypical roles, but a very real, agonizing, and largely insoluble conflict divided among various characters so that it can be seen from every possible angle. Cervantes purged himself of the absolute faith in literature that seems to be Don Quixote's madness, to which he radically opposed his own reasonable faith, a faith compatible with a lucid vision of reality. But this first doubling is not sufficient because Don Quixote's madness, absolute as it is, does not prevent nature and society from claiming their due and affirming their rights to both his mind and his body. The existence of Sancho, formed from the elements of a reality Don Quixote categorically refuses to recognize, answers to the requirements of this new opposition, an opposition no longer played out between the madness of Don Quixote and Cervantes' sanity, but now between the mind and the body, between the absolute rejection of the body and the naïve acceptance of its needs. Charged by Cervantes with the responsibilities of art, Don Quixote shifts the baser responsibilities of his nature to Sancho. Thanks to the squire's enormous belly, the Don himself is exempt from the need to have a stomach and spared the shame of yielding to its demands; he is allowed to be thin and pure, miraculously freed from natural necessities, almost disembodied. At least so he imagines; naturally, he is mistaken. He has split himself and transferred in vain to Sancho's person all his embarrassing flesh, for the *need* still assails him, proving in the most urgent way that he has a body and that it is wasted effort to deny it. In these

moments when the need breaks his enchantment,[2] Don
Quixote's heroic resistance, his obstinate efforts to preserve
his unity, are perfectly useless. Forced to satisfy the corpu-
lent Sancho, whom he thought he had safely left behind, he
himself is doubled.

In this way, Don Quixote reinvents the old folklore
theme of the double, which, if it loses some of its obviously
demonic character, gains in exchange a quality that might be
deceptively reassuring. For the demonic in this apparently
innocent case lies precisely in the fact that we do not know
who or where the devil is. Is Don Quixote the tempter of
Cervantes, the demon he tries to exorcise by writing his
book? Is the Don, as he himself fancies, the victim of an
enchantment worked by his author? Must he be seen as the
devil who effectively seduces Sancho with false promises?[3]

[2]The wonderful passage in which Don Quixote is brought back to his
house in a cage, believing he is enchanted, and finally succumbs to a pressing need that Sancho cannot satisfy for him, does not merit the modest
reservations it generally incurs. Its triviality is not an ordinary comic
technique but part of quixotism's larger plan, which is above all to throw
into question all the moral and spiritual hierarchies that are described as just
and unimpeachable by books.

[3]With the authority that his exceptional affinities with quixotism gave
him in this matter, Kafka settled on the hypothesis that conceives of Don
Quixote as Sancho's demon. His commentary provides an indispensable
insight into the way he perceived his own Don Quixote, namely K. and all
his avatars.

Without making any boast of it, Sancho Panza succeeded in the course of years, by
feeding him a great number of romances of chivalry and adventure in the evening and
night hours, in so diverting from himself his demon, whom he later called Don
Quixote, that this demon thereupon set out, uninhibited, on the maddest exploits,
which, however, for the lack of a preordained object, which should have been Sancho
Panza himself, harmed nobody. A free man, Sancho Panza philosophically followed
Don Quixote on his crusades, perhaps out of a sense of responsibility, and had of them
a great and edifying entertainment to the end of his days.

("The Truth about Sancho Panza," by Franz Kafka, translated by Willa and
Edwin Muir, in *The Complete Stories,* ed. by Nahum N. Glatzer, Schocken
Books, New York, 1971.)

Or, on the contrary, as the victim of the demonic squire who always leads him astray, ruining his enterprise? In the system of successive doublings that governs the composition of the novel, all these questions can be examined, but none are definitively answered by the author himself. And from a strictly quixotic point of view they must remain unanswered, the devil here being the agent of division itself, the principal obstacle to unity that the novel wishes to present without distortion. Nowhere can this be more clearly seen than in *The Castle,* where the devil splits everything in two, creating a crowd of doubles among whom K. futilely tries to establish a hierarchy, though he has no recognizable identity himself. Is K. really destroyed by the assistants he takes for low-level demons; or, as their name indicates, do they really assist him? Is Barnabas, who attracts him as much as the assistants repel him, and yet resembles them, truly his aid or, as K. suspects at the end, the treacherous instrument of his destruction? K. never learns anything on this point, which is so crucial to his very existence (and pivotal for interpretations of the novel). Since he cannot renounce self-knowledge, however, he can only pursue relentlessly the strange quixotic dialogue with his doubles in which, as Kafka says elsewhere in order to define his thought,[4] "reasoning goes hand in hand with sorcery." But reason never triumphs over enchantment, nor does magic fathom the depths of logic.

---

[4]"His reasoning goes hand in hand with sorcery. One can escape from reasoning by taking refuge in magic and from sorcery by taking refuge in logic; but one can also eliminate them both at once in such a way that they become a third thing, living magic, or destruction of the world that does not destruct but constructs" (from *Wedding Preparations in the Country,* Cahiers in-octavo). This aphorism, which follows the fragments on the biblical Abraham, defines the quixotic word (la verbe donquichotesque), which is invocation and critique, conjuration and radical probing, both one and the other with their risks and perils.

Simulation

THOUGH the very purpose of quixotism binds it to the novel, it can nonetheless be conceived as having close affinities with the theater, for quixotism, too, is based on a dramatic imitation drawing upon all the resources of play and illusion. Our two authors were, of course, powerfully attracted by the stage. Cervantes wrote more plays than novels, and although Kafka left only a fragment of a play, which he did not value very highly, the surprisingly theatrical quality of his novels points to a passion for the theater confirmed by many entries in his *Diaries*.[1] In any case, the strikingly dramatic organization of their works continually attracts writers who are convinced that they can transform the novels into plays with very little effort or loss. This is not the place to discuss the legitimacy or usefulness of such adaptations, but it must be said that these can never be strictly faithful to the original works, no matter how serious or successful the adaptor might be. The stage versions rest upon the unquestionable presence of a ready-made dramatic subject in the novel that presumably needs only to be lifted

---

[1]Besides the single extant act of "Guardian of the Tomb," Kafka wrote a play at the end of his life whose subject is unknown and that Dora Dymant burned along with other manuscripts. See in the *Diaries* his numerous notes on the theater, and especially on the Yiddish theater, which at a certain time (1910–11) played an important role in his life.

out of its context to become a realized drama. The presence of this "theater" in the novel, however, is precisely what defies adaptation, since the quixotic drama is never an end in itself, which it becomes on stage, but rather a means whose power is entirely in the service of the novelistic argument. As an imitator, the quixotic hero frequently appears in theatrical guise—masked, and rigged out in borrowed clothes, words, and gestures that emphasize his willing surrender to the drama. He is an actor born of the doubling process only in order to represent his side of the charmed argument by which the author pleads his own case. When he is transferred to the stage or screen, the quixotic hero is necessarily deprived of the literary nuances that imperceptibly influence our reading and convince us that his actions are, in fact, reactions. Moreover, he is completely severed from his author, who has no role in the realized drama. By contrast, the fictional drama of the novel lends itself, largely, to the author's purpose. Rendered naturalistically, the presence of the quixotic hero and all that goes with it gain a certain power of conviction that can no longer be questioned, since the theater has no way of dramatizing the active commentary that constantly runs through the novel. An *acted* Don Quixote coincides so perfectly with his mask and seems so *natural* that we are bound to take him at face value. Yet in the novel, clearly, he *acts* in order to underline the distance that has to be maintained between himself and his performance. The suppression of this distance has the serious inconvenience, among others, of transforming Don Quixote into a caricature and reducing the novel to the proportions of a pleasant but limited satire. When he is presented to an actual audience with the solidity demanded of true dramatic characters, Don Quixote is seriously im-

poverished; when he is no longer the powerful agitator who
shocks everyone with his words and questions, his subversive purpose is lost and he is degraded to the level of parody.

We might object that it is understandable why theatrical
adaptations mistakenly follow the facile road of satire.[2]
They might well be led astray, on the one hand, by Cervantes' assertions that his only aim is to ridicule the chivalric
romance, or on the other by the narrative tone, the grim
humor of situations in which the hero seems to be the innocent victim of an enormous absurdity. But the proliferation
of commentaries proves that the satiric thrust of *Don Quixote* and *The Castle* is so ambiguous that it must be labori-
ously explained. No doubt the impression that the two
novels denounce something is correct, but what is it? What
are they for or against? A satire that does not answer these
basic questions departs from the genre and, in a sense, betrays it. But the quixotic text contains no codifiable message. Does Cervantes sympathize with Don Quixote's cause

[2]This critique, of course, is addressed strictly to adaptation and not at all
to the drama as an original art form. Theater has all of the requisite tools to
make rich use of the endless resources of imitation, provided that it develops adequate material of its own. Brecht has done this by reserving the
right to choose and invent the elements of his epic drama. He has been
condemned for his theory of the adaptor's total freedom with texts, but this
liberty is not self-indulgence or nonchalance; it is necessary for the task of
distilling the borrowed subject, not in its original form (this would hardly
be worth the trouble), but the *problematic* that the original can only intimate
or sketch out. The imitator's "sovereignty" (the word is Brecht's) clearly
excludes the kind of literary piety that, as we have seen, leads to the worst
embarrassment for the adaptor of a quixotic work. Such a work is, by
definition, irreverent and unfaithful and does not scruple to appropriate all
of literature. In a sense, pillage, plagiarism, alienation from the common
good, are aspects of its enterprise. From this point of view, Brecht shares so
much with quixotism that he should have had a place in this study. I have
had to refuse him one, however, because I did not want to toss the novel
and the theater together indiscriminately. The technique of theater,
perhaps more than any other, demands a specific analysis.

while pretending to attack it? Does he crusade against chivalric romances and then believe that he can actually reform them? Does Kafka take K.'s side against the Castle, or is it the other way around? We can only conjecture, at best, because the answers to these questions vary, or rather, there are no answers. All certainties are premature and insidiously raise new questions. Quixotism is indeed related to satire precisely by its qualities of observation, its comic gifts, and its predilection for questions; but this relation only throws into relief the originality of the quixotic method. As with all unique literary phenomena, nothing better illustrates a method than comparing it with the genre it approaches but never becomes.

Satire, in fact, assumes a way of seeing and thinking that, for all its caustic bitterness, remains essentially optimistic, confident of the final triumph of some kind of order (reason, nature, health, or simple good sense), and it remains, above all, convinced of the authority of its own message. It carefully divides wrongs from rights and puts everything it denounces on one side—scandals, abuses, eccentricities—and the author as witness on the other, where he is exempt from error, disinterested, lucid, and of course above suspicion. With the positive clearly separated from the negative, one side is used to discredit or to validate the other, so that the imaginary world of satire is no more than a foil for reality, a means of judging without describing. This is the meaning of satiric *displacement,* which, in the guise of imaginary voyages, exoticism, and fantasy, provides an agreeable message that is more easily assimilated because it bears upon a reality selectively filtered in advance. To transport Gulliver to Brobdingnag or Lilliput, Robinson to a desert island, or an inhabitant of Sirius to earth, is a way of using contrast to stimulate criticism of a given state of things—in France or

England of the period, for instance. But on the pretext of unmasking reality more effectively, the narrative action is transferred to an inaccessible realm, where it is, in fact, protected from the risks of immediate observation. And these are the gravest risks, after all, because we are less afraid of being condemned than of being *seen*.

Satire can be bold, even courageous; we are inclined to believe it may contribute to the reform of mores and institutions. Yet it is based on an aesthetic method that supports evasion as much as lucidity and conceals a truly destructive thrust. This particular cowardice throws into serious question the relationship of satire to reality. Gulliver's travels actually have little in common with the "sallies" of Don Quixote, and Robinson Crusoe's shipwreck is not comparable to the plight of the Land-Surveyor, cast up without hope of regaining his bearings. A Gulliver moves from the real to the imaginary world without transition or effort, transported by an essentially magical operation that frustrates his plans and as a result blocks his capacity for sober judgment. The quixotic protagonist, however, follows a very different, more tortuous path. His mere appearance provokes a tremendous conflict that leaves its mark equally on the world of imagination that he forces into life and on the real world that he enchants with his dream. He meets no extraordinary beings, no giants, no floating islands or monsters. Only the enigma of daily existence: the unrevealed mystery of the known.

Satire may constitute a censorious yet clement tribunal for social and moral reality, but it is not meant to hear the case of literature, which Cervantes and his successors held to be the principal witness, if not the chief suspect. This in itself suggests the narrow limits of satire. It exploits the many charms of a conventional genre such as the traditional tale,

for instance, without engaging in any self-conscious prob-
ings of its own method, that is, without asking why the tale
is a genre peculiarly suited to the purpose of satire. The
miraculous is simply replaced by the rational, opaque images by facile ideas, folklore by philosophy or morality, and
these transpositions are supposed to root out superstitions,
obsolete tastes, and any other remnants of the past. Yet
whatever literary elements it employs—parody or pastoral,
caricature or pastiche—the thrust of the satiric method is to
mutilate its model while avoiding any serious confrontation
with it. The idea that a declaration suffices to extinguish the
influence of the past is precisely one of the serious delusions
that quixotism attempts to destroy—not with derision, but
with piety *and* irony, respect *and* humor, admiration *and*
criticism, compassion *and* rigor, replacing the categorical
either/or of satire with a distressing *and* carried to the limits of
the absurd.

By its refusal to pose mutually exclusive alternatives,
quixotism resolutely turns its back on the satiric method.
Paradoxically, it seems to be much closer to ordinary imitation and has been called insipid, pious, and servile with
some justification. For indeed, insipidity, piety, servility,
are things that truly engage quixotism, touching it so deeply
that they must be mimicked rather than tackled head-on.
Like those insects who protect themselves against their
nearest and strongest enemies by a mimetic ruse, quixotism
apes the manner, tone, and gestures of its anonymous adversary, whose indifferent, self-interested or simply lazy
conformity it perceives on all sides. Here, however, the
tactic of simulation is not only a defensive consideration, it
is a formidable weapon. How can the born yea-sayer refute
Don Quixote's massive *yes,* so immediate and absolute that
it crushes the dignity of its object? In the course of things,

this pious *yes,* which introduces into the narrative a kind of recollection of wisdom, of idyllic times, of childlike innocence, is so hedged in on all sides, challenged by suspicious questions, that it soon evaporates completely. Finally, the reader wonders whether this "yes" does not strongly resemble a "no," yet he has never noticed the substitution.

Clearly, the unoriginal imitator hasn't the least notion of what inspires Don Quixote, for he imitates out of impotence in order to bask in the reflected glory of his model, to satisfy the current demand for familiar subjects, or for other reasons having little to do with literary considerations. His productions are parasites, always plentiful in every age and equally transitory. And of course they are not comparable to *Don Quixote* and *The Castle,* works of such unfettered genius that the usual concept of imitation is inadequate. Today, imitation is considered the opposite of creation, and here the judgment of common sense is even more severe than that of the literary manuals, which sometimes speak of "brilliant imitations," not glorifying the process, but at least allowing it the license of wit. In current usage, however, imitation is a frankly degraded activity, mimicry on the one hand (man creates, apes imitate), and on the other something distressingly close to the ersatz, to forgery or plagiarism. We judge it, after so many centuries of uncontested reign, morally suspect and historically condemned.

An epoch so infatuated with novelty and originality (increasingly confused with newness) indeed has every reason to proscribe imitation, at least theoretically.[3] When there is a

---

[3]Today's contempt for imitation does not prevent us from admiring works of art that issue directly from it. Witness Brecht, Picasso, Stravinsky, whose works are simultaneously repositories and critiques of history, anthologizing and revolutionary. Yet these "new" works of imitation are innovative precisely because they transcribe the special situation of the artists in their own time.

demand for works capable of reflecting the times, a manner of writing that reinstates the past and discards the new in the name of a revered and immutable authority must be automatically suspect. Yet, to be precise, it seems clear that what we reject is not so much the literary formula, which after all has generally proved its worth, as the imitator's implicit convictions. Indeed, we feel that an author who makes imitation his preferred method inadvertently betrays a host of facts about himself: his relations with others, his ideas, his feelings, many things not openly expressed in his writings. Hence we despise imitation because it attempts to impose on us unawares nothing less than a conception of the world.

Basically, contemporary readers reject imitation for exactly the same reason it was accepted by past generations. Both audiences recognize the interconnection between a system of writing and a system of thought; taken as a whole, these were sanctioned in the past and are now discredited. This seems logical enough. Yet how can we arrive at any serious conclusions about the justice of these respective attitudes that derive their rationale from the times, not from ideas? The claim that what was once true no longer is, or the inverse, simply lands us in the centuries-old quarrel between the ancients and the moderns. The quarrel was not settled, it merely subsided; the question remains: who is right, those who believe that there is "nothing new under the sun" or those who believe in the endless possibility of original invention? How can literature extend itself helter skelter in every direction without any loss of its power to endure?

Such a question does not require a definitive answer, of course, except in settling matters of sensibility or belief. Yet qualified answers are no longer satisfying, since in the present case we must make a choice. Quixotism takes the only course of action that, given the importance and impossibility of the choice, can change a partisan argument into a real debate: it breaks out of the trap of shackling alternatives. That is to say, instead of accepting imitation *along with* its ideological support, it dissociates them in such a way that it can imitate obsolete forms *in order to* weigh them against the fragile, questionable claims of the new forms it is in the process of creating. This perfectly controlled simulation, which provokes the most bitter academic arguments, allows the quixotic author to write *as if* he shares the ideas of the imitator (to some extent he does share them and the simulation is only partial). He is then free to parade openly all the affirmation of authority and implicit values that imitation carries in its wake. In this way he turns imitation against itself and forces it to recognize the dignity, the force, and the urgency of the present.

Naturally, Cervantes and his progeny could not have justified their work if the respective value of the old and the new had been established by solid arguments. The only value recognized with any certainty is one of strict chronology; beyond this, the new and the old continue their battle, so enmeshed that their respective virtues are blurred. Properly speaking, they are not antithetical because they are structured on a mutual dependence, but this parasitism is not mutually advantageous. The old is able to discredit the new by absorbing it and claiming the unquestionable right of priority. The new, however, is precarious and doubtful; it has not been tested or confirmed, and its very nature is unknown. Furthermore, in the face of the enormous mass of events, facts, actions, and words that are literally its *precedents,* it is tempted by borrowings, conscious recollections, and repetitions, that aggravate its fragility. This continual tension explains the extraordinary and unexpected importance of imitation, in which quixotism sees the essential drama of all writing and all language.

Imitation seems to be the single ubiquitous source of the most sophisticated human activities, the most archaic, as well as the most effective, educational tool, and the fundamental element of play, theater, and art. Everyone must therefore be subject to this law that helps man shape himself and largely determines human psychology, whether we are conscious of it or not. Imitation, then, appears to be a timeless act binding the writer to the whole of humanity and fashioning him in the image of all: the child, the teacher, the player, the actor, the artist.

Imitation must also satisfy a deep, universal need that touches the writer even more acutely than others, since his task is precisely to break the hypnotic power of imitation even as he fears it. Banal as it is, yet mysterious in its connections with the timeless and subversive world of the unconscious, imitation is a vast subject for meditation that the contemporary writer, who is the late-comer in a long history, can escape only at his peril. Don Quixote's immediate and unswerving commitment to this age-old subject, with all its banality and mystery, must be considered the beauty of his genius. This genius—modest, observant, serious, like all great revolutionary conceptions—works with the debris of knowledge, life's asides, which are repugnant to people of taste and serious intellect. Don Quixote's genius, in fact, is to discover what everyone has known all along but no one has had the inclination, courage or folly to pursue in a new way.

The effect of Don Quixote's meditation is not explicitly revealed, but it is not too difficult to reconstruct it from his plan of action, which, like a child's game or the inspired imitation of a believer, reveals both its effect and its psychological motivation. The child or the believer imitates out of love, admiration, or piety, finding no better way to pay homage to his ideal than to make himself over in its image. In doing so, however, he diminishes the sanctity, the perfection, of his model. He begins in the fervor of devotion but soon violates the limits defined by his own humility, and the model, used as a measure of his own achievement, no longer inspires respect or fear but rather a growing sense of competition. The pious act becomes heresy, and the ideal, no longer protected by absolute faith, is exposed to the profanation of scrutiny and criticism. Little by little the complete harmony with the loved object is broken by ironic indulgence, mockery, or lucid appraisal, all signs of a hostility that is still timid and highly qualified, but none-theless irrepressible. The objective status of the imitator, of course, has scarcely altered.

This extreme ambivalence toward its model is one of the chief qualities of quixotism, as it is of the child who plays at being an adult or of the believer who imitates his master in order to understand what creates the bond and the distance between them. Only in this case the model is literature itself, which recapitulates all possible models. Quixotism clearly and promptly affirms the universal literary inheritance[4]— everything that men have ever thought, said, and written, which is the given patrimony of each new writer, who is free to use it or reject it (if he dares), but not to disregard it as ·

[4]This inheritance benefits all men, regardless of their cultural refinement; this will be confirmed by good sense and an ordinary feeling for reality. Cervantes and Kafka were both voracious readers, but they were not scholars. Their relations with literature were passionate and did not grow out of specialized knowledge, though such knowledge always inspired Cervantes with secret envy (see the Preface to *Don Quixote*).

if it did not exist. The beginning of the seventeenth century, when quixotism was born, saw an enormous accumulation of books and their increased circulation through two centuries of printing. Cervantes, who is modern precisely in his acute consciousness of his historical situation, not only finds these facts encouraging, but regards them as proper subjects for his writing. His *yes* here is logical: the isolated individual hasn't the right or the inclination to refuse a gift whose value and extent he cannot measure. If he were to refuse it, he would profit from it anyway, fraudulently, and so would forfeit any right to speak. But Cervantes' response is also a warm gesture of sympathy with a marvelously uninterrupted effort that was realized at an enormous price.

Don Quixote is distressed, even a bit crushed, by the existence of this continuous chain of works. Yet he intends to add his own to it, nonetheless, for he considers all books equally valuable, the most artless as well as the most sublime. They all represent for him nothing less than the shifting and immutable dream of mankind. In a profound sense, all books are true: this is the first principle that Don Quixote angrily defends against general disbelief. When he is contradicted on this matter, his indignation is comic: "Do you mean to tell me that those books that have been printed with a royal license . . . are but lies?" (I,50). At the same time, he displays a generosity and a kind of wisdom to which others are often attracted. Quixotism, by virtue of the affirmation that it grants to the universality of the literary phenomenon and that it stakes on an irrefutable truth, acknowledges its debt by the most immediate means at its command: it exhibits its borrowings openly, announcing that in a sense it owes everything and creates nothing new. The quixotic work is a memoir and a tribute, an act of humility and a reminder of the historical situation of its birth in a period conscious of having nothing to say that had not been said before, nothing to create except variants or clever rearrangements. This may be a melancholy view, but it is not a discouraging one. As we have already noted, Don Quixote is still ready to make his own contribution.

The truth of books lies in the sum of knowledge, fantasy, and experience whose transmission they assure. This, however, is not their intention but rather the notion of a later reader for whom their history awakens nostalgic reflections. Books themselves offer their lessons as if they were still as true today as they might have been fifty or a thousand years ago, and the older the literature the more it claims permanent validity for the convictions that it propagates or spontaneously invents. Here Don Quixote's *yes* assumes a nuance of doubt; for if the literary legacy has a general human value that makes it precious to whoever writes, nothing says that every book forever remains an infallible source of edification. Yet this is what books tacitly affirm under the cover of aesthetic feeling or simple pleasure, and the hidden power of their didactic ambition is even more irresistible than if it were exercised openly at the risk of inviting criticism. Indeed, great books appear to have no purpose other than to charm. But it takes little effort to perceive that they seduce the reader in order to impose a philosophy or a morality that is simply garbed in the enchantments of epic, legend or tale. All traditional or conventional literature, in fact, spontaneously applies Cervantes' formulation that "The best aim writing can pursue is . . . to charm and instruct at the same time." And success can be measured by the ease with which the reader is charmed into accepting instruction. So literature is suspect in the eyes of the quixotic author, who is always ready to be fascinated but is not at all disposed to accept a vague truth difficult to verify, especially when it is communicated through deception.

What is the real, immediate, practical value of the lessons books teach? We can concede that contemporary readers must have found these lessons good and serviceable, and that subsequent generations found them admirable, moving, and even worthy of respect. But there is no reason to grant them an absolute value that places them outside history. What makes these ideas problematic, even more than their widely varied substance and their equivocal relation to aesthetic principles, is this extravagant pretense to permanent validity in the midst of a changing world. The slightest scrutiny reveals them for what they are: at best, survivals having historic interest, at worst, anachronisms that any intelligent person should promptly dismiss. What man today, unless he is Don Quixote himself, could live in harmony with the teachings of his childhood? No one, surely; yet everyone reads books that insidiously propagate such teachings as if they always had practical application. Two alternatives emerge from this paradoxical situation: either fictional truths are eternal, in which case we must not only admire them but shape our daily lives by them as well; or they are threadbare and anachronistic, and the best we can do is to discard them so that we can find new truths better adapted to the needs of the times.

This is the dilemma that Don Quixote poses and clings to with the tenacity of a madman, and he has good reason to do so. For it illuminates an ambiguity that weighs heavily on language in general and is therefore of universal concern. Popular books, as well as serious literature, are implicated here, for in spite of their modesty or mediocrity, it is clear to Don Quixote that these books also aim to *charm* and *instruct;*

they merely simplify the lesson and multiply the means of seduction. We can readily see that chivalric romances, adventure stories and mysteries, Indian tales and children's books, simply disguise their message in order to reveal it more effectively, as do all traditional genres that exploit pure fiction for a didactic purpose. Hence the quixotic author recognizes no essential difference in literature between nobility and vulgarity, sublimity and naïveté, beauty and mediocrity. Cervantes imitates the insipid romance of Amadis, though actually he holds Homer, or rather the epic in general, responsible for creating a great but ambiguous literature that transmits, even in its most degraded forms, the marvelous capacity to charm and instruct that largely accounts for the tremendous prestige of books. For this reason, the epic can represent literature as a whole and provide imitation with a model truly worthy of its enterprise.

And just as the epic, the chivalric romance, the tale, and the adventure story convey an unperceived and therefore unexamined message, so current locutions, proverbs, and aphorisms infiltrate everyday reality, carrying shreds of knowledge or instruction that are unthinkingly assimilated. Cervantes illustrates the way current language promotes the most elevated purpose of serious literature by making the sanchesque mania for proverbs an indispensable foil to the quixotic mania for the romance.[5] And indeed, the very banality of comparisons, metaphors, and literary associations confirms literature's continual encroachment upon the realm of daily life, where, though it has no apparent func-

[5]This is still something that astonishes critics, even when they do not reproach Cervantes for it. Sancho's sententious language is perfectly justified, however, and its meaning is quite clear if we take *Don Quixote* for what it is: a dramatic and impassioned treatise on the relations of literature and language with life.

tion, it rules with a tyrannical force. Hence the names of familiar characters, impressions of their manner, and their adventures are used to describe people and objects that then seem imbued with an even more convincing reality. With his justly celebrated ingenuity, Don Quixote invokes this anomaly as the basis of a solid argument supporting the living truth of his favorite books: "So true is this that I can remember how my grandmother on my father's side used to say to me when she saw a lady in a venerable hood, 'That one, my grandson, looks just like Dame Quintañona . . .'" (I,49). The very absurdity of this childish and brilliant argument is irresistible. If we reject it, how will we explain the need to recruit Dame Quintañona to describe the first respectable woman who comes along? Or the fact that a strong man is made more convincingly powerful if he is compared to Hercules, and a long perilous journey made more dramatic as an odyssey? Does this suggest that life imitates art and not the reverse? But then, what is the nature of this reality that requires a second language to describe it and make it comprehensible? And what is the nature of the literature that seems indispensable to life? Is it simply an indulgence, a parasite, or, on the contrary, a higher, independent law whose purpose is to illuminate things, to reveal them to themselves and lend them a certain dignity? Don Quixote's not so naïve belief in Dame Quintañona raises these pressing questions, questions that are so inscrutable to the enemies of quixotism. Unless modern literature is to be counted among these, it must be the last to judge such questions trifling.

Don Quixote, then, is not preoccupied with the inadequate reality or surreality of things, but rather with the excess of literature that saturates them. His real torment, which he tries to purge by writing (the only discreet way to investigate and complain about it), is caused by his perception of the complicity between the fictional and the real, though he does not know why it exists or who profits from it most. On the one hand, the imaginary world is and declares itself to be subordinate to the things it represents; nevertheless, it implicitly claims certain qualities of permanence and immutability that confer a kind of transcendence. On the other hand, the real world rightly affirms its autonomy, even though the most prosaic language carries an infinity of literary borrowings that contradict that autonomy. Quixotism is an attempt to gage the benefits and disadvantages of a process that seems very like influence-peddling, or rather trading in words. It begins by stating a problem that is ordinarily suppressed in the interests of literature: namely, that the raw material ordered by fiction does not exist in everyday reality, nor is the opacity or transparency of things immediately perceptible and amenable to direct transcription. What does pervade reality is a mixture of objects and words, nature and images, truth and idealization, brewed slowly by language over the course of the centuries into an insoluble unity.

In order to comprehend this singular situation, and if possible resolve its chief ambiguity, the quixotic imitator begins by invoking the enormous mass of books that impose an invisible screen between himself and real things. At the same time he warns the reader that what he describes is not reality, that his novel is not a faithful reproduction but a fictional construct based on one of the exemplary books in which the real world* sees its own reflection. He imitates quite openly and has no intention of dissembling his complicity with all those oral and written lies that pass themselves off as objective description. By this strategy, he un-

*That is, Western culture

doubtedly avoids the danger of unconscious imitation. His primary concern, however, is that he should not mistake for reality itself the images and judgments time has attached to its surface, fixed there by habit, interest, and intellectual laziness. Imitation here does not challenge the objective reality of the external world but rather its accessibility, the possibility that it can be penetrated and possessed. To the naturalistic or realistic novelist's calm certainty about the real world, the quixotic imitator opposes a doubt that can best be expressed by imitating that certainty. He cannot act as if he were dealing with a pure, instantly revealed world, and so he indicates through imitation the only reality he can recognize, a reality encrusted with words, idealized and dusted over by centuries of literature and aphorisms. But the melancholy aspect of this gesture should not disguise its true meaning. For although the quixotic author's long detour through books seems only too like the obvious ploy of an embittered fantasist, it nonetheless results in the free, arduous act of a mature mind that is translated, literally, into the context of a realist work.

The same mixture of nostalgia and rigorous realism is found in the quixotic imitator's conception of his own historical situation. He is the last link in an imposing chain of works and men whose beginnings are lost in prehistory. It would be ridiculous for him to act as if his mere appearance could annihilate the past or as if he were the first to imbue the new world with a purity of vision and language. For all that, the situation of epigone is of no particular merit; he is distinguished from the rest of humanity only by his acute self-consciousness and would regard any special consideration as misplaced and inappropriate. For his work in the making, however, he has understandably mixed feelings. Before the enormous power of the literary inheritance he feels as weak and helpless as the child born into a ready-made world that is organized, thought-out, and written by others. He is both protected and reduced to impotence by the number, value, and authority of his precedents. At the same time, he must quickly destroy this perfect harmony with his forbears in order to make his own development possible. The serious game of imitation offers him the means to do so.

The quixotic adventurer imitates exactly the way children play to wedge themselves into the larger adult world. He takes on the role fitted to the measure of his desires, saying "it might be said that . . . ," and at once he is the perfect knight, or perhaps the liberator of an enchanted village. And he plays these roles with such passionate conviction that he would seem to forget—though in fact he doesn't—that he himself has contrived his triumph, and that his sham is only a compensation, a last resort, from which it would be vain to expect more than an illusory pleasure. Quixotic childishness—witness the constant maternal care Sancho lavishes upon his master or the endless rebuke the villagers heap upon the Land-Surveyor as though he were an insufferably inquisitive child—is preserved from puerility, however, by the author's mature and lucid intelligence. In order to express himself fully, he mingles the tone of childish demand with the severe or bitter tone of adult criticism. Thus he manages to express simultaneously faith and skepticism, devotion and hostility, without attempting to reconcile his feelings with his ideas. He protests that he admires the *old* ideal, but in his tone, respect just barely outweighs mockery. On the other hand, the Golden Age—which inspires Don Quixote's eloquence and Cervantes' disaffection—is invoked in a voice of regret that imperceptibly becomes a whine. Who is right in this duet of two voices that are equally strong and clear: the childish soul claiming its right to dream, or the adult intelligence that finds its only hope in the gloomy assertion of reality? Quixotism does not presuppose a decisive answer to this question, and this is what makes its mission so urgent.[6]

Sovereign imitation, then, creates a figure that comprehends both the child who wants to grow up without losing the Golden Age, the "once upon a time" of stories, and the adult who would follow his dream without renouncing his clarity, who concludes, "this is how it is today." The imitator, who seriously plays the role of preserver and restorer of the past, has on his side an allegiance to the "good old days," the beauty of fixed things, the power of legend. The observer has on his the sad privilege of discernment, the obligation to restore the dignity and charm of the present, to unearth the reality that has been buried under a mass of books. At first, observer and imitator stake out carefully defined areas for themselves; but these areas soon begin to overlap, so that whatever Don Quixote does is rectified, challenged, or measured by everything that Cervantes observes. Soon the observer and the imitator cooperate so closely that it would be difficult to sort out their respective roles. Inseparable and irreconcilable, they are eventually reunited in the character of K. the Land-Surveyor, who tries earnestly, though in vain, to satisfy their contrary demands. In this last, most rigorous, and perfect issue of quixotism, there is neither brutal conflict nor any posing of alternatives, but a collaboration of two wit-

[6]This is why quixotic imitation differs in an essential way from more parodistic forms that are related to it, but in which, from the very beginning, disrespect outweighs veneration and piety. The whole difference between Joyce's *Ulysses* or *Bouvard and Pécuchet* and *Don Quixote* rests in this refusal to make choices and offer conclusions, which allows the drama of faith to be played out to its logical conclusion.

nesses, each recording his version of the facts and stubbornly clinging to his separate conclusions. In *The Castle,* a
work almost pedantic in the way minutiae displace the
power of action, the epic has assumed the neutral tone of an
administrative report, while the description of daily reality
proceeds with the clarity and discordance of a nightmare
dreamed in times of uncertainty by an anonymous sleeper.

The quixotic work not only reanimates and attempts to
judge the quarrel of the ancients and the moderns, it also
tries to settle the dispute between realism and romanticism,
which it treats as an internal, not external, conflict. The
quixotic intelligence is enamoured of romanticism's respect
for the past, its faith in the myths of childhood, its belief in
an eternal recurrence—a consolation for the inability to live,
for the fear of the present. The quixotic adventurer also
believes in the ideal, in love and unity; nothing attracts him
like nocturnal adventures, plunges into a shadowy world
where he can lose himself in nothingness, death, madness.
As a great reader he delights in all tales, tales of fairies or
witches, even old wives' tales—any fabulous invention,
however bizarre, is to his taste. But what he loves best of all
is to tell stories himself; in fact, he is so distracted by his own
tales that he completely forgets life—which is a kind of
discreet revenge. Always drawn backward, the quixotic
character hopes for a return to a primal state that would
destroy history and restore primitive purity and unity. And
he asserts these regressive tendencies with a somewhat
ironic satisfaction. Indeed, Don Quixote might be taken
for the brother, even for the true spiritual master, of all
romantics.

But quixotism has another dimension. It may share this
romantic nostalgia and desire, but it also constitutes a
critique of romanticism, a recognition that its irresistible

nostalgia has no legitimate force in real life. Unlike the romantic, who makes a virtue of necessity and disguises as a choice his incurable inability to live, the quixotic figure feels it imperative to see himself as he really is: chimerical, irresponsible, dissatisfied. It is his torment, and the good fortune of his work, that he does not believe he can change the world by a simple act of imagination. He wants to penetrate reality, to shake it by the power of his vision and, *in spite of everything* (which is, finally, his motto), to carve out a place for himself. Clear sighted and naturally discerning, he is always led—by curiosity, respect, love of the very thing that keeps him at a distance—to tighten his slack ties with life. For him, then, antiromanticism is not a matter of conviction, but an unfathomable internal debate that he can settle only by allowing himself to speak as the romantic he is without restraint or dissembling. What he gains by this are his realism, his gift for description and concision, and his sense of proportion. These qualities not only contribute to the precision of his art, but serve, he hopes, to redress the wrongs he has inflicted on reality by turning it into literature. Yet this very act of reparation, conceived as a gesture of simple justice, ultimately reveals a romanticism so pervasive that, finally, it is inaccessible to any criticism.

THE NEW ODYSSEY

I discover my origins in the
book I knew by heart before knowing how
to read: *Don Quixote*.
FLAUBERT

The Plot

"Cervantes . . . starts out well and ends up
nowhere."   THE CURATE
                                      I, 6

Don Quixote does not immediately strike us as one of the
great and lasting works of literature, for the few other instances of this order of literary achievement would seem to
be distinguished not only by their endurance, but by their
unique choice of subject as well. Calling to mind the basic
plot elements of the *Divine Comedy, Faust,* or *Hamlet,* for
example, we begin to wonder whether Cervantes was truly
ignorant or simply contemptuous of the rich fund of impressions and ideas that had nourished Western literature
since ancient times. Dante, Goethe, and Shakespeare treat
serious subjects touching upon universal, recognizably significant human problems. The pitifully improbable story of
Don Quixote, by contrast, consists of a trivial plot that is
anecdotal, scant, and rather foolish. We might even be
tempted to ignore it entirely in our pursuit of the true meaning of the work.

The full magnitude of this unusual disproportion between the stature of the work and the triviality of its subject
becomes clearer if we can imagine a novel written today
solely in order to ridicule the enthusiasts of a certain kind of

literature, for example, the readers of detective stories or science fiction. And we would have to imagine such a limited book achieving the very highest popular and literary acclaim with almost every generation during several centuries. An impossibility, we contend. No book could gain such stature without some fundamental human value that was capable of engaging the interest or passion not only of so many of its contemporaries, but more importantly, of subsequent readers. Yet Cervantes accomplished precisely that, and he did it without resorting to trickery or disguising the poverty of his subject.

Readers and critics have always been impressed and embarrassed by this discordance, since they expect at least some minimal connection between a work's apparent subject and its meaning. Two kinds of explanations, in general, have been recruited to resolve the difficulty. Unfortunately these explanations lead to radically opposed readings. Critics who follow the first approach take the subject of *Don Quixote* quite seriously and consider the novel's depth and richness, its vigorous intelligence, to be simply matters of chance, in no way attributable to the writer's skill. These readers are the partisans of Cervantes' imbecility, they see him as *un povero uomo,*[1] a kind of wildly inspired idiot, incapable of comprehending what he created. Critics in the second category—and admittedly these are in the majority and have made the most important contributions—deal with this thorny issue by flatly denying the real subject of *Don Quixote.* They contend that the business of the chivalric romance is only a pretext, and that we should follow the example of Cervantes himself, who seems to have given it little importance (and mocked everyone, with good reason). The true subject of the novel, they maintain, is an

[1]De Lollis, cited by Americo Castro in *Cervantes,* Rieder, 1931.

esoteric one that can be discovered only by those who know how to decipher it. Based on this viewpoint, an exegetical movement has developed that holds the letter of the text to be infinitely less important than what it conceals, allowing unbridled speculation to supersede any consideration of the facts. Americo Castro quite rightly observes that,

> Cervantes has given birth to a whole literature that might be called superstitious. In it can be found evidence of every science, from geography to medicine. But superstition, properly speaking, even madness, prevails in the work of those critics who would attribute to every line of *Don Quixote* an esoteric, religious, political, or simply enigmatic significance. They have even discovered anagrams. . . .[2]

The fact is that a good part of this literature on Cervantes contains more superstition than critical judgment and, as a result, does more damage, despite its richness and the brilliance of its insights, than the less popular thesis of the *idiot savant*. Most remarkable, however, is that the two explanations are so radically opposed only because they share the same premise, or rather the same prejudice, about the manifest subject of the novel: That it is unworthy of a great writer. Therefore the masterpiece must be either a miracle or an accident whose real author is unknown, or a brilliant construction, the real meaning of which exists only for the benefit of the enlightened. Its paltry fictional plot, they imply, is simply a bone tossed to the vulgar. The two conclusions both follow nicely from their shared premise, and though contrary, they have the same effect. Whether the subject of *Don Quixote* is considered trivial and stupid or simply dismissed as a deliberate disguise, the flesh and blood of the book is conjured away, and with it the only justifiable object of inquiry.

[2]Americo Castro, op. cit.

Quixotism, as we have seen in the first part of this discussion, is peculiarly vulnerable to the most damaging kinds of miscomprehension. Certain readers believe its essence can be grasped only when it is reduced to an abstract intellectual principle. But in fact it is a literary matter, an endeavor to portray the struggle of the writer with writing and through this the problematic relationship between books and life. This confusion may be understandable in the case of Kafka; by his time, this relationship had assumed such complexity that literature as a subject in fiction had to be disguised or presented only as a narrative allusion. It is surprising, however, to find this misunderstanding of Cervantes, especially since he announces quite clearly his intention to do battle with a literary genre and could hardly do more to inform his readers. *Don Quixote* treats the chivalric romance as another book might treat a love story or an historical event, the only difference being that these create an illusion of reality, while the chivalric romance in Cervantes' book flaunts its purely fictional character. The chief difficulty of the book, in fact, is not in deciphering the arduous problems ostensibly posed between the lines, but rather in the strictly literary nature of its subject, which places an unexpected obstacle between the reader and his own habits of thought.

In *Don Quixote,* nothing happens with the natural simplicity characteristic of the realist novel, which pretends to mirror life. On the contrary, everything undergoes a primary literary elaboration that is quite openly displayed. Instead of lifelike characters, we encounter only prescribed *copies,* created through a series of variants that the reader is invited to appraise for the sake of critical comparison. (There are at least three drafts: one by Amadis, one by Cid Hamete Benengeli, the fictional chronicler, and one by the last compositor, Cervantes.) The worst misunderstanding in this case is to base an interpretation of the novel on a belief in the realistic dimensions of the plot. The novel can be understood only in terms of the different versions that are cleverly cast by their last author to underline the fictional nature of the actions. We would therefore do well to shift the focus of a critical, and not credulous, reading of *Don Quixote* to the chivalric plot itself, which is the first model, and hence the real subject, of the novel.

The genre of the chivalric romance, of course, did not attract Cervantes by its outstanding literary qualities. It is probable that he chose it rather for its capacity to bring alive the worlds of fantasy in which imaginary creations emerge, so to speak, in a pure state. We already know the subject of these works. They endlessly sound the same themes and share with children's books the privilege of being fantastical yet perfectly familiar, always fascinating and at the same time incredibly monotonous. Battles, abductions, enchantments, courtly love, black and white knights, highborn ladies, marvels, fabulous conquests—these are the usual ingredients, infinitely varied but completely unoriginal, involving little psychology or verisimilitude. The chivalric romance was given its impetus by the heroic achievements of the Middle Ages and is related to the cycle of Breton romances as well as to European folklore, which is the source of its marvelous elements and of various motifs. In its final flowering, the chivalric romance seems to have been the most precious and decadent form of escapist literature.

Cervantes himself thrived on this literature (indeed, he avidly read anything and everything; he tells us that he even devoured scraps of paper found in the streets). One might suppose that in elaborating his excessive predilection for this rather shabby but fascinating minor genre, he wanted to stigmatize a widespread mania, innocent in itself, but dangerously contagious. Such a conjecture, however, could have no validity, for although entire generations had gorged themselves on chivalric romances, Cervantes' contemporaries were in no danger of doing so. At the time of *Don Quixote*'s publication, such novels were 30 years out of date and were no longer published at all—a sure sign of public disaffection. Cervantes' detractors—Lope de Vega, Gongora, and Avellaneda, his parodist and plagiarist—had an easy time mocking a satire so deprived of its object. And as spiteful as their argument is, it carries some weight. Does it make sense to wage a war with such force and ingenuity against something the public no longer wants? If, as he says, Cervantes wanted to wean his contemporaries (and he could only address himself to them) away from a literature that was, in his experience, pernicious, his enterprise would be scarcely less aberrant than Don Quixote's; for the books in question, far from exerting a corrupting influence, had long been forgotten. From the beginning critics have proposed the alternatives already mentioned: either Cervantes was a pathetic fumbler, or, driven by the force of his ideas, he seized upon the first subject to present itself, which, of course, led to certain incongruities that, considering the power of his genius, should not be held against him.

One might hold either position, but this curious preference for anachronism must still be explained on grounds other than stupidity or thoughtlessness. Cervantes could not have been so insensitive to his time, which was hardly an era threatened by an excessive passion for the chivalric romance. Politically, it was the Spain of Philip II, the disagreeable and niggling bureaucrat king, who was certainly more skilled in the intricacies of red tape than in the virtues of heroism. On the literary side, it was the Spain of the cynical *picaro,* a sort of antihero who prevailed in a disillusioned world. Cervantes did not live like a hermit and knew better than many what this prosaic Spain was all about; if he spoke out of rhythm with the times, offering his contemporaries outdated dreams, such a gesture must have answered a personal need and served some determined purpose. The chivalric romances were certainly not a collective menace, but for Cervantes himself they represented a very real danger and fascination. Describing them was his way of resisting temptation, or rather of succumbing to it with a certain elegance. And clearly he did succumb. By exhuming these unfashionable books from the recent past, he was pursuing his own pleasure rather than fostering the moral education of a few enthusiasts like himself. Under the pretext of rectifying public taste, he adroitly managed to revive *in extremis* a moribund and forgotten literature, something that perhaps no one else would have dreamt of doing. This revival, of course, was not his ultimate aim, but it offered him a unique opportunity to settle in one sweeping gesture his battle with words and his complicated account with the times.

Certain critics have accurately discerned some of the conclusions that might be drawn from this ruse, through which Cervantes surreptitiously revives what he pretends to destroy. They are particularly struck by the obvious association between an outmoded genre and the period when it flourished, and they deduce that through the vehicle of these harmless books Cervantes quietly voiced his regrets for the time when *Amadis de Gaule, Tirant lo Blanch,* and the litany of *Palmerin* enchanted not only the masses but the elite as well—even such celebrated persons as Charles V and Saint Theresa, who read them as daily entertainment. Indeed, the splendors of the imperial age might well have inspired the

regrets of a man infatuated with greatness, who thought of
Cortez, Pizarro, and the emperor himself as heroes whose
ideas had been as vigorous as their deeds. Cervantes was
only seven years old when Philip II ascended the throne, so
he could not have known this glorious epoch except
through family reminiscence; yet he must have felt all the
more vividly the pettiness, the bureaucratic aridity of his
own age. By the time he wrote *Don Quixote,* the gulf had
widened between a recent past, exemplified by the strength
of its achievements and ideas, and the new spirit, embodied
by a gloomy regime whose meanness Cervantes knew only
too well (being a military hero with a very meager pension).
The impressive accomplishment of Charles V, creator of an
immense empire symbolizing an all-embracing unity, was
followed by a phase of reaction heralding crushing defeat
and pervaded by the pessimism of decay. At the distance of
nearly half a century, the emperor could become an
idealized figure, especially since he seemed able to reconcile in his person political power and the power of the
imagination.

In the absence of biographical data, we cannot state
categorically that *Don Quixote* was inspired directly by the
legacy of Charles V and the traditions associated with his
reign. This does seem possible, however, since we know
that Cervantes always spoke of him with admiration and
respect. We might even be tempted to say it is probable,
considering certain characteristics that suggest an unusual
resemblance between the emperor and Don Quixote.
Charles V was fifty-six years old when he renounced power
and the world, Cervantes' hero is fifty when he repudiates
his past life. They read the same kind of literature in pursuit
of the most visionary compensation for their disenchantment. Finally, they were both unhappy (melancholy is

perhaps the most plausible explanation of the emperor's abdication, which still puzzles historians today). There is one major difference, however, that might overrule any analogies—namely, that Charles V truly transformed the world, whereas Don Quixote had to be satisfied with dreams.

A reading that links the chivalric romance to the epoch of its greatest popularity leads us to understand *Don Quixote* as a kind of exalted tribute to the recent past, a past that awakened Cervantes' nostalgia for grandeur and heroism and might have seemed an inaccessible refuge from the present. This reading is supported by many of the Don's statements, which make no mystery of his judgment on his own time: "And considering this, I would willingly say that I am dismayed from the bottom of my heart to have undertaken this knight-errant's task in a century as detestable as our own." Or again: "Sancho, my friend, you may know that I was born, by Heaven's will, in this our age of iron, to revive what is known as the Golden Age" (I,20). Don Quixote presents himself here as one of those men, born too late, who have no place or role to play in a disappointing time. Displaced by an error they attribute to the will of heaven, they derive the conception of what they call their "mission," and the strength to accomplish it, precisely from this original mistake. If Don Quixote's speculations about the Golden Age were the only point of view expressed in the novel, we would certainly have to think of Cervantes as one of those men whose alienation is a cause for sorrow but also the chief resource of their genius—which leaves aside, of course, the ironic insight that Cervantes turns against himself to describe and condemn his escape.

The nostalgia for the *recent* past may be expressed in the novel, but it does not represent the deepest level of meaning, which, as I have already emphasized, remains irreducibly ambiguous. In fact, Cervantes does not present us with an idealized past but rather with a ridiculous survival, which is described rather maliciously through the vehicle of a minor and somewhat shabby literature. It is clear that if he had wanted to express his feelings of loss for the pageantry of the empire, he might have chosen more convincing means. Most readers take his regrets to be pure mockery. Once more we run up against the irritating question of Cervantes' intentions, a question that has been continuously debated by an enormous literature and still remains unsettled.

The new image of a reactionary Cervantes who scorned his own time in the name of an impossible dream of the past may be effectively opposed by the more convincing image of one of the first revolutionary writers to engage in the bitter intellectual struggle that is still raging after three centuries, and in which the author of *Don Quixote* still plays a remarkably active role. This version of Cervantes makes sense if we consider the chivalric romance no longer from the angle of its historic situation, but rather as the object of Don Quixote's *devotion*. Cervantes exploits his model in two ways, first, by reproducing a literary form and its contents, which in themselves evoke dreams of a past time; and, more obliquely, by making this literature the object of a cult—an unexpected response to the chivalric romance, but one quite appropriate to sacred texts. In this way he establishes the equivalence of the two kinds of books; the result is a subterranean displacement of genres whereby the profane romance is endowed with the exclusive characteristics of sacred or didactic literature. Don Quixote himself behaves less like a common maniac than a foolish believer. By taking this analogy to its logical conclusion, we could replace the word "chivalric" each time by the word "theological" or "sacred" and so translate the entire novel.

The character of Don Quixote actually seems to demand such a translation at many points. First, his relations to the chivalric romance are modeled on those of the devotee to his sacred books, for these offer him both an example and a discipline. He believes blindly, swearing an unlimited allegiance to the letter of the texts, which he knows by heart and consults at every important juncture. In this respect, indeed, he goes well beyond the capacities of an ordinary believer and seems more like a theologian or a scholar. More remarkable still is the effect of this devotion on his character. He is ordinarily good, intelligent, humane, and conciliatory, but he is entirely transformed by the magic name of his favorite books. Suddenly he becomes credulous, intolerant, unreasonable, violent, and excessive; in other words, he displays all the most obvious symptoms of fanaticism. He is beside himself at the least contradiction, acknowledging only the argument of authority, which, as far as he is concerned, resides wholly in the past and in tradition. Moreover, he is inspired by his intransigent faith to convert others—by force, if need be—and indeed to sacrifice his own life in a gesture of extreme abnegation. It would be reasonable to infer from this that Don Quixote's beloved romances prudently mask texts of a rather different sort. The romances are so trivial, in fact, that one begins to wonder whether Don Quixote does not hide behind his appearance as a harmless maniac the dreaded figure of the "inspired" fanatic, the persecutor and crusader who was so familiar to his contemporaries. At the very least, we have good reason to suppose that by so closely meshing these secular and sacred books, Cervantes figured to compromise the religious texts without too much personal risk. He takes such evident pleasure in this meshing of texts that we can scarcely accuse him of naïveté.

In any case, the association of the chivalric romance with

books of a religious nature was neither fortuitous nor Cervantes' invention. His contemporaries had already been introduced to this idea by the author of the *Life of Theresa of Avila,* Father Ribera. According to his account, the devil launched his attack upon the celebrated Spanish saint by means of two principal temptations, bad company and chivalric romances. "Gifted as she was in the realm of the mind and the imagination, she was so imbued with this kind of literature that she and her brother Rodrigo de Cepeda composed, over a period of a few months, a chivalric romance with all the adventures and fictions proper to such compositions . . . ." Don Quixote, who would have become a writer joyfully ". . . if his thoughts had not been constantly occupied with other things of greater moment . . . ," would have very much appreciated this transition from reading to composition, or better, from consumption to production, that his favorite books seemed to encourage. And he would have savored even more the entirely quixotic way Saint Theresa "sallied forth" one day to transform literature into life, to put into practice the acts and conduct of the saints as they are recorded in *The Tales of the Golden Legend.*

The heart of the young Theresa was inflamed by the stories of the suffering and death of martyrs . . . and soon she began to desire a death like theirs, to win the crown they had obtained. This desire was so ardent that finally, taking a few provisions, she and her brother left their father's house, resolved to travel to the land of the Moors, where they would suffer beheading for the love of Jesus Christ . . . .

Father Ribera hasn't enough hard words to condemn Saint Theresa's pernicious reading habits, yet he cites this last incident as proof of her precocious vocation. He sees no connection between the two, but then how could he? It would not occur to him that all books demanding faith and obedience (the practical implementation of their law) are of equal value, and that therefore the transition from reading to pious or saintly acts does not fundamentally depend upon the reality or value of the literary model. A pious theologian could hardly entertain the blasphemous notion that the young Theresa's heroic mission and the ramblings of Don Quixote amount to very much the same thing.

It is likely, however, that Cervantes harbored just such a notion. He does not flaunt it openly, but he does all he can to provoke the open-minded (if not free-thinking) reader's suspicion. The fact is that Don Quixote's adventures would scarcely be affected if, instead of devouring nonsensical romances, he gorged himself as immoderately on sacred books. His mission, for example, which is undertaken so suddenly, as though it were mysteriously commanded (hence its resemblance to Saint Theresa's escapade), would have the same consequences if it were represented from the outset as the fulfillment of a religious vocation. It does, after all, entail disciplined acts of piety (Don Quixote's mortifications in the Sierra have their analogues in all the religious literature); a holy crusade (he wants to restore the Golden Age and to convert his contemporaries, by persuasion or force); dangerous trials (the descent into the cave of Montesinos and, even better, the adventure in the lion's cage are variants of a well-known hagiographic motif); and finally a quest, through which the chosen hero must secure the possession of a mystic object (in this case Dulcinea). Seen from this angle, Cervantes' novel seems to be a compendium of theology, doubtless somewhat confused, but dominated by a personality whose chief virtues make him the equal of the most celebrated saints. Like them he is humble, obedient, pure, faithful, always ready for martyrdom; he is usually

gentle and patient, but he is intractable where his faith is
concerned and furious should the article of that faith be
questioned. In other words, Don Quixote has everything
necessary for a career in sainthood except an ideal that conforms to established norms.

And now we glimpse the treacherous question Cervantes
clearly wished to plant in the minds of his readers and
which, for a number of critics, suggests its own answer. If
the adventurer, the madman infatuated with a bizarre idea,
so closely resembles the rarefied creatures called to sainthood, isn't the converse also possible? What becomes of
sainthood then? Or, to put it in more familiar terms, what is
the value of an ideology that cannot be judged on rational
grounds, but only by its intentions and a certain number of
practical applications? Don Quixote's intentions are pure,
and as for applications, he can support comparison with any
canonized saint. Of course his ideal is risible, his motives
futile, his faith worthless and comic; yet it is precisely the
inanity of his efforts that makes the ideal, the motives, the
true faith of religious orthodoxy appear in a dubious light.
And Don Quixote's eccentricities, the senseless penance he
imposes on himself for reasons that are purely illusory,
cruelly illuminate the eccentricities of Saint Theresa, who
enters the refectory of her convent with a load of stones tied
to a rope around her neck.[3] There is no third possibility:
either Don Quixote and Saint Theresa are equally justified
by the sublime madness of faith, and we must conclude with
Unamuno[4] that Cervantes did not understand the grandeur

[3]The comparison with Saint Theresa and the theological references that
follow are borrowed from L.-P. May's "Cervantes, un fondateur de la
libre-pensée," in the collection *Descartes, Pour la Verité,* Paris, 1947.

[4]In his book, *The Life of Don Quixote and Sancho Panza,* Unamuno compares the saintliness of Don Quixote to that of Loyola, the founder of the
Jesuit order and the father of the theology that, according to free-thinking
critics, was precisely Cervantes' target.

of his own creation; or Don Quixote's foolishness seriously discredits religious thought and practice, and this is, finally, the meaning of the book.

This last view can be convincingly supported by facts that have been eagerly retrieved by L.-P. May.[5] In his estimation, Don Quixote is not merely a legible caricature of piety in general, but he speaks and often behaves in a most devious way, as if he meant to engage the reader in the theological quarrels of his time. To this effect he takes wine for blood (in the story of the goatskins), thereby settling the question of the real Presence. In the affair of Mambrino's helmet, Don Quixote denies his perception of the object (in this case a barber's basin) for the sake of an imaginary thing whose existence rests on a name and the mention of this name in a book. This may be quite absurd, but it conforms to the theological system that governed the religious thought of the time and that, by granting the image as much power as the object, transferred to the name the very substance of the thing itself. Don Quixote in general behaves like a zealous student of the theologians who reject sensory evidence, maintain that the invisible world of faith is more real than the palpable world, and finally establish a total equivalence between image and object. This is not just a figment of the deranged mind of Cervantes' hero, but the belief system of the whole Medieval cult of image-worship. Don Quixote cannot witness a performance, for instance, without immediately confusing theater and life and thrusting himself into the action. The marionettes of the puppet-master Pierre are not dolls for him but living beings called into existence by the immediate power of the image. There is no difference between reality and its representation: the historical event and its figurative image are identical. Therefore, if the marionettes unite to commit some dreadful act, they must

[5]L.-P. May, op. cit.

be massacred on the spot. (The masses of the Middle Ages reasoned in just this manner when they ran to the ghetto to murder the descendants of Judas after participating in a performance of the Passion.) So Don Quixote does not trust his own perceptions, even those most necessary to his survival—recall his unhappy perplexity and the way Sancho comes to his rescue in the story of the lion's cage. He does not *see* anything, or rather he passes through the world as though it were not his business to perceive what takes place, but rather to decipher *the book of the universal order of nature and things* whose existence is posited by a celebrated theologian.[6]

This is certainly the explanation of Don Quixote's aberrant behavior. For him "the universal order of nature and things" is a sealed book, something that in itself has no intelligible meaning; but it can acquire such meaning thanks to the contents of another book, namely Amadis' romance, which is his guide, his science, and his bible. We can see here that the substitution of a highly profane text for the sacred one skirts sacrilege, and that with a bit more penetration Cervantes' censors would have had material for a proper trial. Of course he covered his tracks with the most intelligent precautions. For instance, he condemns the Canon, the representative of orthodoxy, for attempting to persuade Don Quixote to give up *his* bible for the true Bible by urging that, after all, the Holy Scriptures will quite adequately satisfy his taste for the marvelous. "If, however, carried away by your natural inclination, you feel that you must read of knightly exploits, then turn to the Book of Judges in the Holy Scriptures, for there you will find great deeds recorded, and as true as they are valiant" (I,49). Cervantes' tactic is clear, but it is a bit too underhanded, since Don Quixote himself invokes the biblical argument to support

[6]Raymond Sebond, translated by Montaigne, cited by L.-P. May.

the truth of his favorite stories. If one denies the existence of giants, for example, he is prepared with the best retort: "The Holy Scriptures, which must be true, teach us that there are . . . [giants]." What can be said to that? Instead of leading Don Quixote along more orthodox paths, the evidence of the Bible only leads him further astray, for he has no sense of a hierarchy of truths. And he does not give an inch. If we believe in Goliath, we must also believe in the story of the exploits of Felixmarte of Hyrcania, who "with a single backward stroke cut five giants in two around the middle . . ." (I,32). If we believe in the saints and their relics, we must admit the historical existence of Pierres, of the Cid and Roland, ". . . seeing that to this very day, in the royal armory, one may behold the pin—a little bigger than a cart-pole—with which the valiant Pierres guided his wooden horse through the air, while alongside it is Babieca's saddle [.] And at Roncesvalles there is Roland's horn, the size of a beam" (I,49). If we can believe without flinching that at the battle of Muret, on September 13, 1213, "more than twenty thousand of the enemy perished, while, according to the testimony of historians, the Catholic army lost only one knight and eight soldiers,"[7] we have no reason to doubt the fabulous fictional battles in which evildoers always perish but the good are miraculously saved.

Belief must at least be consistent. Improbability is not a matter of size or number, and we cannot arbitrarily label one thing a miracle, another a mirage. For after all, it is a matter of faith, not reason, and faith is unconditional. Don Quixote gives his public fair warning: the mysteries he believes in are not things whose existence can be proved with any finality. If we presume to examine them, we will be obliged to verify other mysteries as well, which the Don, at least, has the modesty not to mention. In other words, it is certainly per-

[7]The legend of Saint Dominic, cited by L.-P. May.

missible to ask for proof of Dulcinea's positive existence, but we cannot do this without similarly becoming engaged in proving the reality of revelation itself.

Don Quixote fails to raise his literary Camelot to the heights of a theology, but—rather insidiously—he succeeds in another direction. The chivalric romance may gain nothing by the association with theology, but religious orthodoxy stands to lose much of its dignity. This secondary effect of the quixotic imitation serves to support the humanist critic who sees in Cervantes primarily a man of the Renaissance, a pioneer of modern rationalism who engaged his mind and his talent in a secret struggle against the obscurantism of his time. "Cervantes," says Jean Cassou, "the first of the moderns before Descartes, more or less knowingly wore a mask . . . . He recalls a passage from *The Deeds of Persilis and Sigismund* in which Cervantes seems to explain his position: "I follow the customs of my nation, at least those that seem reasonable. As for the rest, I pretend to observe them, since dissimulation can be profitable . . . ." Here the ruse is even half confessed. There is speculation that Cervantes had a bone to pick with the Inquisition of 1587, whose vigilant officials excommunicated, pursued, and imprisoned him. If this is true, we can imagine his need to disguise his real thoughts with the greatest prudence. According to this view, Cervantes wrote *Don Quixote* as a convinced rationalist in order to enlighten his contemporaries and to make them laugh at their own puerile superstitions. His controversial novel would be precisely "the coded expression of free thought in the Spain of the Inquisition, *that stream of truth* according to Pascal . . . ."[8] Or, as it is put by an author of the last century,[9]

[8]L.-P. May, op. cit.
[9]Émile Chasles, *Michel de Cervantes, sa vie, son temps, ses oeuvres politiques et littéraires,* Paris, 1866.

an exercise in the high criticism of ideas, by which Cervantes hoped to break openly with all the chimeras of the public mind . . . to flush out false ideas, factitious sentiments, and contagious errors; and having accomplished this, to bury the poison of the effeminate romance, the anachronisms of feudal pride and the mania for chivalry . . . . All this in a fight for the truth that he believed more beautiful than beauty itself . . . .

One is tempted to adopt this reasonable humanist interpretation at once without worrying too much about whether it excludes or inadvertently adds anything to the text. What it does exclude, however, is quite obviously the unwavering radiance that emanates from the person of Don Quixote himself alone among the characters in the book. The novel may be a call to revolt against a superstitious, authoritarian, and intellectually degrading system, but it does not necessarily follow that Don Quixote is the incarnation of benighted obscurantism, or Sancho, by some inevitable opposition, the model of enlightenment. Far from it. Sancho, the natural man of the people, may possess a firmer grasp of reality and more plain common sense than his master, but he is not so free of the prejudices and superstitions of his time. Indeed, he occasionally falls prey to them wholeheartedly enough to compromise his "philosophical" dignity. His sound relations with his body and nature are evidently the counterpart of Don Quixote's morbid asceticism, yet this rustic good health has nothing to do with rectitude and strength of judgment. The final proof is that he blindly believes the false promises of his master, and, reasonable as he is, allows himself to be half converted to Don Quixote's cause.

It would be as rash to make Sancho a pioneer of the philosophy of the Enlightenment[10] as to identify Don Quixote with single-minded fanaticism. If this had been

[10]L.-P. May identifies him with Bacon.

Cervantes' intention, he could have painted his protagonist more crudely than he did. The contrast between the two companions is striking, but it is not the violent antagonism of irreconcilable ideologies. On the contrary, their differences are the source of the affection, devotion, and fidelity that bind Don Quixote to his squire and give such charm to their common history. The true fanatic would not have Don Quixote's forbearance and essential benevolence toward what he condemns; and on his side, the militant rationalist would entirely lose the thrust of his argument if he responded to his adversary's misdeeds with Sancho's indulgence and tenderness. The schematic division of these issues into black and white is a misrepresentation of Cervantes' profound intuition, which never separates or opposes but strives to restore everything to the primary unity of life and thought. Centuries of theology had destroyed this essential unity for the sake of a spurious spirituality cut loose from the real world and driven by its very spuriousness into collusion with the worst tyrannies of Cervantes' time.

The new humanism, however, does not seem to have been much more engaged in contemporary events, although it roused far more hope. No sooner was it born than it created a scholarship in which the gathering, classification, and inventory of ideas took the place of real thought. The vagaries of mysticism were supposed to be dissipated by the meticulously drafted catalogue. But such an abstract repository, though it may satisfy man's rational side, is powerless against the need for belief, the pursuit of a compensating ideal, the hope of salvation. Furthermore, by separating reason from the rest of life, it opens the way for new mystifications when the old have not yet been unmasked. This situation is described with prophetic precision in the Montesinos episode, in which Don Quixote accepts the company of a young man who offers to guide him across the lagoons of Ruydera toward the mouth of the famous cavern. Questioned about his activities, this young man declares that his profession "was that of a humanist composing books for the printers, all of them of great public utility and very entertaining . . . ." He has written a work on liveries in which he describes seven hundred and three "with their colors, mottoes and ciphers . . . ." He is preparing another book that he calls *Metamorphoses, or the Spanish Ovid,* and has, in addition, composed a *Supplement to Virgilius Polydorus* that deals with

"the invention of things and is a very scholarly work and one that cost me much study. In it I set forth in a pleasing style, with due proof and explanation, certain things of great moment that Polydorus neglected to mention. He forgot to tell us who was the first man in the world to take unctions for the French disease, all of which I bring out most accurately, citing the authority of more than twenty-five authors. From this your Grace may see how well I have labored and may judge for yourself as to whether or not such a work should be useful to everyone" (II,22).

This humanist is not portrayed in a very flattering way, and if he is supposed to represent the new philosophy, as his name would indicate, he betokens a rather sad future. Of course we cannot determine the degree to which Cervantes intended him to be representative, but he marvelously embodies the smug self-righteousness and mental laziness that takes thinking to be the juxtaposition of badly selected data on secondary subjects.

This collector of trivia certainly cuts a poor figure by comparison to Don Quixote as he appears in the revealing episode of the cavern. The Don is mad, and his tendency to dogmatism might make him harmful were it unchecked by

his natural goodness and, still more, by his complete impotence. But he is inspired. He sets out to explore the abyss
with a poetic or prophetic passion that is more valuable than
the results of his expedition. These passions, of course,
make no practical sense—at least no more nor less, perhaps,
than poetry and prophesy themselves. It does not matter
that this abyss is only a hole and that afterward Don Quixote
has nothing more to tell than a confused and trivial story of
sleepwalking. Still, isn't it true that all revelations defy
expression? Isn't "the most awesome abyss" always described in terms of the overwhelming experience of the descent and an ineffable vision? The story of Montesinos is
probably a fiction that Don Quixote has simply invented or
modeled from his inexhaustible fund of tales. Perhaps it is a
dream or the result of a momentary epiphany. Who can say?
Nor is it important, since no answer would belie or verify
the authenticity of the vision, except for those who are
closed to the value of poetry. This is basically Sancho's
position, though the fact that he is moved by the bizarre
grandeur of his master somewhat mitigates his myopia. The
humanist, however, is a more glaring example. He is incapable of wonder, admiration, or even irony, and sees Don
Quixote's adventurous descent merely as an opportunity to
glean a few bits and pieces of knowledge (about local geography or the invention of the pack of cards). This future
savant has no regard for the strange apparition of Don
Quixote, when "finally, after a considerable length of time,
he at last regained consciousness, stretching himself as if he
had been roused from a profound slumber," manifesting all
the signs of a state that could be either mental paralysis or
ecstasy. He has scarcely recovered his speech when the
humanist plies him with questions, for, after all, the man's
métier is to exploit the discoveries of others. His deadly seri-

ousness, the way he pedantically records the least of Don Quixote's hazy musings for his next book as if they were scientific information, his lack of imagination, and indeed his stupidity, indicate rather unequivocally that Cervantes intended this humanist to be seen as a vulgar pedant.

The historical exploration of the chivalric romance, then, cuts a path between two interpretations, each of which contains a basic truth, but becomes false when raised to the level of a generalization that imposes ideas foreign to the narrative or excludes what might prove embarrassing. *Don Quixote* cannot be read as a kind of swan song to the glory of Charles V and his time unless we deliberately ignore Cervantes' bitter critique of the intellectual, spiritual, and social foundations of the same period. For it was not only the epoch of the emperor, but also of the Jesuits and Dominicans and the Inquisition, which was based on a system of thought as much as it was on political power. On the other hand, if it is true that the book takes issue with contemporary theology of the kind imposed by the worst constraints of Dominican and Jesuit orthodoxy, a reading that reduces *Don Quixote* to a profession of humanist faith denies half its substance. Such a reading may partially reflect Cervantes' ideas (only partially, however, as witness the humanist in question), but it fails to account for the expressions of regret and disenchantment that so powerfully determine the novel's affective coloration. Certainly Cervantes promoted the "high criticism of ideas," but this is not proof of his militant rationalism. It is rather the vehicle of a truth beyond beauty and reason that cannot be articulated but only seized in the assemblage of its scattered fragments. This truth obliges Cervantes to state, for example, that the marvelous is a lie, platonic love a hypocrisy, the effeminate romance a poison, feudal pride and the mania for chivalry anachronisms; but he is also obliged to admit that all of these nearly obsolete and yet dangerous illusions fascinate and attract him in a way that neither his enlightenment, his respect for reality, nor his love of truth have ever been able to prevent. We are speaking here not of an ordinary concern for objectivity nor of a neutrality that permits a consideration of opposed points of view. This is a matter of a poetic necessity that compels reason to plead the case of the irrational. In the novel, both Jesuits and humanists receive their share of barbs. But Cervantes cared less about being even handed than about formulating a clear distinction between the cave of Montesinos, in itself an insipid fiction, and the irresistible desire for the descent, for a trial—the fascination of the unknown. These deeply human desires have perhaps a greater reality than the most enlightened and rational aspirations.

Cervantes' treatment of the chivalric romance, after all, cannot please partisans of the genre (and ideas associated with it) since they must find the hero indefensibly grotesque; but then neither can it satisfy the humanists, who surely sense the novel's marked aftertaste of mysticism. Clearly Cervantes did not intend to settle the matter. ("'Cervantes,'" he says in the only place in the book where he names himself, through the mediation of the curate, "'starts out well and ends up nowhere.'") He takes masterful advantage of the distinction between *desire* and the *object of desire;* indeed, it is precisely on the basis of this distinction that Don Quixote sets out on his adventures. His object is futile, crude, ultimately false, but his impulse to pursue it, even though it procedes from a grave error in judgment, springs from a very real desire. Deranged as he is, this desire strongly corresponds to a universal need and to the very law of poetry itself.

Now if desire cannot be calculated by the actual worth of the thing desired, there is nothing to prevent us logically from conceding that the ideal of the chivalric romance is paltry, while defending the genre for the authenticity of its poetic impulse. This is demonstrated in the brief that Cervantes presents through the canon, who is probably his spokesman in this episode. The brief begins with an accusation and concludes, in the most preposterous way, with a vindication; in fact, it contains more praise than blame. This would be difficult to understand if Cervantes meant to discredit theology by exposing it to an angry broadside attack. Polemical pamphlets are not usually concluded with an enthusiastic description of the adversary, and as Cervantes did just this we can assume that although he took a few swipes at it, theology was not his primary target. Indeed, Cervantes needn't be conceived as a militant humanist to account for the theological aspect of *Don Quixote*. It can be explained quite adequately by the simple fact that theological books are basically like other books, only they are more useful to the quixotic enterprise because their nature is to bind writing to piety. Although piety is the first subject of its inquiry, *Don Quixote* does not lay blame on religious books in particular, but rather blames all books. The point being that every written text is sacred, every printed *letter* claims its share of faith. This fact is never mentioned but is always exploited by literature; and so it is questioned by Cervantes, who would like to clarify the connections between words and faith.

In the general context of the novel, the chivalric romance does not allude to theology, as one might infer, but its pervasive theology alludes to literature, specifically to the kind of books that by virtue of their endurance and simplicity usually mark the starting point of critical inquiry. From this

point of view, the canon's apparently lame reasoning assumes the necessary rigor and clarity. We must condemn
chivalric romances because they belong to a degenerate epic
genre, as their imperfections clearly demonstrate. They
have lost the secret of proportion that informs their models
and seriously violate principles of order and measure:
"'Never,'" concluded the canon, "'have I seen any book of
chivalry that held the body of a story completely with all its
members so that the middle was consistent with the beginning and the end with the beginning and middle. Rather
they are made up of so many disparate members that it
would seem the author's intention was to create a chimera or
a monster rather than a well-proportioned figure'" (I,47).
These monsters are "in addition . . . crude in style, unconvincing in the exploits they relate, lascivious in the love
stories they portray, uncouth in their efforts at courtliness,
prolix in their description of battles, absurd in their dialogue, nonsensical in their accounts of journeyings, and,
finally, destitute of anything that resembles art . . ." (I,47).

In other words, like all decadent genres, the chivalric romance is excessive, ill-proportioned, an insult to art, and a
serious offense to truth. Nevertheless—and here the canon
explains the subtle quixotic dialectic a bit coarsely—these
degenerate compositions have some redeeming features. A
gifted writer might still use them to good advantage and
with their help possibly become the equal of Homer. We
must therefore defend these books and openly support their
revival, since they offer the writer "'a broad and spacious
field'" and can "'depict shipwrecks, tempests, encounters,
and battles . . . a valiant captain with all the qualities requisite to such a character . . . now a lamentable and tragic
event and now some joyful and unexpected occurrence . . . .'" In these texts, the epic survives with an undi-
minished power that can still achieve a panoramic vision of

the world. Nature, history, man's place in the natural order, his historical destiny, society, the passions—the chivalric romance evokes all these on a grand scale, and this in itself is instructive. The author of books of chivalry has almost unlimited means of expression at his disposal. He can display the most diverse knowledge and "'might further show himself to be an astrologer, an excellent cosmographer, a musician, a student of statecraft, or even upon occasion, if he chose, a necromancer'" (I,47). He can relate anything convincingly, "'. . . the astuteness of Ulysses, the filial piety of Aeneas, the bravery of Achilles, the woes of Hector . . . ,'" etc. His task is to re-create for the present what the epic created in former times for the benefit of posterity, namely a literature with universal appeal. The prose nature of the chivalric romance is no obstacle, "'for,'" says the canon, "'the epic may be written in prose as well as in verse.'" *Discursive writing* is even a freedom that makes possible the variety of tones we find so appealing in a modern work.

As the somewhat attenuated heir to an imposing literary tradition, the chivalric romance is still rich enough to inspire books today, to answer the needs of the writer and the contemporary public. Revive it and we will see that once retrieved from the exile of general disrepute, it will recover seriousness, grace, fantasy, all the qualities necessary to navigate the gulf between the new and the old, the past and the present. And having checkmated his own accusations with such an unimpeachable argument, the canon cannot possibly hope to lead Don Quixote back to the path of reason. But was this ever his real aim? In any case, Don Quixote is incorrigible. In Part Two, when the canon launches into his long discourse, he confines his comments to what Cervantes himself has been doing through his novelistic practice.

Epic Truth

All men owe honor to the poets—
honor and awe, for they are dearest to the Muse
who puts upon their lips the ways of life.

HOMER[1]

CERVANTES would seem in complete agreement with the ancients about the universality of the epic and its singular capacity to entertain and instruct. Homer's first readers and commentators, we know, made his poems the basis of all truth and knowledge. As early as primary school, the young Greek copied out, as a model sentence, "Homer is not a man but a god . . . ."[2]

Heraclitis the Rhetorician[3] writes that "From the tenderest age the naïve mind of the child is nourished by Homer . . . It is quite appropriate that as babes in arms our souls should imbibe the milk of his verse. We grow up and he is always near us . . . We cannot leave him without thirsting for him again. It can be said that our commerce with him finishes only with life itself . . . ." Homer is a god, then, the father of all knowledge, humanity's guide. At

[1]Homer, *The Odyssey,* translated by Robert Fitzgerald, (Book 8, 11. 460+), Doubleday & Company, Inc., New York, 1963.

[2]H.-J. Marrou, *Histoire de l'Éducation dans l'Antiquité,* Paris, 1948.

[3]Félix Buffière, *Les Mythes D'Homère à la penseé grecque,* Les Belles-Lettres, Paris, 1956.

the same time he is the nurturing spirit who knows how to convey a sense of mystery and poetry to the little child. For the poet's function is not only to stir and shape the intellect; his stories, his fabulous adventures, his fantastic voyages, the exotic color of his folk tales inspire the childhood dreams that leave a lasting mark.

This grateful attachment to Homer seems uncommonly resilient. It has withstood the most violent attacks of philosophy, and even Plato himself, who has always symbolized a systematic hostility to the cult of the poet, presents the argument for the epic's superior pedagogical value. Protagoras[4] argues that to enforce this value effectively, the model teacher "provides his students with works of good poets to read as they sit in class, and are made to learn them off by heart; here they meet with many admonitions, many descriptions and praises and eulogies of good men in times past, that the boy in envy may imitate them and yearn to become even as they." Plato suggests that the pedagogue adopts the very doctrine Don Quixote articulates to justify his imitation of Amadis:

Thus, he who would achieve a reputation for prudence and long-suffering must and does follow in the footsteps of Ulysses; for in describing his character and the hardships that he endured, Homer gives us a lively picture of the virtues mentioned. Similarly, Virgil, in the person of Aeneas, portrays for us a dutiful son and the sagacity of a brave and intelligent leader. And these personages, be it noted, are not depicted or revealed to us as they were but as they ought to have been, that they may remain as an example of those qualities for future generations (I,25).

As for the centuries that the epic poet intended to instruct, their time did come. It was precisely the era of Don Qui-

[4]Plato, *Protagoras, Plato, 1V,* ed. & tr. W. R. M. Lamb, Harvard University Press, 1924.

xote, who testifies that for a true disciple like himself, time has only served to confirm Homer's exemplary virtue and his wisdom.

In this light, Homer becomes the object of general belief and imitation, providing a code of morality, a summary of wisdom, indeed, a compendium of the most diverse knowledge. And he is equally a storehouse of practical information. Every discussion can be settled by reference to him. Anything can be glorified: islands, hair, the nobility, even flight in the face of the enemy,[5] by the fact that Homer mentions it somewhere in his work. This too is Don Quixote's method: he celebrates melancholy, for example, because it is sanctioned by Amadis. The Homeric precedent is conclusive evidence even when it serves to bolster two perfectly contrary opinions (on the nobility, for example, which may be defended or attacked according to the same Homeric reference). The poet is thus infallible and all-encompassing. He has seen everything, known everything, said everything. His work is a complete encyclopedia, a bible on which all thought and life, indeed all literature, must be patterned.

Homeric infallibility could not be questioned without provoking the suspicion, if not the judgment, of sacrilege. (As far as Don Quixote is concerned, Amadis' infallibility derives strictly from Homer's.) Very soon, however, this dogma came to seem shocking to those disillusioned or embarrassed by the national myth who preferred to uncritical devotion a careful—often picayune—study of the texts. Believers might simply close their eyes. Yet the slightest scrutiny of the two Homeric poems reveals errors, fallacies, and scarcely plausible, even foolish, statements. This, for zealous and even somewhat malicious critics, was quite

[5]Cf. F. Buffière, op. cit.

enough to shed serious doubt on Homeric infallibility and omniscience. For instance, Achilles unleashes his celebrated anger at mules and dogs, which is ridiculous, since these beasts cannot be considered responsible agents. In the *Odyssey*, Odysseus fasts 10 days consecutively when he is shipwrecked; this is scarcely credible. And how can we believe that, following the battle with the Kikones, he accidentally loses precisely six men from each of his ships? There is so much imprecision, so many glaring superstitions and suspect turns of plot, that we begin to wonder if the epic events themselves—the Trojan War, the voyage of Odysseus—are not also purely fictitious. This is the opinion of John Chrysostom, for example, who sets out to prove that Troy was never taken and that Homer is wholly unreliable, since he records events he did not witness firsthand. (The objection is familiar to Don Quixote and makes him furious. Nonetheless, he reserves the right to use it against Sancho, who is neither inspired nor deeply rooted in a tradition and therefore can only babble invented nonsense.[6]) How can we speak of truth and knowledge when we are confronted with a tissue of fictions in which the author's caprice, ignorance, heedlessness, and the requirements of versification clearly play a greater role than attention to reality and logic? We can certainly read Homer for pleasure; but since he tosses together truth and falsehood, the historic and the imaginary, precise facts and superstitions, it would be foolish to turn to him for instruction and even more so to hold him in adulation.

[6]In the story, "Misfortune comes to him who seeks it," Sancho mingles many folk elements. Listening to the portrait of the shepherdess Torralba, "a round, fat girl . . . with a faint mustache; I can almost see her here," Sancho exclaims. "Did you know her, then?" asks Don Quixote. It is the only time that he shows himself to be skeptical, and it is true that Sancho's authority here is questionable.

Here we find the principal argument of the curate and the barber, who endlessly confuse epic *truth* with the author's *veracity,* the *accuracy* or *verisimilitude* of the events described, or the authenticity of an eyewitness report. Naturally, nothing exasperated Don Quixote so much as this confusion, for he understands that epic truth is not dependent upon demonstrable proof. If we are incapable of feeling it and living it, and if we insist on lumping together truth, veracity, verisimilitude, and verifiability, then we must extend to Homer the censure we reserve for the chivalric romance (which has been rendered defenseless by the rather cowardly contempt of scholars. For Amadis offers the same kind of truth we find in the *Iliad* and the *Odyssey.* If we think the romance "is a lie, then it must be that there was no Hector nor Achilles nor Trojan War nor Twelve Peers of France nor King Arthur of England who to this day goes about in the form of a raven and is expected to reappear in his kingdom at any time" (I,49). (We should note in passing the accuracy of Don Quixote's judgment, which establishes the historically precise correspondence between the Greek epic, the French *chanson de geste,* and the Breton epic cycles from which Amadis effectively derives.) With the sure intuition that guides all his literary insights, Don Quixote divines that Homer was attacked long ago by the same curates and barbers who now make him suffer. Therefore, he has even more reason to affirm his solidarity with the writer he considers the inspiration of all poetry.

The logical critique of Homer must of course be accompanied by a moral critique if the gods and heroes are to be divested of their vital function as paradigms. Most of the Greeks reasoned spontaneously, just as Don Quixote does. They were not much concerned with scrutinizing the exemplary value of the epic too closely. They felt it and believed in it by virtue of the exceptional epic *situation,* a situation in which everything is on a grand scale and consequently beings and objects are revealed by an appropriate mark of grandeur. Once we reject this tacit correspondence between the scale of the model and its real value, the whole exemplary function of the epic is called into question. Having pointed out Homer's illogic, we are led to marshal proof of his immorality, an easy enough task, since, as we know, his gods and heroes are not exactly paragons of virtue. Odysseus is a liar and his lies cannot always be excused by necessity, though they might pass for the underside of his resourcefulness. What of his celebrated courage? At least once, he is routed by the enemy, though admittedly he is the last to flee. His life's ideal—"nothing is more beautiful than a table piled high with bread and meats"—hardly deserves to be admired and imitated forever, and it is doubtful that a Renaissance reader would have found him a convincing model of temperance. As for the other Homeric heroes, they completely lack firmness of character and are generally self-pitying whiners. Achilles weeps at the affront he suffers from Agamemnon; he weeps for Patrocles as Priam weeps for Hector, with as little self-control as the sailors of Odysseus, who pull their hair out at the least adversity. Odysseus himself is given to hysterical outbursts. At Alkínoös' palace he dissolves into tears while hearing the story of his own misfortunes, and with Circe he sobs, tossing on her bed. Where is the manliness, the courage, the spiritual power of these poems, which are deluged by the tears of heroes and, if anything, encourage a flabby sentimentality? (Don Quixote is ravished by these transports of epic suffering and imitates them as best he can.) Where is the morality of the author who evidently revels in the impropriety of his stories?

Nothing is more scandalous than the loves of Zeus and Hera for Ida. In fact Homer dwells in his descriptions on certain circumstances that make these episodes quite simply obscene. And what of the adultery of Ares and Aphrodite, unleashing not the reprobation but the laughter of the gods?

Indeed, Homer's immorality is flagrant, and, what is worse, goes hand in hand with impiety, for in his tales the gods seem bent on rivaling the concupiscence and depravity of men. They quarrel, deceive each other, reduce each other to mutual bondage, perjure themselves. They commit adultery and incest (Zeus, after all, is married to his sister Hera); moreover, they are entirely capricious, meddling dilettantes and heedless liars. They are also vulnerable—Aphrodite is wounded by a mortal, Diomedes—and self-pitying—Zeus gives a painful performance in weeping over the death of his son like any simple mortal. Finally, they undergo the most improbable metamorphoses, comparable only to the tricks of a bad magician. And not only heaven is demeaned by Homer's description. Hades is a soulless place, dull and miserable, scarcely an attraction for the warriors who are supposed to be happy there. Anyone with a sense of grandeur and divine dignity must be profoundly shocked by Olympos and its customs, marked as they are by such degrading anthropomorphism. Homer must therefore relinquish any claim to general veneration. Indeed, he deserves our contempt and a punishment befitting his crimes. (Pythagoras, according to his biographer, claimed to have seen the soul of Homer in hell, suspended from a tree surrounded by serpents, doing penance for his impiety.) Outraged moral critics are quite right then to consign the two Homeric poems to the fire.

Even so briefly summarized, the ideas of antiquity illustrate the two diametrically opposed concepts that will subsequently dominate literary history. According to the first,
the written text demands a naïve faith independent of its
contents or pragmatic value. Paradoxically, the strongest
champions of epic truth are those who care least about its
application to real life. (This paradox is precisely the point of
departure for *Don Quixote*.) The opposite view is that literature in fact has nothing at all to say about life. The illusions it
creates are dangerously seductive, but the literary work is
not *true*. It is just "literary" in the pejorative sense. Homer's
works are declared as contemptible and as ineffectual as any
romance, yet paradoxically his influence is regarded as pernicious. By a contradiction that is not clear, literature is both
impotent and insidious, no more than an occasion for error,
or worse, sin. Even today, the total, spontaneous faith that
literature inspires is sometimes threatened by logic and
puritanism, those two enemies that remain stubbornly resis-
tant in spite of Don Quixote's heroic efforts.

One must note, however, that the scales are not equally
balanced between Homer's apologists and his detractors.
The apologists may sometimes reason badly, but they tap
unconscious forces that always favor the poet. Their adversaries, on the other hand, are weakened by a residue of faith
that they must fight in themselves. The most honest
philosophers are ready to acknowledge this. Socrates, for
example, admits in remarkably quixotic terms that reasoning requires great effort in order to "prevent a man from
lapsing back into the passion for imaginings that enchanted
his childhood and still enchants the masses . . . ."[7] Against
this enchantment, which plunges every man back to his

[7]Plato, *Republic III.*

origins and to the legendary beginnings of his people, philosophy is finally powerless. It can criticize the epic, but not destroy it; for the individual and the human family that created the epic are bound to it by primary and indissoluble ties.

Plato himself, however, conducts a most vigorous simultaneous defense of philosophy, religion, and morality. Surely his indictment of the epic had a significant influence on the ideas of his time. Indeed, he forced the apologists to revise their argumentation, or rather devise a new and more persuasive method of interpretation; for the accusations against Homer were too serious to go unanswered, though it was dangerous to undertake their refutation and particularly difficult to do so coherently. If one wanted to save Homer, it was necessary to think of more effective ways to end a debate that by its nature was already verging on sacrilege.

Happily, two such means were found: the theory of poetic inspiration and the method of allegorical exegesis. By an extension of the Platonic argument, the notion of poetic inspiration allows a complete and fairly consistent explanation of Homeric perfection. The poet is in direct communion with the Muses or Apollo. He participates in the divine. He does not contemplate the external, empirically perceived world, but the world of the immortals from which he receives his vision. Doubtless inspiration is not a permanent state, and even Homer, the most inspired of poets, sometimes finds himself at the mercy of his imagination and sensibility (only in these cases falling under Plato's censure). For the most part, however, he communicates with the divine and then reports his vision, though he often disguises it in rather crude material form. Thus the loves of Zeus and

Hera for Ida and the adultery of Ares and Aphrodite represent mystical love, and not, as the poet's detractors believe,
a lewd low comedy. Although episodes may seem shocking, they nonetheless contain a revelation that is ultimately
divine in nature. We know this from the *Odyssey*. Demódokos, the bard who is a self-portrait of Homer, and
Phemius, who "knew the works of gods and men," are said
to emerge from the very bosom of God to enlighten
mortals—hence their infallible knowledge and truth.

The second expedient adopted by Homer's apologists has
had extraordinary good fortune over time. The allegorical
method allows most of the problems posed by textual
analysis to be resolved, or more accurately, to be eluded. Its
flexibility and its seductive capacity for generating meanings that cannot be verified are two qualities that probably
explain the favor it has enjoyed not only in ancient Greece
but in the later interpretations of sacred Jewish and Christian
texts and subsequently of the secular literature of the West.
Allegorical exegesis was truly Homer's salvation. All objec-
tions based only on the letter, or the apparent meaning, of
the texts could be silenced by insisting that the hidden meaning alone constituted an expression of the poet's real intentions. Once the essential relationship between the image and
the real object is discovered, with the help of an appropriate
code (which evidently varied according to the case), Homer
could be justified, for one could prove that he had actually
written scientific, philosophical, mystical, even political
treatises, all in the guise of fictional narratives. Of course the
ordinary reader, engaged (in the double sense of the word)
exclusively in the story he is being told, cannot possibly
understand the allegorist's disdain for every concrete aspect
of the work. The rupture between the allegorist and the

average reader is complete. Heraclitis the Rhetorician[8] speaks on the side of the exegetes:

If there are ignorant fools who do not hear the allegorical language of Homer; who do not know how to penetrate the mysteries of his wisdom; who are incapable of discerning the truth and reject it; who do not recognize the voice of philosophy and engage themselves in the appearances of fiction: let them clear out of our way. For we who are sanctified by the sacred waters will proceed along the path of the holy truth, taking our two poems as our guides . . . .

For the initiated, Homer is more than a guide and a master, he is a saint representing the highest spiritual authority. But at the same time his poetry is relegated to the rank of a trivial fiction, suited only to trap the ignorant. The canonisation of Homer, then, involves the debasement of literature, which, being no more than a useless trompe-l'oeil, might as well cease to exist.

Homer then must be read as a prophet who articulates the very doctrines and beliefs on which Greek man based his spiritual life. His work is a secret treatise on nature and the spirit, providing the answers to all human problems and all the rules needed for the right conduct of life and thought. Naturally, each reader interprets this treatise from his own perspective with the tools provided by his particular formative experience, his convictions, or the doctrine of his school. The "holy truth" has many unlikely faces, but no one is very disturbed by this. (And the later exegetes, who knew the work of their predecessors, limited their contributions to rather anomalous pastiches of the earlier readings.) In the course of the centuries, the scholars of antiquity[9]

[8] Cf. Buffière, op. cit.

[9] Cf. Felix Buffière: I have abundantly drawn from this frequently cited work. This valuable book shows the general tendencies of Homeric exegesis that have set the pattern for literary exegesis, and, in particular, for the commentary on *Don Quixote,* as we have already mentioned.

came to recognize that Homer had equalled or surpassed later specialists in his treatises on physics, astronomy, medicine, geography, and history. Further, his two poems were read as a complete doctrine of the soul, a book teaching the knowledge of good and evil, a manual of right living, a political treatise on the relations between the individual and the city-state, and finally a theological work, a mystical poem revealing not only the nature of the material world, but the laws and mysteries of the beyond. While the *Iliad* is most frequently the actual subject of naturalist exegesis, it is the *Odyssey,* with its Sirens, its Circe, its monsters, and its suffering heroes, that has consistently nourished mystical speculations. The two books, then, embracing the totality of human preoccupations and knowledge, offer each man that portion of truth suited to his situation and his spiritual needs. By the end of the Hellenistic era, Homer had endured so long and achieved such immense prestige that it was natural to consider his poems sacred and eternal.

Taken as a whole, Homeric exegesis seems remarkably parallel to the "superstitious" criticism that is directed at Cervantes and that seems fated to play a part as well in the posthumous destiny of every truly quixotic work. It displays the same intellectual disorder, the same apologetic enthusiasm, the same tendency to generalization and absolute statement. Excessive, perhaps even anomalous, it rests, nevertheless, on a conviction of the ancients that has often been supported by the vast research of modern scholars and philologists. With a tenacious if befuddled intuition, antiquity almost unanimously identified its own thought with the belief in the epic's "holy truth."

Curiously enough, an analogous notion has come to enjoy some currency in relatively recent times. In the last century, the Brothers Grimm interpreted the epic as unimpeachable testimony to the life of a people in that remote, mysterious epoch when history and poetry were still one. "The epic assimilates all that a nation has undergone, whether in reality or in the imagination, all that an occult tradition has bequeathed it. The epic does not compile facts, but seizes upon aspects of reality that bear witness to the spirit. This exalted way of interpreting the real world is uniquely its own, indeed its very essence . . . ." [10] The holy truth here, in this Romantic view, is the privilege of the entire people, the inspiration that enables a human group to express itself in its collective totality: "I can never imagine," writes Jacob Grimm, "that a Homer actually existed, or an author of the *Nibelungenlied* . . . . It is the whole people who created the epic. It would be absurd for an individual to contemplate such a creation, since the epic must evolve organically and cannot be written by any single poet . . . . [11]

This conception of Romantic philology, in which the divinely inspired poet is not a man but a people, was to revolutionize the scholarly world and spark innumerable controversies that are still far from settled. The romantic view would probably not have shocked the sensibility of the ancients, who perceived that such an encompassing work, speaking so directly to the collective soul, must exceed the possibilities of the individual. After the Romantic revolution, which put the emphasis on the Aryan origins of the epic and established close concordances between all the European epic cycles, [12] Homer became the stake in an intellectual battle that continued into the twentieth century, though perhaps by now it has lost some of its violence. The

[10]Joseph Bédier, *Légendes épiques,* Champion, 1921.

[11]Bédier, op. cit.

[12]Cf. Marthe Robert, Preface to *Contes de Grimm,* Club Français du Livre, 1959. The German philologists, obsessed by the idea of the unity of all European literatures, have attributed to a common source the folk tales in the epic and the German tales that they collected themselves.

remarkable thing is that whether modern scholars propose a collective epic creation or choose to see Homer as an author in the modern sense of the word, whether they consider him responsible for one or both poems, they nonetheless support the idea of an epic truth, inferring a kind of transcendence from the epic's mode of transmission. "The epic," says Joseph Bédier,[13] "develops by the play of an internal and essential dynamic. The people produce it in the days of their childhood and youth, and thus it preserves the integrity of their primitive customs. The epic, therefore, is completely unsophisticated; it has a purity, a perfection, at each stage of its development. . . . The epic is revealed truth. . . ." Even a writer who attributes the *Iliad* and the *Odyssey* to different authors, and therefore cannot completely accept this thesis of "revelation," affirms the singular authority of the epic, an authority that seems to be almost a generic virtue of the work itself rather than a result of the poet's gift. G. Germain[14] says that the *Iliad* is "The true war, the truth of all war." The Homeric prophecy, in other words, supersedes history, transcending both past and future.

What scholars have advanced through laborious research has also been affirmed by imaginative writers as an immediate intuition. Péguy's Homer is purity incarnate and Claudel's biblical commentary on the *Iliad* is cut from the same cloth: "But here is Priam who leaves the incomprehensible City. He leaves the Father of the incomprehensible city. He leaves God who comes to ask pardon of his creature. He leaves the Father who comes to reclaim his son."[15] It is only natural as well that a philosopher should identify

[13]Op. cit.
[14]Homère, Editions du Seuil, 1958.
[15]Preface to the *Iliad* in: *L'Iliade illustré par la céramique,* de Notor, Bordeaux, 1950.

the casting of Achilles' shield with the creation of the world. ("Achilles' shield is embellished with thoughts, the Homeric reverie begins. The world is newly created, as it is, as it will be. Here is something greater than the Bible, since the externalized god [le dieu séparé] could create the world only once . . . ."[16]) And if the *Odyssey* is compared to the *Book of Job*,[17] Odysseus is rated above one of the most revered figures of the Bible. The moderns, in their own way, have arrived at an attitude of piety and gratitude toward Homer fully equal to that of the ancients.

With the tools of scholarly critique and the intuitive insights of imaginative writing, exegesis continues to enrich our understanding of Homer. Modern readers, like the ancients, try to penetrate the manifest level of the poems to reach their hidden truth. Only such a truth, it seems, might be profound enough to explain Homer's universal prestige. We can assume that the first allegorists would not have found absurd Victor Bérard's geographical commentary, or even the psychoanalytic interpretation of mythic themes that treats the plot as a puzzle—not a significant departure from the early exegetical tradition. The epic truths have undoubtedly changed their aspects according to the various sciences that have underwritten them, but no one has thought of denying them. On the contrary, new uses are discovered for them in the most diverse realms of intellectual inquiry. Just as philosophy, metaphysics, mathematics, medicine or astronomy once did, today the humanities exalt the Homeric epic and its secret, tantalizing message which may be considered a profound psychological truth or the expression of a certain stage of culture, allowing us to reconstruct a society complete with its beliefs, its customs,

[16]Alain, *Propos de litterature* (cited by Buffière), Hartmann, 1942.
[17]G. Audisio, *Ulysse ou l'Intelligence,* Gallimard, 1945.

and its technology. In any case, the idea of epic meaning goes far beyond the apparent contents of the epic plot and pervades all of Western literature, largely determining the way it sees itself. This literature has been able to brook periodic disfavor and contempt, persuaded of the legitimacy of its heritage and of its own capacity to become as pure and as true, as in those early, legendary times when poetry effectively occupied a middle ground between entertainment and ritual. Hence the belief in a "mission," a "message" of art, the "vocation" or "inspiration" of the poet—all concepts drawn from a specifically religious vocabulary. We can discern here the close ties between literature and an external law that literature seems to invoke in order to insure its own glory.

This singular complicity between secular literature and religious authority is exhibited with unparalleled frankness and cynicism in *Don Quixote,* and is at the root of all the ambiguities that stem from the Don's confusion. This complicity is not just a capricious invention that Cervantes devised to ridicule a certain conception of literature or to embarrass the Catholic Church. Its existence in the ancient epic is incontestable, and in spite of the relative silence that surrounds the subject, its symbolic value has been recognized for centuries. Further, the bond between literature and religion so solidly informs the epic that one wonders if it did not have firm historical foundations. At any rate, this opinion is supported in a book of the last generation[18] that attempts to bring solid historical facts to bear on a coherent theory of epic truth. The author, who bases his work on archeology, etymology, the study of myths and religions, and the simple considerations of good sense, claims that the epic, though

[18]Charles Autran, *Homère et les origines sacerdotales de l'épopeé grecque,* Denoël, 1943.

not divinely inspired, can give that illusion, since it was born of a close collaboration between poets and priests, a fact that is inferable if we take an unprejudiced look at the language of the epic and the personality of its heroes.

First the language. Autran argues that unlike the moving but vague versions of the Romantic philologists, Homer's language is carefully constructed, rigid, and archaic,[19] an elevated language reserved for use in certain specialized milieux with which the bards probably had regular contact. This language was not spoken in any particular region of Greece; it was a composite mélange of dialects and is characterized chiefly by the formulaic style that guaranteed its immutability. A highly literary language, it was neither created nor used in a spontaneous fashion. According to Autran's argument, the bard could only have received it from the priests and prophets, who, by tradition, reserved it exclusively for themselves. As for the heroes, Autran notes that historically speaking they are a rather strange lot, neither very consistent nor very humane. Eliminate all hagiography from the *Iliad* and we are left with a tale of dreary battles, a banal chronicle of conflicts that take place somewhere in Asia between tribal chieftains who were little more than pirates. In the same way, the *Odyssey,* stripped of its pretense to edification, is only an adventure story with a rather tame hero who suffers all sorts of frustrations and mishaps at sea that keep him from home.

On the other hand, there is the miraculous intervention of the gods in the affairs of men that for some elevates the

---

[19]Ortega y Gasset, who, to my knowledge, is the only author to have drawn a connection between Don Quixote and Homer, exclaims in *Meditaciones del Quijote* (Madrid, 1914), "The origins of poetry consist of an archaeological fiction."

trivial epic anecdote to the level of a unique primordial event that must be remembered and repeated, passed on to subsequent generations. But it must be admitted that the truth in question here is purely a matter of edification, even of propaganda. The epic, if we follow Autran's line of argument, appeared in its own time as a collection of pious legends designed to perpetuate the continuity of the great heroic families who took care to establish their divine affiliations. This explains the extreme importance assigned to the names of family heads, always carrying ritual epithets, and above all the stress on genealogies and epic catalogues, which prove by continuity of lineage the theocratic origins of the aristocracy and royalty. The epic, in this view, does not deal with historical reality transformed or distorted. It is a *sacred* history whose purpose is to propagate and revive the cult of the heroes who are actually half-gods or divine hypostases. (Agamemnon is one of the ritual names of Zeus, just as Helen is an avatar of the Mother Goddess and Achilles a young god whose death is mourned yearly.) Composed on command and according to absolutely fixed rules, the epic contains only the truth of the priestly caste on which it depended. This caste exploited the prestige and influence of poetry, and expressed in turn its solidarity with a political and social system—the aristocracy—identified with the order of the world.

There is no need to accept whole cloth this seductive, highly controversial thesis to acknowledge that at least at one point Homer himself corroborates it. In the *Odyssey,* the Homeric bard clearly plays the role of intermediary between gods and men, precisely the role incumbent upon the priesthood. His song is a direct expression of the universal order, not of a particular truth.

> All men owe honor to the poets—honor
> and awe, for they are dearest to the Muse
> who puts upon their lips the ways of life, . . ."

Odysseus says to Demódokos; hence the poet's privileged place among men. For a mind shaped by theocratic thought, it is not so important whether the epic poet receives his "divine song" from the gods themselves or from the authority of the priesthood. What matters is the essential capacity of the poet to *recite* "the ways of life." This is not a talent, but a property of his function. To prove that his song is both extramundane and part of the earthly order of things—therefore doubly precious—Demódokos has only to recite perfectly from beginning to end the history of the Trojan horse, the episode that plays a major role in the establishment of Achaean order. The recitation of the epic event is in itself a celebration of the organization of the world (by which we understand the Achaean world, rather grandly identified with the cosmos), though the meaning of this celebration is never explicitly defined. Recalling heroic exploits, designating things by name, enumerating and cataloguing, investigating etymology and constructing genealogical lists,—these activities are in themselves acts of piety,[20] a ritual participation in the human and divine order fixed by those very figures who are the subject of the epic. The champion himself, if he has the *memory* and the knowledge of names, filiations, and precise formulas, can sometimes become a poet, as Achilles does at a critical moment in the *Iliad*. Achilles takes up the zither and sings the glory of heroes as Patrocles stands silently before him, unwilling to violate the sacredness of this ceremonial recitation.

[20]Cf. Adolphe E. Jensen: "To recite the myth is to perform an act of piety." *Mythes et cultes chez les peuples primitifs,* Payot, 1954.

The epic does not, properly speaking, have a message to transmit. It is itself a message. It declares, affirms, verifies, conferring existence upon what it chooses to express and leaving the rest to silence.[21] The epic never registers an opinion of institutions, men, or qualities, contrary to the view of the exegetes. Within a Homeric statement there is never a concealed judgment. Let us consider, for example, the nobility. Homer speaks about the nobility, names its members, exhibits and classifies them, recalls their origins and achievements, their families and disputes. And as his recitation almost completely omits other social categories, it has the immediate force of a limiting vision of the world, operating more like a legal system than an opinion or idea. The ancients certainly understood this and could find in a few, apparently random lines of the *Odyssey* or the *Iliad* the justification of the object, the phenomenon, or institution *named*. They were more perceptive than their adversaries, for the epic does glorify by articulation. In the same way, its silence is fatal. This is indeed the mystery and simplicity of its instruction: its *designations* (by implication, opposed to its silences) instantly confer an ideal meaning on objects and a lasting renown upon men.

All literature, even the most degenerate forms, shares this remarkable quality. The epic recital establishes, perpetuates, and prescribes an overarching order that, in turn, praises the epic above all else and in this way underwrites its power. This has proven to be a mutually profitable political

[21]This mode of epic communication inheres in a basic property of language. "Language," says Roland Barthes, "ordinarily does not permit a distinction between the simple enunciation of a thing and the affirmation that it exists (in this case, what it signifies). Naming always confers existence; to undo existence it is necessary to add the special device of negation." *(Système de la Mode)*

exchange of long standing, the more so because the epic doesn't flaunt its bias. It simply condemns to nonexistence everything it does not admit to its purview; that is its only partiality. The Olympian order simply *is*. The epic establishes this by naming the gods, recalling their individual biographies, their customary behavior, their preferences, and their love affairs, as well as their divisive conflicts and political maneuvers. All this without any compromising apology. Olympos is neither good nor bad; it is not even a mixture of vices and virtues, as Homer's detractors believe. It *is,* in an absolute sense. Although it can fall prey to disorder (this is notably the case during the Trojan War) or be overturned by passion and torn by conflicts of interest, it continues to embody and promote the regularity of the world. In itself Olympos is not a particularly peaceful, harmonious place, but it possesses a regulating force by which it absorbs irregularities and assimilates monsters and freaks, bringing chaos itself within the bounds of order.

In the moment captured by the epic, this divine order has long ceased to be at the stage of creation. (This is why Achilles' shield, though it represents genesis, is only a commemorative image, a relic on which the already accomplished act is frozen for posterity.) With the world already created, the divine task is now purely administrative; the gods are no longer demiurges but functionaries[22] who manage the various sectors of nature and human history that are portioned out among them according to their particular place in the hierarchy. In this way, the order of the material world is based on the divine order, which is not so much a

[22]We will see later what Kafka has made, in *The Castle,* of Olympian bureaucracy. But we can recall here the story of his *Poseidon,* become a highly placed functionary who passes his life in paperwork and has never visited the sea.

mystery as a repository of examples and precedents. In its organization, its conception of human relationships, and its social and political structures, the world below is a replica of Olympos, except with regard to rites (the gods have evidently dispensed with these) and, of course, immortality. As for the rest, the important business of life in epic society (the Achaeans and the Trojans have a remarkably similar organization), it is completely determined by Olympos. This is true not only of its fundamental laws but also of its mores and customs, its tastes, its etiquette, and its special character, which persisted for centuries. The members of the aristocracy below imitate the gods quite legitimately, since their divine origin is often directly attested to (Achilles is the son of a goddess) or indicated by mention of some remote connection in the chain of generations. By virtue of their birth, the nobility are, like the gods, free and equal, owing allegiance only to a chief (Agamemnon), who presides over their assemblies as Zeus presides over the divine councils. The terrestrial monarchy, of course, is not so absolute nor so solidly entrenched. Agamemnon is treated like a king, but his authority can be threatened by the intrigues of factions or the ambition of princes—Achilles, for example, though his strategy miscarries. Yet Agamemnon is not much more beleaguered than Zeus himself, who, though he reigns uncontested over the immortals, can do very little against the projects of Hera, Aphrodite, and Athena. Actually, the fall of Troy restores the authority of the divine monarch, which in turn consolidates the still more precarious foundations of royalty among men.

The resemblance between the two systems makes the visible world continually dependent upon the invisible in exchange for security and permanence. (The epic aristocracy hope to last as long as Olympos, and in a sense this hope is not groundless.) Hence the epic tends to place persons and objects within fixed categories that dictate their names, functions, and qualities. In fact, the human order conforms to the Olympian hierarchy only by sharing the horror of the gods for contingency and surprise and by proscribing improvisation, innovation, everything that might wrench it from stasis and threaten it in any way. The epic hero is named, classified, and furnished with attributes that cannot be modified by time or the actions of men. The epithet attached to his name precludes his moral and even his physical development, just as it prevents any change of his place in the hierarchy or his acquisition of some new, essential skill. His stability is the fundamental element of the epic, for which the very idea of change is heresy. Since it is not conceivable that the gods can ever modify their aspect, their attributes, or the human spheres that ultimately fall under their jurisdiction, Achilles on his side must play out the role assigned by his name (the Achaean), and Odysseus, the man of a thousand ruses, is always bound to conform to this definition. Neither can ever change. The only alteration in his condition that Achilles can experience is death (this is to be expected since, after all, he is not immortal). As for Odysseus, he may be changed by his 10 years of wandering and suffering, but in the end Athena makes him young again, restoring the changeless face that is the sign of his person. All the Homeric heroes have in common this incapacity for growth that protects them from regression as much as from progress. It limits their possibilities for development, but at the same time it is the sign of their ultimate perfection. For them to remain static, everything must be given them in advance: beauty, intelligence, fortitude, courage, a vigorous youth or an old age full of wisdom and strength. They must have sufficient ambition to succeed, without which nature, time, or the jealousy of others might deprive them of their birthright. The principle of stasis that governs them obliges the epic author to reconcile for them all of these conditions. Nature protects them from decline by adjusting the hardest laws of life to their requirements. It kills them, often prematurely, but never allows them to deteriorate or become fatigued or broken; they are made to endure physical suffering, but never to the point of utter defeat. In the same fashion, society places them at the top of a pyramid to which they alone have access and from which they cannot be dislodged. Though they lack immortality, the heroes enjoy a status in nature and history so close to divinity that it would be difficult to imagine a position more stable or secure. In later centuries, the literature of the romance attempted to recover these advantages for the benefit of the elite.

Nobility and divinity, the two words that offer the key to the language of the epic, explain each other and indeed seem to be relatively synonymous. The nobles are the "nurslings" or "outcasts" of the gods. The Olympian deities, for their part, are aristocrats who have won their supremacy over a crowd of popular divinities, suppressing rival cults by force, patience, or trickery. (Witness, for example, the banishment of Dionysos, the most popular of the Greek gods, whose absence in the Homeric poems is often noted.) The gods and the nobles have taken possession of power under analogous conditions. The bard does not merely imply this, he suggests a connection—nearly a causal relation—between the establishment of the great Olympian families and the establishment of the heroic clans who founded their earthly dynasties according to divine decree. The epic poet is so absorbed by the spectacle of this double triumph that everything else escapes him. Of the divine

world, he sees only the summits of Olympos; the mul-
titudes of lesser deities who do have an autonomous existence are lost for him in the mists of anonymity. His knowledge of the world below is limited to the aristocracy and the
warrior caste, who are made to embody all of humanity,
with the exceptional and rather intermittent mention of individuals of low birth who are in a way carnal extensions of
the nobility because they serve or nurture them. The "divine" swineherd Eumaios and Eurýkleia, Ulysses' nurse,
because of their alimentary functions, have a kind of con-
substantiality with their masters and so find a privileged
place in the *Odyssey,* whereas the foot soldiers of the Trojan
War remain a faceless, nameless mass with no history and of
no interest.

The solidarity of these two orders is carried down to the
smallest details. Nothing happens in the human sphere that
is without its archetype on Olympos. Human actions and
situations are all marked out in advance, and it is the epic's
chief function to recall these precedents. Achilles, the great
lord who sometimes takes on the role of poet, knows
exactly what conduct pertains in the case of mourning, for
example; therefore he disapproves of Priam, who in despair
over the death of Hector refuses all nourishment, though
piety commands him to eat after the example of Niobe herself on an analogous occasion. This is the bard's knowledge
and his indispensable function: he defines the legality of acts
and cites the great examples to inspire a humanity who
cannot know them firsthand. From the invisible to the visible world the traffic is intense, but it moves in only one
direction. The immortals may voluntarily descend among
men, but even those human beings who have the rank of
demi-gods have no access to Olympos; the slope and the
path are equally forbidden. The bard, however, would have
us believe that he possesses special license to circulate in both

realms, human and divine. Of course he does not say that he has himself witnessed the amorous frolics of Zeus and Hera, but he does describe them in great detail, even what happens to the divine lovers behind the sheltering cloud. Not only is he the witness of events, but he is so knowledgeable about Olympian projects that we must suppose he is mysteriously informed, or even that he participates in divine deliberations. Finally, he accomplishes in the human realm what Athena, Aphrodite, and other immortals do in the divine: he establishes communication between the two spheres that would otherwise have only an imperfect knowledge of each other. This remarkable activity wrests him from his condition and places him in some sense above the limitations of caste. If he works for the glory of the gods, respects their laws, and serves them as go-between, the gods on their side are not ungrateful: they go so far as to kill men in order to provide him with new sources of inspiration. Alkínoös says to Odysseus:

> Tell me why you should grieve so terribly
> over the Argives and the fall of Troy.
> That was all gods' work, weaving ruin there
> so it should make a song for men to come!"
>
> (Book 8, 11.577–80)

Understandably, the warriors whose posthumous destiny so narrowly depends on his favor are eager to pay tribute to the poet's extraordinary powers.

Viewed from any perspective, the epic always exhibits the same energy in its purpose. Its parts, its material, its composition, the verbal form of its narration, the stereotypicality of its formulas—all of these converge in the articulation of order that is its first and perhaps its only objective. Written in the ideal preterite, the tense of a past eternally present and eternally resumed, it rehearses—that is, it recalls, commemorates, celebrates—primordial events that, once achieved, must be perpetually repeated by men. In the world of the epic, surprise is the thing most inconceivable (even a sudden meeting with a god is foreseen). Nothing happens for the first time, the particular refers to the general, and what is just occurring harks back to the continuous past that alone gives it an intelligible meaning. In this way, the uniqueness of beings and things is negated, or at least absorbed, by the common order: the new is declared forbidden; the unusual, the unproved, impossible. On the other hand, certainty is absolute. Beauty, goodness, truth are certitudes sharing precise lines of correspondence that can be instantly known and verified.

It is true that in spite of these assumptions the epic poet sometimes allows us a glimpse of his nostalgia for the time antedating order, a time without laws or governments or rites, when life, if we can believe the descriptions in the *Odyssey,* still had the charm of an idyllic anarchy. In Homer's depiction of the Lotos-eaters, who feed exclusively on flowers and seem to lead a paradisiac existence, or even of the Cyclopses, primitive godless anarchists ignorant not only of technology but also of breeding and agriculture, one discerns the regrets of the civilized citizen for that pastoral Golden Age. Many centuries later Don Quixote is inspired by the same regrets to become a shepherd (even on this point Cervantes scrupulously follows the romantic and archaistic tendencies that already characterized the epic). But if Odysseus' sailors are seduced by the primary innocence of this rather utopian realm, their captain is not, and he gets them back aboard by force, apparently without the slightest fear for himself. As for the Cyclops, his fate is well known. But Odysseus' cruelty is not only revenge. It is a punishment inflicted upon a free creature, strong and intrepid enough to defy the prevailing order and shrug off the assistance of the gods. Everywhere his adventurous voyage takes him, Odysseus comes in contact with the fabulous powers of the pre-Olympian age, which for his sake revives its Sirens and Cyclopses, its charms and its terrifying monsters. He never allows himself to be seduced or frightened by them. His *odyssey,* which rudely forces him to the edge of time, is an experience he did not invite, but he tries to face it coolly in order to profit from it as much as possible. Flung to the far latitudes of magical realms that deploy their oldest tricks of sorcery before his eyes, he explores all this novelty, new for him *because* it is ancient, though he is not a dreamer or a believer in utopias but a man of action and reason, fully conscious of his responsibilities.

This world may be captivating, but Odysseus aspires only to regain Ithaca, the symbol of moral, social, spiritual, and intellectual order of which he is the king and legitimate defender. For the *Odyssey* the pre-Olympian age is no more than a vague memory, a dream peopled by chimeras and monsters still met in far away, uncharted places at the outer edges of the Greek world. Odysseus marks out by his presence this last frontier; beyond it there is nothing but anarchy and the unknown. He is the advance guard in a territory that none of his people has tried to cross. This is his primordial task, which explains the necessity of his long voyage round the world: to prevent the old chaos from insidiously invading the present. He encloses it within strictly delimited geographical boundaries. This done, he can go home and punish the troublemakers, servants, and pretenders who have for too long and with impunity scoffed at the order of his house. Once the Olympian hegemony is restored, as it must be, in nature and among men, Odysseus' epic mission is accomplished and there is nothing left to prevent him from peacefully enjoying his wife and his earthly goods.

Book and Life

"Do they not have every appearance of being true? Do they not tell us who the father, mother, relatives of these knights were, the name of the country from which they came, their age, the feats that they performed, point by point and day by day, and the places where all these events occurred?" DON QUIXOTE I,50

THE EPIC attempts to make the order of mundane reality conform to the ideal order of the gods, a task that in some sense is in the service of realism. By linking its fortune and its purpose to the epic, however, the quixotic enterprise encountered enormous difficulties that were due primarily to the special conditions of its time, for it became the agent of an epic order that no longer corresponded to any living reality. This order had long since been replaced by a state of things ordered after a fashion, perhaps, but so complex and confused that its underlying design could not easily be grasped. So the fiction-maker had two choices: he could copy his model, behaving *as if* nothing essential had changed since the time of Odysseus and Achilles; or he could conduct a search for the true order of things. Doing the first, he was free to appropriate the epic's sublimity, beauty, and serenity—in other words, he could lie, for he might have read about such things in books, but he had certainly never seen them. And by choosing order at the price of reality, he would necessarily create a shallow, empty work devoid of both. Following the second course, he could take stock of his actual situation and recognize that the sublime mode of the epic was inappropriate to his own literary effort. Yet if he wished to respect the fundamental correspondence between life and literature, which is the epic's most binding law, he was also forced to reject the epic's spontaneous affirmation of the life it portrayed. It was a betrayal in any case, whether he reduced the epic to an academic exercise or derided it by burlesque parody. He betrayed his model even when he took his task seriously and replaced the certainty of the epic with mere possibility and doubt, at the risk of toppling his own edifice.

Cervantes was obliged to resign himself to this last form of betrayal, for he saw the world as a jumbled patchwork, a chaos of appearances, an impossibly tangled skein of possibilities, causes and effects, beliefs and judgments. In this complicated world, the unity of faith, shattered long ago, is no more than a memory piously preserved by books and culture. The lovely Homeric certainties must be declared trifles or lies, conformity regarded as laziness and conformism, beauty, truth, and justice considered no more than the jargon of hypocrisy. The need to articulate the order of things is still every bit as urgent. Yet this confusion makes the perception of order so unreliable that it can be forced to reveal itself only if one goes about describing the chaos and anarchy that appear in its place.

In *Don Quixote,* Cervantes energetically affirms the epic certainties even as these crumble or vanish completely in their headlong collision with reality. The novel is constructed on foundations that were firmly based in the world of the epic, both externally—the legend of its genesis, for example—and internally, where language is spontaneously organized to deliver a clear, legible message. *Don Quixote* begins by appropriating the tools of exposition that contributed to the epic material: the science of names and lineage, the method of composition, and meaningful narrative themes. Then it brutally runs them up against real life, where, of course, epic law does not pertain and can have only a comic effect at best. Split in two from its first pages, the novel is a theater where the ideal book it wanted to be, messenger of order and truth, continually collides with what it is, perforce: a black book of the lessons life scribbles every day with a child's clumsiness or the malevolence of a demon. This schism, and the violent encounter it generates, form the basic plan that the novel scrupulously follows throughout until the moment when Don Quixote breaks the diabolical circle of repetitions by taking leave of both book and life at once.

Logically, then, the first point of certainty that the *New Odyssey*[1] borrows from the old touches on the genesis of the poem that justified the exorbitant credit the bard enjoyed with his public.[2] The bard could not simply express the

[1] We will see in the course of this chapter that, contrary to what we might think from Don Quixote's bellicose humor, he imitates Odysseus much more than Achilles. Witness the roles of the two heroes in relation to the established order: Achilles compromises it momentarily, whereas Odysseus restores it.

[2] What is meant here by the genesis of the epic is what Homer reveals of it within the poem itself and not, clearly, the highly problematic process that scholars have attempted to reconstruct. In the context of our discussion, it is not important whether the *Iliad* and the *Odyssey* are the work of a single man or of one of those fraternities, like those that appeared later under the name Homerides. What matters is the way that Homer shored up his work against disorder, on the one hand, by invoking the Muse (which is not only a rhetorical convention), and on the other, by introducing the representatives of tradition, the two bards Phemius and Demódokos, who so deeply and thoroughly possess the whole cycle of Trojan legends.

vision generated by his feelings or imagination. He could not even begin until he had established that what he was about to relate was not an arbitrary invention but the fruit of wisdom legitimately acquired from approved sources. This is why he invoked the Muse, daughter of Zeus, goddess of Memory, who provided him with the necessary endorsement of his narrative. The Muse is the person best qualified to certify that the poet sings "the ways of life." First, she knows by heart what he is going to say; if she is not the first author of the story of Odysseus, for example, she is certainly its agent, since at any given moment she can recite one or another episode on demand ("Tell us, O daughter of Zeus . . ."). Thus Olympos provides a sort of vindication of the *Odyssey,* a divine model that the human book mirrors. But the Muse does not confine herself to testimony; she enters actively into contact with the men she judges worthy to receive her wisdom, men who will transmit the epic under her supervision and are thus, in a sense, her representatives on earth. These men are the predecessors of the Homeric bard, forming a fraternity that is charged with overseeing the preservation of the text and controlling its lawful use. Whoever participates in their corporate body enjoys an uncontested authority, unless he suffers a failure of memory that would result in an alteration or mutilation of the text. This would be an unpardonable eclipse of the given order and, literally, a grave sin against art. At such a juncture, the Muse comes one last time to the aid of her disciple. She furnishes by heart the precise details of the heroic act, so that the poet has only to repeat them scrupulously after her. Thus, secured beforehand against error and forgetfulness by the divine prompter, he can rely on the justice of his purpose and believe in his own infallibility.

This situation is highly attractive. The quixotic author who would establish his work on a solid epic foundation cannot easily give it up. Yet he is not, like the bard, part of an organization whose members, by virtue of tradition, are at once protected by and protectors of the established order. He is a man alone, with no guarantor but himself, his experience his only law, intuition his guide. The Muse cannot help him, since he does not *recall* but *invents,* and to invent he can depend only on the precarious and intermittently available resources of his mind. Furthermore, he is liable to indulge in all sorts of digressions that would be unimaginable in the epic. For his book is not already written inside some divine head. It does not exist, but must be created, a pure idea whose utility or truth cannot be demonstrated in advance, even by its author. Having no Muse to invoke, no tradition to follow, no divine model to copy, he necessarily creates a new work—subjective, original, and hence invested with that eminently personal quality that is precisely what is not proper to the epic. The only means he has of expressing this isolation and his desire to escape from it is to transform his imitation into a crude counterfeit in which the lonely and precarious nature of his work will be mirrored.

This, in effect, is the meaning of the invented genesis of *Don Quixote* which is so intimately bound up with the novel's intrigue. That device supports the epic pretensions of the *New Odyssey* even as it demonstrates the uncomfortable situation every modern work must face. According to this fiction, Cervantes is not the author of his book. He has contributed to its elaboration, and of course takes credit for it; but in all honesty he is simply, like Homer, the editor who arranges and presents to the public an old, familiar story. He finds the completed work already written; his task is merely to transcribe it faithfully in the most attractive form. At first glance, the existence of this prototype seems to be a distinct inconvenience, since it considerably limits the author's rights to his creation and diminishes his glory. But in fact it is his passport to the epic heights, where, for good or ill, he is determined to cling. Thanks to Cid Hamete Benengeli, to whom he delegates the functions of divine Memory, Cervantes assumes a position at least comparable, if not equal, to Homer's. From the outset, we might conjecture that he won't maintain this position for long with such a mentor, a rootless foreigner and lawless heretic who is scarcely an authority having anything in common with the Muse. Cid Hamete belongs to the race of "lying and perfidious" Moors whose presence alone is an open wound in the heart of Spain. He is an unknown author, whose work, presumably, has not found many readers among his own people either, since Cervantes discovers it by chance strolling through the ghetto of Toledo and barely manages to save it from the fire. Cid Hamete does not call himself a writer of romances but an *Arabic historian,* no doubt hoping to give his story some basis in historical fact. But we cannot take this claim seriously, considering the eccentricity of his subject and his complete neglect of references and sources. A figure so obscure and probably untrustworthy seems an odd choice to father the *New Odyssey*. He does it, nevertheless, and unlike those fictional authors who usually disappear after a few pages because the real author has dropped them along the way, he plays his role without faltering to the very end; indeed, he has the last word.

Cid Hamete is invented expressly to elucidate the epic origins of the book—just as completely as do the Muse and her lawful delegate in the Homeric poem—so that *Don Quixote* should not seem to be simply an ordinary, subjective novel spun out of its author's head. Of course Cid

Hamete does not perform this function at all. On the contrary, everything is complicated by the very fact of his appearance, which is rather tardy besides, since he is first mentioned in the ninth chapter of the novel. Until then, Cervantes behaves like any other novelist who wants to inspire belief in his tale, taking care not to muddy his subject with technical information about its origins. He respects the usual conventions of the novel in his treatment of Don Quixote's first adventures: the burning of his library, the tilting at windmills, and the adventure along the road to Puerto Lápice. Here, however, the narrative abruptly changes shape, or rather it is interrupted in the middle of the memorable encounter between Don Quixote and the Biscayan. Cervantes suddenly pulls up short. The two adversaries are there, facing one another "with swords unsheathed and raised aloft, about to let fall furious slashing blows which, had they been delivered fairly and squarely, would at the very least have split them in two and laid them wide open from top to bottom like a pomegranate" (I,9). But nothing happens; the heroes are mysteriously paralyzed, fixed in their aggressive posture as if some enchanter had placed them under a spell. This *freeze frame* not only suspends the battle, but transforms it into a book *illustration,* flattening the lifelike heroes onto the surface of the page.[3] This puzzling shift clearly needs some explanation.

---

[3]Here we witness the passage from life to literature, which is as ultimately mysterious as all literary creation and which Don Quixote can only explain by the intervention of an enchanter. In Sancho's improvised story, "Misfortune comes to him who seeks it," where there is a question of making sheep cross a river, the obverse emerges: the story cannot be finished because the listener, in this case Don Quixote, does not recall the exact number of sheep that have crossed over. Without life, the *literary act* cannot be performed; consequently, literature must seek the active participation of life and even insist that life keep its records straight.

Cervantes admits that he is unequipped to finish the scene because until this point he has been following an anonymous author who has, unfortunately, left the story unfinished. And, like a good bard, Cervantes refuses to invent the missing pieces. Rather than mutilate the truth with his own fabrication, he prefers to leave a furious Don Quixote, sword raised, in eternal combat. Cervantes professes to remain on the lookout, however, for a more complete version, if such exists, with an authentic conclusion to the episode.

The adventure of Puerto Lápice is one of the crucial moments when life blocks literature, the inverse of the more strictly quixotic moments when it is the other way around. Moreover, this episode allows us to reconstruct the genesis of the novel with a certain precision. Cid Hamete Benengeli is by no means the first author of *Don Quixote*. He has been preceded by others, in particular by the anonymous and negligent author from whom Cervantes borrowed the first chapters. This implies that the story has a long history, that it has already been widely circulated, though one cannot trace its exact path. In any case, Cervantes knows the story, at least in part, or otherwise he would have no reason to undertake such strenuous investigations to recover the integral text. He insists on this point, so we are justified in viewing him not primarily as a writer, but as a reader, an *amateur* partial to a particular genre, almost a collector of curiosities. He even gives the impression that his devotion to his work as archivist comes not so much from the need for self-expression as from the wish to share with others the immense pleasure of his reading.

So we know at least three authors of *Don Quixote:* the anonymous author who has dealt only with several episodes; Cid Hamete Benengeli, who apart from a very

few regrettable lapses furnishes nearly all the material of the
novel; and Cervantes, whose role is limited to collecting and
ordering the texts he has acquired. But these are not all.
Others have collaborated on the work, notably the
Spanish-speaking Moor whom Cervantes recruits on the
spot to translate his manuscript, and the authors of the
parchments, which are found by the merest chance in a lead
box and concern the ending to the first part of the book.[4]
These parchments are quite damaged and partly illegible,
"for the text was motheaten," and have to be patiently de-
ciphered, a task undertaken by an academician who spends
many wakeful nights at his labors. Of course the parchments scarcely inspire confidence in their authenticity. Even
Cervantes seems to think they are apocryphal, which in fact
they must be, since they describe Don Quixote's sepulchre
and epitaphs when he is still very much alive. Yet they must
be preserved, if only because they provide a precious link
between the process of creation and the mutilation of the
text. Perhaps when Cervantes takes refuge behind Cid Ha-

---

[4] It is thought that Cervantes ended the first part of the novel in a rather
primitive way by leaving the reader in doubt about Don Quixote's ultimate
fate. There is the rumor of a third expedition, but the author knows nothing about it. Some think Don Quixote has died, but this is not certain. The
novel has lost its hero along the way and is completed by vague rumors that
give it, once again, the suspect character of hagiography. Yet this false
ending is entirely in accord with quixotic logic, and we find it again in *The
Castle,* which leaves the destiny of its hero a matter of pure conjecture.

In any case, Cervantes' refusal of the fictional dénouement had unexpected consequences. The hero he had abandoned to legend was taken in
and exploited by another author. And so Cervantes had to write the second
part of the book quickly and kill Don Quixote in order to put an end, once
and for all, to any further attempts at plagiarism. By an admirable irony of
fate, *Don Quixote* spawned an apocryphal book that, in turn, determined
the course of the authentic book. Cervantes suffered a great deal on this
account, but he could not have invented a better way to complicate and
illustrate his besetting idea of the relations between books and life.

mete and all the other authors, editors, and translators who are supposed to have collaborated on the composition of *Don Quixote* he is only imitating the authors of chivalric romances. Yet fashionable or not, the pseudonymous disguises invented by the chivalric authors[5] do quite well as equivalents to the legends of the epic's genesis, for these, too, generate the paradox of a work that is at once anonymous and signed by a single author.

Without going into a discussion of the opposing scholarly viewpoints on this particularly obscure issue, we can believe that Homer was not the first to have known and treated the material in his poems. He himself clearly intimates as much by scrupulously repeating the recitals of the two bards who figure in the *Odyssey*. They are contemporaries of the sack of Troy and are necessarily his predecessors, perhaps his remote masters. In the same way, Cervantes is simply one of those who have worked on the material of *Don Quixote*. Indeed, he seems quite willing to efface himself, and even to sacrifice his most legitimate rights as author, in order to accomplish the transformation of the novel into an epic work. For a collective *Don Quixote*, circulating mysteriously like those ubiquitous folk tales that seem to date back to the origins of the world, surely carries more weight than an ephemeral contemporary novel. Like the *Iliad* and the *Odyssey*, this *Quixote* has no known beginning or foreseeable end. Never born, it also will not die.

Cervantes does not go so far as to credit some divine source or the special patronage of the Muse with the idea for

[5]It would be interesting to determine if this conventional procedure, like all those invented stories (of discovered papers and inherited manuscripts) that explain the origin of the novel by means other than the imagination and choice of the author, does not indicate a desire, conscious or not, to recover the primary source of the epic work, which always springs from a common, anonymous base.

his novel. He simply replaces the *divine* with the *obscure*, respecting his true situation while preserving a useful feature of the epic. It is not the goddess or a recognized master who inspires him, but Cid Hamete, an unknown Moor who represents every imaginable obscurity, as if to symbolize the hazardous and troubled circumstances that preside over the birth of art at the end of the Golden Age. His native land, his religion, race, and above all his language, which Cervantes does not speak or read, separate Cid Hamete from his self-styled disciple. For this reason, Cervantes is obliged to do something that is obviously a monstrosity from the point of view of epic tradition—namely, to make an initial translation of Cid Hamete's text. In this case, translation, which always rather seriously alters the original, is symptomatic of a rift in the unity of language. And it is Cervantes' thankless task to repair the resulting fragmentation, though his work is doomed, at best, to partial failure.[6] We can see that the regular transmission of the epic cycle has been interrupted: instead of the smooth passage of the text from one generation to another, lengthy research must be done to recover its very trace. *Don Quixote,* then, is not a free gift of the gods. Any inspiration it might enjoy is strictly a matter of work and culture.

And it is also a matter of money, a point that is illustrated by Cervantes' purchase of Cid Hamete's old notebooks. Evidently, no one has any interest in these papers, yet they have a certain market value, notably for the silk worker who can turn their basic material to good account. Whatever their value, they must be purchased. Cervantes profits from

---

[6]Moved as he is by the problems of language, Cervantes naturally interests himself in translation. Many passages indicate this interest, particularly parts of the canon's discourse and some of Don Quixote's statements during his visit to the printing house in Barcelona.

the vendor's ignorance, and since he does not pay for the translation in kind but in goods (possibly an allusion to the usual compensation of the Homeric bards), the acquisition of *Don Quixote,* all told, is not a terribly costly affair. The author can congratulate himself. Still, the half a *real* that he spends to buy his masterpiece is not a meaningless expenditure, for with this bit of change, money intrudes into the epic world, where it is forbidden by its very nature. Discreet and unglorified as it is, this first appearance of money is a considerable event, which Don Quixote quite rightly judges incompatible with epic order and therefore scandalous. But try as he may in the course of the novel to deny its power (notably on the question of Sancho's salary), he never succeeds in banishing this mundane medium of exchange.

Thus the personas of Cid Hamete and all the screen-authors responsible for the singular existence of *Don Quixote* allow us to construct a complete picture of the muddled situation that Cervantes recognized as his own, a situation that prevented him from being a Homer, but not from wishing to be. This is the greatness and misery, the comedy and sadness of the *New Odyssey*. The tradition that supported the authority of the epic and guaranteed its regular transmission had long ceased to be the vital inspiration of poetry. It was replaced by dry knowledge, abstract and remote, procured through books and culture. The national epic had once been spontaneously understood by men of the same community because it had offered them a faithful image of themselves that strengthened their cohesion. By Cervantes' time, however, the epic was an alien work whose meaning was seriously warped (Cervantes stresses that this national epic of Spain is written by a Moor), a motheaten, half-finished hodge-podge of the apocryphal and the authentic. The rigidly structured order that generated the unity, society, and literature of the epic had given way to a chaotic world where there was no absolute value and where even uncertainties had to be acquired at great cost and labor.

In order to transcribe this critical situation, which both facilitates and shackles the creation of the modern epic, Cervantes weaves into the plot of his novel the history of his personal efforts. This is condensed, of course, and transposed into the comic mode. He convinces his readers with humor—though humor does not alter the brutality of the facts—that his book is no more than the problematic result of the intellectual and commercial operations every modern author is obliged to undertake, exerting an immeasurable and unavoidable influence on the form and contents of his writing. *Don Quixote* was not compiled and preserved by persons invested with a nearly sacred authority; rather it was manipulated, truncated, adulterated at random. It was lost, sought, found, bought, translated and finally resold according to the law of order or disorder that Cervantes is committed to articulate. It is not so astonishing that the novel, such as it is, must be presented cautiously, for its text is doubtful, riddled, one suspects, with gaps, interpolations, errors, perhaps even deliberate lies. The very name of the hero is purely conjectural: it may be Quixada or Quesada or Quixana.[7] Nor is the order of the Don's exploits solidly established. "Some authors maintain that his first adventure was the one on the road to Puerto Lápice, others say it was the windmills"; Cervantes opts for a third solution, leaving the question unsettled. It follows that the narrator, who is, properly speaking, not the author of the book but its literary editor, must continually interrupt his narrative to appraise the available variants or coordinate earlier interpretations

[7]Surely it must be inadvertent that Cervantes calls him Quixano at the end.

with his own commentaries. The result of this work is a composite mélange of novel and scholarly gloss,[8] something more akin to the Scholiasts' annotated edition of Homer than to the poems themselves. The critical apparatus that bears witness to the book's long history, however, is not contained in the margins or in an appendix, as usage would dictate, but is incorporated into the body of the text itself and can be prised out only by an arduous effort of analysis.

Certainly this interlacing of epic book and commentary enriches the text with all that it has absorbed over time, adding to its enduring value an impressive historical dimension, which, in a sense, gives the modern author, like his readers, a decided advantage over the ancients. On the other hand, the book cannot be understood without additional critical tools, since the commentaries do not explain the work but explicate it by an accumulation of hypothetical and contradictory viewpoints that finally negate each other. In a fervor of self-explication, language exhausts itself and its own powers, giving way at last to *illustration*. Hence the book, which is abundantly annotated and interpreted, is also strewn with drawings; these are, in principle, charming ornaments, but in fact they constitute a terrible confession of impotence. Cid Hamete has personally annotated several passages of *Don Quixote,* but he resorts to illustration to explain one of the thorniest episodes (just as Cervantes has to conduct a long, hard search for its end).

In the first of the books there was a very lifelike picture of the battle between Don Quixote and the Biscayan, the two being in precisely

---

[8]Erudition is one more subject of Cervantes' nostalgia (see The Prologue). As always with something that seduces him against his better judgment, he gives his passion free rein in what might be called a melancholy critique.

the same posture as described in the history, their swords upraised, the one covered by his buckler, the other with his cushion . . . Beneath the Biscayan there was a rubric which read: "Don Sancho de Azpeitia," which must undoubtedly have been his name; while beneath the feet of Rocinante was another inscription: "Don Quixote" (I,9).[9]

All this is not simply to give the novel a sort of visual supplement, but actually to confirm the truth of the story, as we can see from what immediately follows:

Rocinante was marvelously portrayed: so long and lank, so lean and flabby, so extremely consumptive-looking that one could well understand the justness and propriety with which the name of 'hack' had been bestowed upon him.

Alongside Rocinante stood Sancho Panza, holding the halter of his ass, and below was the legend: "Sancho Zancas." The picture showed him with a big belly, a short body, and long shanks, and that must have been where he got the names of Panza y Zancas by which he is a number of times called in the course of the history . . . .

(I,9)

Making visible what language only suggests, the illustration proves the justice of the names "Rocinante" and "Sancho" (although no choice is made between the squire's surnames), for both conform to the descriptions of them in the novel. Thanks to these illustrations, men, animals, and things take on a clarity of form and an immediately intelligible existence that is precisely what language cannot confer. Furthermore, such illustrations give the characters an of-

[9]A similar procedure is found in the episode of Don Quixote's visit to Barcelona. Sewn to the hero's coat is a parchment bearing the words: *This is Don Quixote de la Mancha.* Immediately, people in the street call him by name and he is astonished at the extent of his renown.

We will see in *The Castle* that the story of K. is also illustrated by a drawing in the margin of an official paper, a drawing that recalls the negative function of literature, which is to illustrate life in fixed images.

ficial place in the story. Iconography is the best proof that they have become legend. Yet we are presented with their portraits at a moment when their careers have scarcely begun. Henceforth they are no longer lifelike characters, actors in a drama, but frozen, powerless figures fixed forever on a page in a book. That is the sad underside of their epic ambitions: their immortality is only an abstract design, a naïve drawing.

We can see that although this problematic genesis merely seems to revive a simple convention, it is actually a dynamic element in the novel—less because it is closely tied to the action of the plot, than because it is meant to pave the way for the development of certain contradictory ideas. We are led, without transition, from the divine, or at least the fabulous, obscurity that presided over the birth of the epic, to the obscure, troubled, possibly shameful circumstances that surround the creation of the modern work, a work whose complexity and precariousness may be moving, but which is nevertheless commonplace, hybrid, suspect. *Don Quixote* is split in two by this legend of origins, it is bound to the elevated purpose of the epic even as it remains firmly rooted in the prose suited to its time. Since the epic and the prosaic tend to be mutually exclusive, the novel cannot safeguard its unity by attempting to fuse them. It must either choose between them and inevitably fail, or find an expedient way to profit from their opposition. Cervantes found one by exploiting his own conviction that "the epic may be written in prose as well as in verse," a conviction whose audacity may seem rather blunted today, but which in his time went against general prejudice. If the epic is characterized by a stable and definite structure, it can effectively dispense with the elevated language that, in principle, is supposed to exalt and sustain it. It might be possible, then, to create a new work *composed* according to accepted epic rules and *written* in the vernacular, vulgar or trivial as it is—an accomplishment that is the essence of the contemporary novel.

This remarkable division of labor is dictated, too, by Cervantes' suspicion that, of all the potentially profitable elements in the epic, the ordering of the fictional material is what lends itself best to imitation, for it follows explicit rules that, unlike those of language, remain viable in every epoch. In itself, the mode of epic exposition is not less "modern" than the plot development of the usual novel. The epic's narrative method allows almost everything to be represented, as the canon observes, and it provides a vast, solid frame into which all innovation can be gracefully absorbed, though this may later shake it to its very foundations. With his double principle of elaboration and repetition, Cervantes' "episodic writing" opens up a variety of quite different directions for the novel, leading to Joyce's *Ulysses* as well as to Flaubert's *Sentimental Education*. And while following basic rules, it is rich enough to generate the comic adventures of Bouvard and Pécuchet and also the hellish quest of K., the last hero of an impossible odyssey. In this regard, at least, the epic remains the inexhaustible source of all vital literature, and it is to his lasting credit that Cervantes understood this so soon and proved it with such authority.

Don Quixote, then, is epic principally in its composition, which binds it to Homer despite its prosaic contents and language. The shape of the novel, the unfolding of the action (or what takes its place); the rhythm of its episodes, the narratives enclosed within each other and multiplied as if to defer the dénouement; the complete absence of any evolution of character or progression of events; the existence of apparently superfluous doublings—all these elements evoke the Odyssean poem so powerfully that they cannot be attributed to chance or the simple mediation of the chivalric romance. Of course the chivalric works are written in this "episodic" fashion, to their merit in Cervantes' view. But their "episodic" quality soon changes to prolixity and disorder, while *Don Quixote* rigorously follows the basic plan that contains the whole meaning of the epic situation.

Just as the *Odyssey* is an unlimited sequence of adventures where the hero always finds himself in the grip of the same difficulties, the same enemies, the same problems, Cervantes' novel is presented as an open-ended series of episodes whose number and order might vary without seriously disturbing its essential unity. Like the *Odyssey,* whose entire meaning is contained in Odysseus' first trial, his captivity on Calypso's island, *Don Quixote* might be read in any order (indeed Cervantes even suggests this). It does not develop through situations opening out from one another, becoming more and more complex, but is composed by the accumulation of analogous "sketches" set end to end without any causal links. From the very beginning of its narrative (the shipwreck of Odysseus, Don Quixote's first sally), the epic's actions repeat each other, juxtaposed without gradation and easily interchangeable. Instead of cumulatively pointing toward the dénouement, they seem created expressly to postpone it. Before he is stranded with the Phaiákians who conduct him back to Ithaca, Odysseus might have had many more or fewer adventures; most are duplications not intended to further the action to its climax, but to furnish many possible variants of the same situation. This is exactly what happens in *Don Quixote*. There is no gradual progression from one event to another, but a repetition of identical mishaps that literally condemn the hero to chase his own tail. The battle against the windmills, the adventure of the Yanquesan muleteers, the encounter with the Biscayan, the puppet theater—each is in itself an integral expression of the quixotic adventure. Similarly, Odysseus' sojourn with Circe, his travels to the lands of the Kikones and the Lestrygonians, his resistance to the seductive Sirens and the dangers of Scylla and Charybdis are one and the same trial, differing infinitely in mode but never in meaning. In this perpetual cycle of equivalent events, nothing is aggravated or intensified. The last trial is no worse than the first, nor is it marked by the passage of time; it may be closer to the end, but not for reasons of narrative strategy. Given its own movement, the epic does not tend toward conclusion. It is abandoned to the enchantment of its own circular flow, which can be broken only by a sudden, singular action radical enough to escape the magic cycle of repetitions. That is why the death of Don Quixote or Odysseus' violent revenge comes as such a surprise. These are endings not because they have become inevitable, but because they have no possible sequels or precedents in the narrative.

Yet if we compare the endings of the two poems, we can see, once again, the way that the quixotic imitator distorts everything he touches, even what he is most entitled to borrow. The ending of *Don Quixote* shares with the *Odyssey* only the long temporization imposed by the epic movement. Otherwise it is laughable. It does not conclude a cycle of efficacious actions, but rather one of purely imaginary acts, half comic, half sad, in which not even Don Quixote has been truly engaged. Odysseus wanders a total of ten years, which might be lengthened or shortened at will, and undergoes no distinct transformation of character. But he acts; he has one goal toward which he strives with all his might. He may seem to repeat himself over and over again, but this is finally so that he can avenge his sufferings more effectively and be an even more exemplary instrument of order. His immutability is precisely what makes him superior: he never loses his patience, concentrating himself for his last action. This active stasis is utterly different from the paralysis that grips Don Quixote and that, by a profound irony, is the punishment for his fruitless agitation. It is vain for Don Quixote to behave as if he had to conquer a thousand Polyphemoses, wasting himself in meaningless, impotent gestures to the amusement of spectators. The decision to construct his own supremely ordered world, free of all doubt and becoming, is patently a denial of his time. Hence the *New Odyssey* is condemned to have no sphere of action or concrete human purpose. Don Quixote becomes a knight "errant," but his errantry, his wanderings, only lead him astray into error and folly. And he is alone through his own fault. His solitude is not at all comparable to the momentary isolation of Odysseus, who, whatever he does, always suffers and strives for a common goal. Don Quixote's self-proclaimed struggle is nothing but a purely internal affair that weakens and constrains him: his bravery turns to madness, his patience to stupidity, his perseverance to puerile stubbornness. And he dies like the intractable individualist he is—in his bed, uselessly, and too late to be reconciled with the world he has defied. It is not a death but a sleight of hand, a vanishing, a cruel refutation of his life.

Because of the fixed division of epic and prosaic elements in the novel, Don Quixote is the victim of yet another kind of sorcery that compels him to betray his ideal. This ideal is, by its very nature, poetic and in principle should be expressed in the lofty language that has always been its inseparable ally. But this is not the case. Lost as he may be in his dream, rebellious and estranged, Don Quixote does not speak in verse but in prose. On this point there is no difference between him and the other characters in the novel. Aside from certain lyric digressions, precious transpositions of Homer inspired by thoughts of future literary glory ("No sooner had the rubicund Apollo . . ."), his speech is ordinarily even more prosaic than that of his companions, the amorous shepherds or cultivated gentlemen he meets on the road whose favorite pastime is to amuse each other with songs and poems.[10] Truthfully, no one speaks in such crude language so frequently as Don Quixote does, especially in Part I where his conversations with Sancho might shock even the least fastidious readers. This is not a trivial paradox; for language is the only thing that binds Don Quixote to reality, it is his truth, the root of his faith and his last hope. He can scoff at reality until he is quite mad, but if he does not want to destroy himself completely, he must at least treat words with respect.

So as not to break the fragile thread that still ties him to the real world, Don Quixote accepts the vernacular, though its very existence is an assault upon the sublimity of his idealized edifice. He is prompted, of course, by his faith in the absolute value of the Word, but in any case he cannot afford to be intransigent on this issue. He is not the innocent dreamer he might seem; he is a tyrannical reformer who wants to impose his dream on others, to force them to convert words into acts. If he were satisfied simply to ponder his regrets, he might retreat into a poetic universe. But since he passionately wants to have some impact on his contem-

[10]Cervantes relegates poetry to the order of a novelistic "hors d'oeuvre," in which he allows himself a certain abandon. But the few verses he permits into the strictly quixotic adventures do not modify their essentially prosaic character.

poraries, he is forced to communicate with them in prose, which is the vehicle of their ideas. Torn between his contradictory ambitions, the perfect hero, guardian of the purity of the ideal, becomes the first agent of impurity in his book.

The *New Odyssey* is pulled apart by this conflict between the nobility of its epic movement and its profound commitment to prose. Hence it is the locus of continual collisions of meaning from which the ideal, like Don Quixote himself, issues a bit bruised and worn. As if by magic, everything the novel touches becomes trivial. Circe turns into a town whore, castles become raucous inns, armies are transformed into flocks of sheep, warriors into brigands, heroic battles into vulgar fist fights. The striving toward poetry only increases the demands of the material world, a world often distinctly disagreeable, malodorous, and as Don Quixote remarks, intractable. Even its finest flower, Dulcinea, cannot be successfully purified and abstracted. She still retains the stale smell of the farm that betrays her origins. (Instead of changing men to swine, as Circe does, Dulcinea is celebrated, Cid Hamete tells us, as "the best hand at salting pigs of any woman in all La Mancha" [I,9].) The most earnest desire for purity, the best will in the world, count for nothing. The ideal, so carefully distilled by Don Quixote's labors, has only to come in contact with the world and it is polluted once again, stinking of sweat, work, and the dungheap. The very isolation of the ideal from the mundane makes it vulnerable to life's unpleasant vicissitudes. Don Quixote could not have foreseen his worst punishment: for his rejection of matter, he is condemned to perceive and produce it himself only in its most degraded form, as detritus. His idealism does not liberate him from the material and the prosaic, but on the contrary, immerses him in them more deeply. Rigorously ascetic, he is at the mercy of his body, which publicly humiliates him with untimely reminders of its needs. As a poet of purity and the sublime, he is not only a slave to prose, his best lyric flights invidiously become scatology.

The legend of the genesis and composition of *Don Quixote* may be essential to the epic structure of the novel, yet it would be superficial without the support of a worthy hero. Happily, Don Quixote is an impeccable epic protagonist, and if it were up to him, the *New Odyssey* would be an exact copy of the old, faithful to the last pedantic detail. He speaks like a book, single-mindedly leading a life of peerless heroism; he is the tireless agent of the epic in the novel that he leads with a firm hand toward its destined glory. In a sense, one could say that the function of Don Quixote is chiefly to deflect the novel from its own paths, to deprive it of its usual subject and impose an uncongenial alternative. The world of the novel, if we abstract its extreme tendencies and anomalies, is above all the meaningful expression of meaningless things, or things without intelligible meaning in themselves: the reproduction of purely quantitative givens that, simply because they are reflected in this way, become interesting and invested with a certain quality. The rare, the unique, the incomparable, are not within its province; the only values that determine its choice refer rather to statistics. A trivial fact hardly worth ten lines in a newspaper, the silliest character, the most debunked objects, are not only useful to the novel but can even become representative and refer to a portion of reality that would otherwise remain undifferentiated or incomprehensible. That is why the author of a successful novel has the right to say, with Flaubert: "My poor Bovary no doubt suffers and weeps in twenty French villages at this very hour . . . ." The simplest justification of *Madame Bovary* is furnished by the innumerable Emmas who share the heroine's suffering and her fate. This confirms the notion that the truth of the novelistic narrative resides not in the singularity but in the statistical frequency of the facts described.[11]

We can certainly see why neither Homer nor Cervantes, had they thought of this aspect of their work, could have had legitimate recourse to the same justification. In Homer's time there were not twenty Achilles raging before besieged cities, no brothers of Odysseus shipwrecked at the same moment on every Greek ocean, no Penelopes in twenty villages weaving the shrouds they unraveled each night. During the period when Don Quixote was created, there was certainly not in all of Spain a single likely companion suffering and toiling for reasons even remotely like his. The Don is one of a kind, like the Homeric figures with their unique scale and the cosmic scope of their actions, an utterly unique personality. No doubt there were similar figures to be found in literature, but none in historical reality. Furthermore, statistics are irrelevant in his case, since in the space of the idealized past into which he projects himself— contrary to the novelistic present—what he does happens for the first time. He remains the single example of a human type that never existed before and will vanish with him.

Don Quixote, then, lives in a world disproportionate to the novel. But he is not born to it, he reaches it by dint of effort and constant struggle and has no assurance of tenure. Actually, his origins seem to indicate another destiny. We can imagine that had Cervantes wished, Don Quixote

[11]It is clearly Emma Bovary who, of all Flaubert's characters, lends herself best to statistical justification. Frederic Moreau would be less convincing, and Bouvard and Pécuchet even less so, for they, like Don Quixote, are unique specimens.

might have easily become one of those creatures who move us by the power of their insignificance, significant for the meaninglessness of their lives in which contemporary readers can recognize their own. We can imagine him a kind of older brother to Madame Bovary, restless, devoured by boredom, pitiful, capricious, whose sad life might be followed in detail through the days and years. For indeed, Cervantes flirted with this bourgeois novel from which Don Quixote is in such a hurry to escape; had Cervantes carried it through, Don Quixote's epic career would have been ruined. In the first pages of the book, we become acquainted with the character, the condition, the household, and the occupations of a provincial gentleman called don Quixana, who is representative of an impoverished social class that has been effectively retired from the spheres of power and action. In a few words, Cervantes describes for us Don Quixote's mediocre existence, and we glimpse perhaps his greatest novelistic opportunity:

A stew with more beef than mutton in it, chopped meat for his evening meal, scraps for a Saturday, lentils on Friday, and a young pigeon as a special delicacy for Sunday went to account for three-quarters of his income. The rest of it he laid out on a broadcloth greatcoat and velvet stockings for feast days, with slippers to match, while the other days of the week he cut a figure in a suit of the finest homespun. Living with him were a housekeeper in her forties, a niece who was not yet twenty, and a lad of the field and marketplace who saddled his horse for him and wielded the pruning knife (I,1).

This is Don Quixote's narrow life and he himself, "of a robust constitution but with little flesh on his bones and a face that was lean and gaunt. He was noted for his early rising, being very fond of the hunt" (I,1). Or, put somewhat differently, this is Don Quixote before he deserts his own biography. He is a poor displaced nobleman, half country gentleman, half petty bourgeois, unemployed either by preference or circumstance, but to his distress, cultivated. As he nears fifty, with no hope of any change, he takes stock in a muddled way of the emptiness of his life, of his extreme, apparently unbearable loneliness. And, as is natural in such a case, he looks for some explanation of his failure. For reasons that are not expressed (precisely because his novel stops so abruptly) but that might be inferred, he has remained a bachelor and, women aside, has generally kept his distance from active society. He leads a self-absorbed existence, useless to others and to himself as well (let us not forget that his orgies of reading are chiefly symptoms of idleness and boredom). Being timid and probably terrified of love,[12] he has had to resign himself to an emotional poverty that leaves him quite alone, withered in body and soul and unhappy, because in spite of his impotence he is demanding and gifted with a passionate nature. Don Quixana is afflicted with a similar emotional infirmity, but apparently he hasn't any taste for the fight; everything indicates that he renounced it long ago, out of fear, or perhaps out of weakness. He has certain gifts that unquestionably raise him above his condition and milieu, but the same gifts make him a misfit. In the course of his fifty years, the gulf between what he might have been and what he is has grown wider. Hence his dissatisfaction, the disillusionment that has made him turn away from the world and seek a rather cowardly refuge in books and dreams.

[12]One psychoanalytic sketch (Helene Deutsch: "Don Quixote and Quixotism") attempts to deduce the psychology of the character from the scanty biographical facts furnished by Cervantes, particularly from Don Quixote's secret love for Aldonsa Lorenzo, the future Dulcinea, and from his singular relations with Sancho.

Cervantes blocks out this sketch in just a few pages, and he could have gone on to describe the atmosphere, the milieu, the human and social geography of his character, mingling with such concrete information an account of his hero's spiritual state and his latent inner conflicts. Cervantes could have composed a rich, many-layered work with varied situations, complex characters, all the density of a human life reconstructed in minute detail. But this would be a book without Don Quixote, or at least without the Don Quixote we know, who exists only because he refuses his real life, which is precisely what the novel would force him to accept. From the moment he leaves his house in order to restore the world to the Golden Age of the epic, Don Quixote abandons forever the mundane world of the novel; in a single gesture, he embarks upon a new life beyond the pale of the old. His first "sally" marks not only the beginning of another age, in which biography and statistics will be meaningless, but it can be read as a profession of faith, indeed as an aesthetic manifesto. It is natural, then, for Cervantes to halt his novelistic effort just at the moment when Don Quixote prepares to carry out his plan. These preparations seductively produce a kind of abrupt mutation that diverts the narrative from its normal course (Don Quixote fervently hopes that this change will be definitive; however, he is reclaimed by the novel when he would most like to escape it, at the moment of his death, which is bare of any epic flourishes). The end of fifty years of boredom and spiritual emptiness has come; hence, the death of don Quixana, who must disappear without a trace if Don Quixote is to have some chance of living.

The moment his plan is matured, the hero re-creates himself by stripping off his first flawed shape, killing the old man to give birth to the new. In this sense, he merits the self-styled title *hidalgo:* he is truly the *son of his own works,* [13] even of his "work" in the accepted literary sense of the word. The epic begins where the novel ends, when Don Quixote determines to achieve this spiritual rebirth by annulling his past and even his memories. He begins with the thought of procuring arms and a horse, the attributes that will mark his new state and give his actions a certain legitimacy. Of course, these attributes are not yet his—he would have no need to change if they were. He must invent them with what he has at hand, without examining the end product too carefully. Arms are a relatively simple matter: he has only to clean and refurbish those he inherited from his great-grandfather—"which for ages had lain in a corner, moldering and forgotten" (I,1)—and replace the missing pieces, fixing himself up with a helmet, the ingenious hodge-podge that will be such a vexation to him in the days to come. The horse, on the other hand, poses a thornier problem. No reconstruction or repair is possible in this case, for the object is chronically defective. Don Quixote does have, however, a possible recourse. Since the animal cannot be cured of his infirmities or assume a less pathetic appearance, Don Quixote can administer his usual remedy, namely language, whose magical power transforms even the hopelessly defective. He simply christens his hack to make it worthy of the superior existence it must henceforth share with him. This baptism is such an important act that Don Quixote spends four days reflecting upon it. Since he believes that the name is absolutely identical with the thing itself, he must find one for his horse that will correctly define both the hidden qualities of the animal and its future deeds. Four days of meditation are not too much to discover

[13]According to the etymology accepted by Unamuno (cf. work cited), *hidalgo* comes from *hijos de algo,* son of his works.

the unique term that will indicate, and therefore affect, such a primary transmutation. We don't know how Don Quixote fills these days, but they must be well spent, for they result in the most admirable of his many inventions: the name "Rocinante" *(Hack-before* or *former-Hack),* "a name that impressed him as being sonorous and at the same time indicative of what the steed had been when it was but a hack, whereas now it was nothing other than the first and foremost of all the hacks in the world" (I,1). In former times, Rocinante was a miserable nag—a fact that Don Quixote intends to state honestly; afterward, its base nature is magically purified, it is reborn, flawless and sanctified, for its heroic task. By the grace of this quixotic baptism, and by this alone, the old beast becomes a spirited charger, the equal of Babieca and Bucephalus, indeed the "first and foremost of all the hacks in the world."

The baptism of Rocinante represents, once again, a convergence of the two functions that Don Quixote always confounds. It is a sacerdotal act that guarantees a legitimate passage from the profane to the sacred. On the other hand, it is a specifically literary act that allows the imaginary world to touch reality. As always, Don Quixote is both priest and poet, abiding precisely by the law of the epic, which, as we have seen, does not discriminate any better than he does between these two occupations. With regard to their names, at least, the Homeric heroes are very like Rocinante. They, too, are baptized to satisfy the requirements of the epic purpose and have no name of civic status, except a sort of expressive term that embraces their basic traits or defines their role. We do not know, nor should we, what Odysseus is called before the *Odyssey,* that is, before he could be identified with "the one who flares up or is angered," or, by an etymology touching a play on words, with the man who has made himself *odious* [14] by offending Poseidon. We do not know Penelope's maiden name, the name she had before she was celebrated for her conjugal fidelity; nor do we know the name Odysseus had given to his son before he merited the epithet "the one who does battle far away." The epic, creating its own magnified universe, only gives its heroes first names, meaningful names that lend it and its characters an added aura of truth. [15]

We can imagine that with such good reasons for baptizing his horse, Don Quixote will soon baptize himself (though he begins, nevertheless, with his horse). Since he is about to change the character and sphere of his actions, he must clearly mark the change by denying his family name. This time it takes him eight days, which is not excessive, if one considers as he does that his future name must be the sign

[14] The connection Odysseus-odious is made by Homer himself. In a general way, the Homeric etymologies seem to be the products of fantasy. Some are puns, others more or less adroit attempts to recover the origin of an archaic name that has become incomprehensible; still others are simply transparent (Telémakhos, Demódokos, and Phemius are self-explanatory). The tentative nature of the epic etymologies, however, does not in any way diminish the absolute faith in language that they underwrite by their continuous usage. For quixotism, this faith in the science of words is equally unquenchable and absurd, and it is at the root of the most serious contradictions. We will find it again, no longer naïve but self-conscious, in Kafka, who has a genius for etymologically ambiguous names. We should note, too, that it is preserved in the most debased epic forms—for example, in the serial novel, in which the surname marks the character's place in a closed society.

[15] It looks as though Greek names regularly have the same structure as epic names. But we can assume that the qualities they attribute to the new-born child represent chiefly the parents' hopes and ambitions. There are some cases, however, where these names seem, in a bizarre way, to be fulfilled (again, if one does not bother with surnames). Jorge Luis Borges is astonished that certain historical names (Demosthenes, Tacitus) so perfectly signify the vocation or qualities of their bearer. This does give us food for thought.

and measure of his success. Deeply versed in the epic science, he searches for a term for himself as apt as
"Rocinante," a dignified, sonorous name indicating "what
the horse had been and what he was now." He becomes don
Quijote, or the former Quixana; he is now so welded to his
horse that he confuses himself with a part of its harness.[16]
To perfect his invention, he has only to add the name of his
own country, "for by this means, as he saw it, he was making very plain his lineage and was conferring honor upon his
country by taking its name as his own" (I,1), as did Amadis
of Gaul or Achilles the Achaean. When he brings to an end
this series of baptisms by inventing for Aldonza Lorenzo the
name of Dulcinea, "a musical name to his ears, out of the
ordinary and significant, like the others he had chosen for
himself and his appurtenances" (I,1), he will finally set out
to accomplish his plan.

Permanently flanked by his "appurtenances," duly
named and thereby transformed, Don Quixote believes he
is suitably equipped to rise unencumbered from insignificance to grandeur. This is precisely his mistake. His acts
of baptism may seem quite in order, yet they are no more
than meaningless gestures. He baptizes without the sanction
of any authority; indeed, he performs his own baptism,
which is, properly speaking, a heresy according to his faith.
We don't imagine Odysseus christened by his own efforts,
or Achilles exhibiting himself publicly under the name and
identity he bore before he showed all the marks of his election.[17] Furthermore, the act of baptism cannot figure in the

---

[16]According to a note by J. Cassou referring to a Spanish dictionary of
1911, "quixotic" designates a part of the harness that covers the thighs. The
ending *ote* is a Castilian pejorative. Hence the name seems to contain both a
hint of nobility and a sense of the ridiculous.

[17]On this point, Don Quixote's imitation is closer to the biblical stories
in Genesis than to Homer. In Genesis, the patriarchs abandon their given

epic action, since it is a primordial event, anterior and exterior to the poem. The epic includes only characters already furnished with their attributes, who are in some sense consubstantial with their names. By introducing the ceremony of baptism into his book, Don Quixote not only commits an anachronism, he appropriates a privilege that refers to the right of an ancient and anonymous authority and is not transferable to an individual. He is never farther from his promised land than at this moment, when he believes himself so near. For in reality, his baptism is an act of despair, with no impact on the world or any validity as part of an epic order. He is prompted by a mixture of passion and misguided ambition (to *make a name for himself*, as a man of letters or an actor might want to do) and, of course, by the naïve faith that feeds all mythomania.

Don Quixote's dramatization of his own character tends to have the same effect as Cervantes' interruption of the action with the genesis of the story. And the accumulated commentaries and drawings have a similar effect, burdening the story with the accretions of time. Don Quixote does not like his life, and he protests: this, in itself, is a serious offense against the epic order, in which the individual is not the son of his own works and is never permitted to move out of the static frame of what is. Obliged to pull his "appurtenances" out of nothing, to invent everything himself, poor Don Quixote becomes the author and hero of his world— and its only inhabitant. With unquenchable zeal, he manages to compress within the same time and space heterogeneous events that are often separated by many cen-

---

names to take on those that proclaim and consecrate their purpose. Baptism is accomplished in the course of events: Abram becomes Abraham, Jacob becomes Israel, etc., and these transformations are explained by interpretations of their names. In Genesis, of course, the heroes do not perform their own baptisms, which are evidently the work of Yaweh.

turies. But this is his downfall: the more he acts out different historical roles, the more he dates his acts and demonstrates that he belongs to the very epoch he condemns. By concentrating in his person diverse, anachronistic forces that transform him into a kind of abridged history, he may have the illusion of acting; yet in fact, he simply externalizes an inner drama that does not concern the outside world at all. This is the paradox of the quixotic hero, who is not a hero precisely because he lives in a self-enclosed universe.

Even his obsession with naming does not touch the rest of the novel's population. Sancho, who is Don Quixote's companion and adopted son, should be the first to benefit from this literary sacrament. Yet he takes his name from a different authority. Sancho is not the former *Panza,* as Rocinante is the former hack; Sancho is and will always be the *panza,* the *belly* incarnate. This is a fact that Don Quixote must acknowledge, though it negates his efforts at education and the seriousness of the chivalric initiation. The squire's perfectly apt name expresses his intention to remain just what he is and his ambition to satisfy his appetites more effectively, not to change them. Sancho's stubbornness is all the more aggravating, since his deep folk wisdom, the source of his name, makes him quite superior to Don Quixote's household, who are a particularly frivolous and mediocre lot. But Sancho is fixed in his crude nature, and with his puny size, his knock-knees, his donkey, and his enormous appetite, he can only tramp along the low ground of the last epic frontier (a little like the sailors of Odysseus, except that these are anonymous and have no individual role to play). He is placed a bit higher than a simple servant, but he remains well beneath the society of squires. Don Quixote imagines he can place Sancho there and ennoble him by virtue of association. Yet in spite of the Don's good will and great gifts as an educator, he succeeds only in making Sancho a captive audience, never a real partner or an equal.

The only being who might mitigate Don Quixote's isolation is, by the nature of things, relegated to a corner of his universe. But it is even worse for the other characters, who are totally excluded from the quixotic realm, and don't care to enter it in any case. What would they do in this inviolable space where Don Quixote stands armed and perfectly baffling? They are prodded neither by passion, interest, nor deep commitments to join them there. The requirements of the novel's intrigue may force them to take a step in his direction, but not to pursue him seriously. They want to be amused, to satisfy a sometimes benevolent, sometimes malign, but always superficial curiosity, and above all they want to treat themselves to a good laugh. Even the curate and the barber (who would have had fine careers in the Flaubertian novel that Cervantes did not write) do not go beyond the limits of neighborly decorum. As for the numerous episodic characters who file through the novel, they may be amiable traveling companions, refined aristocrats, or rogues ready to exploit Don Quixote's madness, but they all view him from a distance—as a spectacle, a half-animated statue, a kind of talking-machine shaped like a man. Those among this crowd of passers-by who come closest to Don Quixote are the convicts and their leader, the actors of the Parliament of Death, the Biscayan, etc.— namely, the "enemies" he sets out to correct. They react to the sight of him with fury, physical assault, even sadism (Ginés de Pasamonte, the convict whom Don Quixote frees from his chains, actually becomes the Don's worst tormentor). But their efforts are wasted, Don Quixote remains inaccessible. He simply cannot believe in the reality of his wounds or even in the reality of his tormentors: "For there is much blood coming from the wound which that phantom gave me" (I,17). It is impossible to make any contact with him, even by the radical means of cruelty and violence.

Nor can the people who wish him well hope to touch him by their intellectual arguments or their affectionate rebukes. The only recourse they have that might break his proud solitude is feigning and trickery. Everyone quickly perceives that the only way to become, even tentatively, his companion is to take on the disguise of a false name, a costume, some sort of hastily concocted epic gear. The more crude and improbable the disguise, the fiction, the pseudonym, the more the performance has a chance of success, for its very crudity cancels the inequalities of condition that otherwise divide the characters into sealed worlds. Since Don Quixote cannot descend from his epic wilderness to mingle with the things of the real world, the real world tries to recover him by converting itself into an epic realm. Thus the novel becomes a perpetual theater, undergoing continuous transformations: the roads become street theaters in which people, who come from anywhere at all, can meet at just the right moment to play out their roles. A crowd of false knights, of would-be princesses claiming to be victims of persecution, rush in at every turn in a brilliant display of tinsel and lies. Feigned battles follow upon abductions (Sancho and his master are led to Hades accompanied by a Homeric tirade in which the two heroes are assaulted in the epic fashion, by murderous Troglodytes and Polyphemoses), and Don Quixote is delighted by this peopling of his wilderness.

Is he truly taken in by these endless dramas? Or does he keep silent because he doesn't want to deprive the others of their favorite sport? We cannot know. The knights and ladies amuse him too, but they do not win his heart. Don

Quixote may dream of convincing mankind to share his ideal, but no sooner does he find a brother in arms than he provokes him and fights without mercy, even with malice. And the ladies' efforts are in vain; he does not suspect them openly, yet he is terribly good at exposing their shortcomings. Finally, Cervantes sets Don Quixote in a theater where two characters are seated, who "from the crowns upon their heads and the scepters in their hands, appeared to be kings, whether real ones or not" (II,69). But whether it is fatigue or approaching death or the constant thought of Dulcinea, the appearance of Minos and Rhadamante, and even the resurrection of Altisadore, who apparently died of love for him, leave him cold, if not, perhaps, secretly skeptical. True or feigned, actors or clowns, the figures that surround him are without exception in league with life, and that is enough to make him flee from them the moment they come near.

Don Quixote has no real companions, no one he can treat as an equal except the few characters who pretend to enter his world chiefly for their own amusement. This is why their comedy, despite its amusing facade, is even more brutal than the gratuitous cruelties of others. Don Quixote can rage and struggle against violence, but he is defenseless against the mimicry of those who would transform his splendid imitation into a pathetic parody. He is forced to withdraw more deeply into his solitude, severing completely the novelistic world of his book (where in any case his appearance is only an act of politeness) from the purely epic realm where he is king and sole subject. Indeed, his tragic loneliness is not just a result of inclination or social ostracism. It is caused, quite literally, by the utter lack of proportion between the two narrative plans in which the hero and the other characters respectively evolve. For Don

Quixote is alone just as Odysseus would be if, instead of inhabiting an epic world, he were forced to work out his destiny among a population living in another time and according to different laws, for instance in an operetta by Offenbach or a psychological novel. Such solitude is not simply tragic, but as the result of displacement is comic as well. The hero is not the plaything of fortune but rather the victim of an uncanny oversight, a blunder that makes him simply wander into the wrong book. Don Quixote's comic aspect, then, is not so much a function of the fabled sadness of the clown as of this grotesque and tragic error.

No one can convince Don Quixote that he has effectively mistaken the genre of his book, and that this is the only cause of his "enchantment." He seems, however, to consider this possibility himself when he thinks seriously of giving up the heroic genre for the pastoral idyll, a sentimentalized epic form in which he might perhaps recover a few connections with life.[18] But his thoughts take this turn only at the end when further prospects have already been foreclosed by age, exhaustion, and impotence. Here we see the diabolical way in which things are linked. It is not that Don Quixote lacks the talent or means to act; rather, he is powerless because he has absolutely no rapport with the world of hoodlums, prostitutes, vulgarians, and highwaymen who are perforce his companions. In the company of the Nestors and Helens of his dreams, he might have managed. But displaced into a realm of alien chaos, he is arrested, like a specter, in an attitude both threatening and grotesque.

From another point of view, however, he is very much a part of this alien, decadent world. He shares with it his

[18]Here, too, Cervantes exploits an epic parallel, with the Cyclops shepherds, but this is an archaic motif that is overcome precisely by the action of Odysseus.

gravest defect, the irreparable split between mind and body that has ravaged his intellect, his imagination, and his sensibility. With all his intelligence, his body has withered, and though passionate, he has been entirely paralyzed by his dream. Loneliness has parched his soul. Impotent in the real world, he is every bit as ineffectual in the world of the epic where success requires not only intellect and spirit, but a hearty constitution, an unquenchable vitality, and crushing physical strength. In a moment of realism, Don Quixote seems aware that this degenerate aspect of his character makes him unfit to accomplish his task. He even confesses that the task itself inspires him with a certain repugnance, and that left to himself he would be content to follow Amadis in his retreat from the world, when he changed his name to "Beltenebros, one that was certainly significant and suited to the life he has voluntarily chosen. Accordingly, seeing that it is easier for me to imitate him in this than by cleaving giants, beheading serpents, slaying dragons, routing armies, sinking fleets, and undoing enchanter's spells . . ." (D.Q. I,25). Don Quixote knows himself better than we think. In this moment of contemplation, he understands that he is both seduced and terrified by the cruel reality of the world that he populates with serpents and dragons. Clearly, he prefers his habit of creating optical illusions and fails to recognize the pleasure of lucidity.

Don Quixote is as ill-equipped for epic tasks as he is for the demands of real life. His pitiful body, his clumsiness, his melancholy, all prevent him from acting and, what is worse, from dreaming the dream of action that might give him strength. He knows that the epic deals only with men who are proud of their beauty and strength and have no pity for the disinherited. Clearly he cannot enter this realm by conquest. He can, however, take it by persuasion, for he does have the gift of eloquence, which is valued in the epic world nearly as much as beauty itself. Don Quixote equals the most eloquent of the Greek heroes, even Odysseus himself, when it comes to the respect for language and the control of its rhetorical resources. And he is careful to deploy this gift to advantage, since it is all that can begin to compensate for his disastrous physical inferiority. We have seen him use his gift for language to create his "appurtenances," but he doesn't stop there. He wields his eloquence throughout the book, substituting words for the concrete weapons that might have allowed him to intervene more directly in worldly affairs. As much as he is handicapped by his constitution, he is privileged by his gift, which is so vital to the epic sense of order and the search for truth; and he still believes that an affirmation is equal to an act. An oath, a declaration, a civility, a threat, must prevail over facts. He goes much further in this than Odysseus and his companions, who certainly believe in the efficacy of their verbal formulas but employ them symbolically and sometimes, perhaps, merely as simple gestures of politeness. Don Quixote takes the formulas literally. For him, the spoken word is not a matter of courtesy but a sovereign act whose effect is instantaneous and final. If the common prostitute whom he calls "damsel" says to him, as she fastens his sword, "May God give your Grace much good fortune and prosper you in battle" (I, 3), he is a knight, in so far as one can be, because she has used the appropriate formula, which is in itself ennobling. Standing on his title "Righter of wrongs and injustices," he makes a farmer swear to pay his servant's back wages. The declaration of an ordinary man is good enough for him, and what happens afterward doesn't concern him. (That the servant receives more lashings than wages once his back is turned is not his fault; having *spoken,* he fulfilled his duty.) In most of his adventures, Don Quixote's motto seems to be, not "no sooner said than done," but rather "speaking is enough." And he applies this motto to himself as well as to others, without nuance or qualification, with a faith that happily spares him the consequences. Armed with this faith he sets out on his strange crusade to challenge all swindlers, boors, and unbelievers ignorant of the Word, all the atheists of language whom he has sworn to convert.

The Word is indeed Don Quixote's true religion, a religion he serves with humility and to which he sacrifices his life (or, at the very least, his peace of mind). He practices his faith basically in two ways: first, by exercising his own free-flowing gift of speech; and secondly, by drawing a crucial lesson from words, an arresting and self-evident truth. When he first sees the chained convicts, for example, he is not particularly moved (in general, he doesn't understand what he *sees*). But when it is explained to him that these are the king's *forced laborers,* it means that he has forced certain of his subjects to act against their will. Such violence is intolerable, and Don Quixote must take a stand against it. He must free the convicts, not out of humanity or pity—in other instances he can be quite insensible—but because the words *forced laborers,* as soon as they are pronounced, require it. The liberation of the convicts thus assumes its larger epic meaning: there can be no human justice without the absolute justness of words.

Justness and justice are, for Don Quixote, indissolubly linked. The "righter of wrongs" has a chance to succeed only if he can redress the injury to words, restore their full meaning and their living force. This is a superhuman task. Laziness, habit, ignorance, cynicism, indifference, all conspire against it. One of Don Quixote's gravest disappointments is that his crusade for a just language provokes nothing but indulgent laughter, veiled sarcasm, or spiteful skepticism. He is literally preaching in the desert. The world has no wish to hear this bore who comes to stick his nose into its affairs, prying with such impunity into its best-kept secrets. His missionary zeal might easily make him dangerous if his preaching were taken seriously. Fortunately for him, he has no followers, and so, while waiting to be rid of him, the world can simply turn a deaf ear and tolerate him for a time.

Nevertheless, Don Quixote is not discouraged. He may not be able to create the living word that would change the world, but he strives to preserve precision, aptness, and purity of language at least within his own sphere. Without these, the advent of justice, however distant, is only an illusion. Of course, this activity is rather far from his chivalric ideal and smacks of pedagogy. Yet he carries it out, as he does everything else, with a seriousness and integrity that professionals might envy. The truth is that he excels in this role as guardian of words, which suits him better than the role of conquering soldier and dragon-slayer. On every occasion, he eagerly and unflaggingly pursues imprecisions, unidiomatic expressions, nonsense, and barbarisms. He intends, with grammar as his weapon, to root out evil and injustice where they are accessible. It is a bitter fight in which he spares no one and allows nothing to stand in his way, neither the vulnerability of others, nor his own. Whatever happens, he is always ready to rectify a verbal inaccuracy, to correct a vicious style, condemn an impropriety, replace superficial chatter with a precise phrase. When the curate sees him quite ill and believes he is wounded, Don Quixote tells him firmly: "Wounded, no, but bruised to a pulp, there is no doubt of that . . ." (I, 7). Like a child, he is fond of stories (telling him stories is the only way to calm him), but he is so tormented by nonsense that even against the rules of courtesy he is impelled to interrupt the story-teller. He reproves even crude types like the poor goatherd, who obstinately says "Sarna" instead of "Sarah." (At the same time, Don Quixote is intrigued by new words. In his encounter with the convicts, he is delighted that they call the galleys "gurapas" in their argot.)

As one can imagine, the chief target of his censure is Sancho. The squire loves to talk and is admittedly rather gifted at it, but Sancho does not share the Don's idea of language. What is meaningful for him is less the rigor and aptness of speech than its richness, its color, and above all its unimpeded flow. He is actually fond of redundancies and barbarisms, renouncing them only with great difficulty. So the two are locked in a bitter argument, Sancho defending his freedom to speak the language of the people, Don Quixote protecting the purity and truth of his own speech against the taint of vulgarity. When Sancho ventures to string unlikely proverbs together to support an argument (for his master has said: "I think there is no proverb that is not true"), Don Quixote resorts to an extreme measure: he commands Sancho to remain silent. Sancho does not for a minute intend to submit to this injunction—he would rather die than curb his speech. But since he does not enjoy wrangling with his master, he makes a great effort in the second part of the book to mend his ways. Toward the end, when he hears that his adventures have been written down and published, he is suddenly seized by a literary fit and mimics Don Quixote so well that his listeners are quite astonished. He appropriates the sententious and obfuscating language he thinks is proper to his new character. Yet the effect is simply a droll variation of his comic speech. Don

Quixote has not chastened the world and established the reign of the living Word, but he has chastened—and spoiled—the language of his squire.

Still, it is rather sad that this messenger of the Word is forced to exchange his messianic role for one of a finical, pedantic grammarian. Yet what else can he do? In general, he plays his role with great dignity, for though he has a bent toward tactless pedantry, it is mitigated by a real love for his vocation and a sense of humor (after he has corrected the illiterate goatherd he concedes that "*Sarna*"—the itch—has outlived *Sarah*). Since he cannot carry the flaming sword of the Word, he is satisfied to give *instruction* to the needy.

Misfortune is not the only result of this passion for language, which is perhaps excessive, yet bespeaks his commitment to a kind of truth, therefore preventing him from becoming hopelessly lost in mythomania. Indeed, it is remarkable that with such a highly developed propensity for falsehood, Don Quixote never lies except to bolster his vision. It would be so simple, for instance, to rewrite his life in flattering terms. Yet the name he invents for his own baptism is an ambiguous title that expresses both his passion for nobility and the actual mediocrity of his social condition. In the same way, he could easily have constructed a genealogy for himself and thus eliminated the chief obstacle to his assumption of epic character. But the notion doesn't even occur to him, since the act of inventing his own ancestors would involve cheating with the science of nomenclature, a body of knowledge so sacred that to use it fraudulently would be sacrilegious. Out of deference for names, then, and the order they signify, he does nothing to gild his origins. These remain obscure, despite his chivalric title. This sacrifice to language is all the more courageous, since Don Quixote foresees its consequences. He knows quite well that there is no epic without genealogies, no hero who wins his epic position by merit alone. On this point, however, he ventures a certain innovation. He invents a story, for Sancho's benefit, to illustrate the final success of their enterprise, lingering in the course of this tale over the loves of a highborn princess and a knight, who, obscure though he may be, nevertheless possesses "so much courtesy, gentleness of bearing, and valor" that he must be a "grave and royal personage . . ." (I, 21). The father of the princess will not hear of a marriage, but he is disregarded. The girl is abducted, and either the father listens to reason or he dies. In any event, the daughter subsequently inherits the throne and "in a couple of words, the knight becomes king." (Note here, once again, that for Don Quixote time is reckoned in words, not deeds.)

This theory of value acquired by love and personal merit, not inheritance, goes a long way to compensate for the absence of aristocratic birth. And yet, for all that, Don Quixote is a bit troubled when he thinks of the "sage" who will record his exploits and will have the thankless task of researching his ancestry. So he constructs another theory on the spot: "'For I would have you know, Sancho,' he went on, 'that there are in this world two kinds of ancestral lines. In the one case, there are those who trace their descent from princes and monarchs whom time has little by little reduced until they come to end in a point like a pyramid upside down; and in the other case, there are those who spring from the lower classes and who go upward, one step after another, until they come to be great lords; the difference being that the former were what they no longer are, while the latter are what they formerly were not'" (I, 21). This ingenious explanation is apparently not sufficient. Much later he mentions it again, when his niece reminds him of his chief defects: his age, his weakness and poverty, and his common birth: "'There is much in what you say, my niece,' replied Don Quixote. 'I could tell you things having to do with family trees that would astonish you; but since I do not wish to mix the human with the divine, I shall not mention them'" (II, 6). And then, as if to discount any divine secret, he articulates his democratic theory of the "four classes," a variant of the first theory and even more self-serving. It does seem that he is sincere in refusing the aid of genealogy; he doesn't fret over his place among the people, "who serve to increase the number of the living without any other claim to fame, since they have achieved no form of greatness that entitles them to praise" (II, 6). Still, he feels only too keenly the contradictions between his dream of heroism and the democratic beliefs that impinge upon him, mad as he is, through the irresistible force of current ideas. He is torn apart by this contradiction and conceals it badly by this rather too logical discourse. But he knows how to turn confusion to advantage. It is primarily because of this confusion that he is able to create the new epic, a democratic poem in which the hero, without title or birth, caste or privilege, sets off alone in quest of the truth.

Don Quixote is the first solitary representative of this chivalry of the ideal *without nobility*. He is alone in his novel and he is isolated in history, having no predecessors to bind him to the chain of generations, his solitary private life before his mission marked by a bachelor's hopeless aridity. We can only guess what prevented Don Alonso Quijano the Good (this is the last name he confers upon himself before his death) from taking a wife and founding a family; it is not particularly helpful to assume some deep repugnance to marriage due, perhaps, to a serious psychological disturbance. Whatever the reason, Don Quixote is at fifty a confirmed bachelor, a secret misogynist in spite of, or precisely because of, his jealous devotion to the eternal principle of feminity. On the rare occasions when his adventures thrust him into intimate contact with women, he takes flight. We may even suspect that Dulcinea is chiefly useful to him as protection against real women—there is some concrete evidence to this effect. No fleshly woman could ever equal her perfect, disembodied femininity, so she is a unique bulwark against the temptations of mundane love. Don Quixote remains entrenched behind this absolute principle and simply avoids temptation without shame or effort.

Of all the failings that make him, so to speak, unfit for epic service, bachelorhood with its isolation and serious constraints is certainly the most deplorable and deep-seated. The lack of a wife and progeny, even more than his obscure birth, makes him unacceptable in the epic world, which does not conceive of a hero without family ties, of a quest or conquest that is not a decisive step toward maturity. Even Don Quixote's effeminate romances identify chivalric prowess with a proof of virility. And although passion in the chivalric romance is sentimentalized and insipid, it preserves at least the memory of this profound connection between love and war that for the West is most dramatically embodied in the *Iliad*. A woman may be the goal or a means to the goal, she may save the hero or destroy him, she may serve as an intermediary between man and the dark or divine powers that govern him, she may be ultimately possessed or merely desired. In any case, love is the pivotal experience in the epic adventure, the experience that shapes and matures the adolescent and dictates the return to home and self that is the usual conclusion of an arduous quest. From the top to the bottom of the epic scale, from fairy tales to didactic romances, the core of the story is always the union of two figures destined for each other, whether this union is finally blocked, deferred, or ultimately fulfilled and made permanent. The union of the prince and princess reestablishes the order of things: sorcery is undone, the land becomes fertile again, springs gush forth once more, evil and anarchy are expelled from the life of the community. Natural law, which was disturbed by dragons, giants, and "evil ways," is promptly restored.

When marriage is not the avowed or primary goal of the quest, it nonetheless marks its full success, and in all dangerous quests a woman is closely identified with the trials that the hero must pass through in order to kill the Minotaur, win the Golden Fleece, find the Fountain of Youth, or simply return home. From this point of view, Helen plays the same role as the fairy princess. She is at the center of the *Iliad:* war will cease, and with it misery and chaos, evil and anarchy, only if Helen brings peace to her family and her people by returning to assume her place in her husband's house. As for Odysseus, his age and his character as husband and father do not make him so different from that young man of the fairy tales who must always undergo a thousand trials to be initiated into marriage and assume the fullness of his manhood. Moreover, this is Odysseus' singularity among epic heroes. He is married, but for some obscure reason his marriage seems to have crumbled, perhaps because of his long absence, the drawn-out war, or even because of the impulsive, chaotic way he has lived. At any rate, he must now marry for a second time, but first he has to navigate certain rites of passage that are much more difficult since he is well past the age of initiation. If in the *Iliad* Odysseus is the leader and warrior, in the *Odyssey* he is emphatically the husband. All of his thoughts, all of his resources, are turned to the achievement of this conjugal union that accident, error, or the ordinary course of life has forced him to postpone. Odysseus as he is after the Trojan War could not win Penelope back again. Apparently he must relearn the ways of love through contact with a certain number of women who are not themselves love objects but rather represent degrees of femininity. Circe, who enslaves men and rules over an exclusively female society, keeps Odysseus in a state of complete dependence but finally guides him on his way. Calypso is his self-appointed jailer but also his deliverer. Neither Circe nor Calypso is part of the order of Ithaca where Penelope is uncontested mistress (they inhabit islands at the end of the world, beyond society). But Odysseus must pass through their hands, and in the end the return they impede is in fact their work, the proof of their wisdom. So contrary to the usual moral reckoning, Odysseus reclaims his wife *thanks* to all those women he has known away from her: the two sorceresses, Nausica and Aretea, and above all Athena, the intercessor who guides him toward his end and arrives to lend his second wedding an almost sacramental solemnity. He has only to vanquish the crowd of gluttonous pretenders who have planted a world of barbarous and destructive instincts in the heart of his household. Afterward, he will be able to reign as king and husband, for the sake of his own happiness and the prosperity of all Ithaca.

Nothing is more bitter to Don Quixote than the brief recollection of this amorous odyssey, whose trials would have delighted him and whose consummation would have struck him with terror. On his side, Don Quixote can boast only of a spiritual marriage with a phantom composed of literary fragments. He has sworn eternal devotion to Dulcinea, but it is a vow that requres no spiritual growth or transfiguration. And though he is passionately excited, Don Quixote never steps outside his own frozen universe where he is condemned to nurse his sadness alone. He would say in his defense, no doubt, that he is imitating not the "earthly" heroes like Odysseus, but the "celestial" knights who renounced all pleasures of the flesh to contemplate the Holy Grail. The knights of the Grail, however, are hardly so pedantic—they renounce women in full awareness of their loss. And Galahad, the purest and last of these knights, is chaste because it is the only way to accomplish his mission, which involves curing the wound of an old king and bringing happiness and good fortune to an accursed land.[19] Even in an epic quest tinged with mysticism, the hero's ascetic restraint is not a value in itself, cultivated purely for his personal satisfaction. Rather it is a necessity imposed by a spiritual system to which the entire community submits itself, a sacrifice that one man takes upon himself to reenforce or reestablish the general order. This is the source of the intense energy that flows through the whole quest and also of the renewal, the rebirth, which is assured by the quest's successful end. The mystic hero humbly accepts his trials and deprivations as part of his mission; and if he *triumphs* over his impulses, he becomes at once the savior, or at least the healer of the world.

Don Quixote introduces into literature the asceticism unbound to any obedience and purged of magic that characterizes the quest for a norm, in which the individual follows

[19]The movement from the mundane Quest to the mystical Quest is indeed remarkable. Originally, neither Perceval the Gaul or the Parsifal of Wolfram von Eschenbach was obliged to practice chastity. For the German poet, the Grail quest even has a marked erotic character, since it involves the cure of King Amfortas, whose sexual wound is quite graphically described.

his own self-imposed laws, generating a kind of spiritual anarchy. Alone, uprooted, with no family, condemned to suffer strictly for his own gratification and intellectual pleasure, Don Quixote is the negation of all the Ithacas he wants to revive. He marks the end of an age—the old order—that feeds his hunger for the absolute, and he heralds something that is not a new order but an unbridled individualism that by its very nature slips to the extremes of anarchy. With his nostalgia for the past and his fanatic love of order, he himself sows disorder, shakes the foundations of dogma and certainty, scandalously denounces all conventional bonds— and this, except for a single occasion[20] when he makes an explicit anarchist statement, not by fomenting open revolt but instead by practicing an ongoing interpretation of the world that takes issue with reality. For reality is the only true object of his subversion.

Don Quixote is compelled to interpret because, quite literally, and in both senses of the word, he does not *recognize* what is. Instead of grasping things in the world through observation and experience, he can only compare them to a literary model, accepting or rejecting them according to whether or not they conform to his mental image. It is as if he had never seen the most ordinary objects. A barber's basin, a procession—everyday things disconcert him, and in general his images of the concrete world are unbelievably vague and scrambled. For his own concerns, however, he has a prodigious memory, which compensates after a fash-

[20] "Who does not know that knights-errant are exempt from all justice and judgment, and that their law is their sword, their rights their bravery, and their order only their will? . . . What knight-errant has ever payed tax, duty, fees for the queen's wedding, postage, toll or fare?" We should note, too, Don Quixote's taste for the hearty brigands and romantic outlaws who populate his book.

ion for his utter lack of experience with life. (This contrast between the weakness of his concrete memories and the infallibility of his literary ones frequently has unfortunate results; for instance, when he fails to recognize the Virgin in the story of the penitents.) Just as the Homeric heroes, also gifted with peerless memories, refer to mythic precedents in order to validate their actions and explain even trivial events of daily life, Don Quixote interprets reality in the light of a literary precedent that is freighted with anterior meanings. It is perhaps in this tendency to conform to prior models that he reveals most clearly the deepest motive for his revolt.

Reference to the Olympian world had an absolute value for Odysseus and contemporaries of the epic. Everyone shared the belief that the human world had its eternal prototype in Olympos, that nothing happened here that had not been foreseen there, comprehended and judged. Olympos was not an idea but an immediate necessity for action. It had to exist for Achilles to do battle with Agamemnon, for the Achaeans to disband, for Odysseus to reunite them and lead them to victory. This revelation of the gods allowed the heroes to be afraid, to be angry, to abduct each other's wives, betray each other, altogether to abandon themselves to their passions and fully live out their human condition. Above all, the supernatural world did *not* simply intervene to fire the imagination and make the epic tale more attractive. Its role was quite different—namely, to bind collective life at a moment when it had weakened or was in danger of disintegration. The Achaeans refuse to fight and nothing can make them change their minds; then Ares appears and instantly they rally again. The leaders let themselves go, relax rites and discipline—until Athena intervenes. Then they at once assemble to fight, to rediscover the meaning of custom from which the collective spirit draws new strength. This is not a miracle. At least we do not call miraculous this singular and wonderful energy that works at critical moments to remind a society of the very laws of its cohesion and the individual of the necessary norm of the established order.

Nothing is more revealing than Don Quixote's inadequate but genuinely heroic efforts to recover this epic norm that once sustained the plenitude of life (and art as well), but was gradually lost in the course of the centuries. For Cervantes' contemporaries, such a norm could no longer be entertained, except as some vague cumbersome memory. The rift was complete between Olympos and the real world, between spiritual ideas and everyday reality. Christian doctrine, and various philosophies, dogmas, and beliefs, had gradually eliminated any regular intercourse between the world below and its divine prototype. Man was returned to himself, the supernatural was translated to a purely interior realm and ceased to be a vital source of power and law. It became instead a fantasy, a regret, or an unhealthy longing, something closer to superstition than to truth. Don Quixote is aware of this rift, which goes quite unnoticed by those around him (the absence of norms has become normal). The torment of existence without a viable norm is one of the chief reasons, if not the only one, that prompt him to set out on his adventures.

Don Quixote "sallies forth" in order to restore normative order to the anarchic world of his time, which suffers unwittingly, less from the bankruptcy of contemporary spiritual models than from their disappearance, if you will, into a transcendent sphere where they have become inaccessible. Of course he has identified with the book that to him embodies the perfect order, not a static but a dynamic order capable of regulating reality and infusing it with new life.

By implementing this order, he hopes to put an end to the schism between the visible and the invisible that is the hidden malady of what he calls the age of iron. Literature, he insists, will reweave the broken threads linking the quotidian and the divine; in other words, it will assume, on its own terms, the task that was formerly the province of mythology.

One can anticipate a serious objection: the great value-generating myths of the epic have nothing in common with the mediocre romantic fiction that Don Quixote makes, quite arbitrarily, his touchstone of truth. An abundance of good will—or bad faith—is required to lump together Amadis and his companions with the gods of Olympos, who because they are divine are not comparable even to the most exemplary human beings (from this point of view even King Arthur and the Knights of the Round Table are absolutely "earthly"). But Don Quixote would scarcely refute this objection. He knows perfectly well that Amadis is not Zeus, and that Charlemagne's Peers do not measure up to Olympian perfection. Yet this is precisely why he needs them. These figures who are half-human, half-divine, offer him a viable immediately applicable norm that no doctrine—certainly not theology—was capable of forging in his time. He finds himself obliged to articulate a law that, again, he is the first to formulate: When the divine withdraws to some opaque and distant realm, leaving man helpless and hesitant in the face of the ordinary decisions of life, the fictional world intervenes to afford him some relief, poor substitute though it may be. It is not with a joyful heart that Don Quixote transforms Amadis into a Messiah— Amadis is a silly character from a bad romance. But the knight has no other hero with the necessary qualities (he needs a truly popular story, "known and understood by all little children"), and furthermore this grotesque apotheosis allows him to provoke some audacious questions that no one around him seems to consider. Does an ideal exist for man today that is not fashioned wholly, or at least in part, by books? Is there a single goal of life that is not at all influenced by the authority of literary invention, no matter how it is transmitted? In the mysterious elaboration of ideas, can we still distinguish between spontaneous creation and learned conceptions, between the directly inspired vision of the ideal and the ideal imposed upon the individual by family, education, and contemporary culture? These questions are not posed but are continuously implied in Don Quixote's adventures, and he responds to them with an energetic "No!" Instead of setting out to found a new religious sect (which he might be inclined to do), he is satisfied to recruit followers for a particular literary genre. This is because he perceives that there is no ideal, personal as it may seem, that is not an assemblage of inherited ideas and images for which literature is the most refined and persuasive repository. In a time when everything has already been said, written, and thought, ideals of conduct are no longer purely invented. They are the result of an indeterminate blend of imitation and creation. Literature, then, is no longer merely a collection of pleasing images. Vulgar, mediocre, decadent as it sometimes is, it provides a range of striking and interesting models. Don Quixote's quasi-religious elevation of Amadis is therefore quite logical: for lack of anything better, the most insipid romance takes on the function of myth.

By raising this serious and far-reaching issue, Cervantes confronted the reader with a new fact and its obviously problematic consequences. Because of circumstances that were in part unavoidable, in part exploited by literature itself, books held out the promise of an unprecedented fate—perhaps a magnificent achievement, perhaps a resounding failure. Cervantes did not predict the future of literature, for as we know he was determined to draw no conclusions. But he allowed his hero to act, and that was enough. For Don Quixote is clairvoyant in the true manner of the prophets, which is to say that he not only reveals the future, but by his acts he unmasks the meaning of the present. In the era when he set out to bring literature to the streets, specialized religious writings spoke of charity, truth, justice, and salvation, but no longer had anything to say about the concrete decisions of life: how to unite thought and action without compromising one or the other, how to make justice actually prevail, how to invest the truth—for those who believed they possessed it—with the force of law. Yet Don Quixote absolutely has to know these things in order to live. He requires precise rules of conduct, a code that will allow him to distinguish in practice order from disorder, truth from illusion, not in an abstract way but here and now, at each moment.

Amadis thus becomes his personal bible, the substitute for scriptural authority to which he can calmly refer at critical moments. This model fulfills a number of functions. Sometimes Don Quixote asks the chivalric hero to intercede for him, to bring him aid and enlightenment; sometimes he combs his memory of the book for precedents pertaining to a particular decision; sometimes he treats the narrative as a whole like a sacred text, each letter divinely inspired. He consults it, reasoning like a doctor of law, parrying difficult points so that he can honorably settle embarrassing situations that for him are simply confused by life. For example, he has too many contradictory notions to be consistent in his relationship with Sancho. His kindness and innate sense of democracy would lead him to tolerate his squire's gossiping familiarity, which his ideals and his self-respect clearly oblige him to condemn. Happily, the law is precise on this point: ". . . for in all the books of chivalry that I have read, and they are infinite in number, I have never heard of any squire talking so much to his master as you do to me" (I, 20). He simply refers to his favorite texts to find an appropriate model of severity. Whatever is contained in his book has the force of law, and, equally, what is omitted does not exist. Since money matters are never mentioned, for instance, they are systematically denied. Amadis' earnings and expenses are never discussed, any more than Odysseus' financial dealings. It must be assumed, therefore, that he and all other knights-errant had no need of money. Since the Don does need money all the same, he puts Sancho in charge of his finances and thereby salvages his own integrity. Reasoning in the same way, he feels entirely justified in refusing to compensate Sancho for his services: "I should be glad to give you a fixed wage if I could find in the histories of knights-errant any instance that would afford me the slightest hint as to what their squires used to receive by the month or by the year" (II, 7). If Sancho were prepared to hear it, Don Quixote might support his argument by citing Homer, who does not say a word about the pay of Agamemnon's footsoldiers or the salary of Eumaios, Odysseus' faithful servant. The admirable disinterestedness of the Don's ethical conceptions, however, causes Sancho to retract his claims and declare that he is ready to serve his master all the remaining days of his life. Don Quixote is triumphant: epic law prevails, which sorts out the primary from the secondary and creates for future idealists of all persuasions an airtight and invaluable precedent.

It would be a mistake to imagine that Don Quixote is simply an idealist in his own interest. He is somewhat stingy, of course (this miserliness, like his pedantry, separates him clearly from his illustrious models who have no dealings with money). But he never confuses his everyday self that makes calculations with his rigorous doctrine. Not only does he think there is no harm in serving without pay, he is sincerely persuaded of the contrary, for he defines the good as the absolute conformity to the law he has chosen for himself. To pay Sancho would be to commit a grave sin against the tradition that wisely denies squires both money and the right to free speech. Don Quixote is careful not to fall into the hands of the "ruffians, rogues, and bloodsuckers" who try so treacherously to extort money from him with their agreeable talk. Sincerely shocked by the way Sancho uses words to get his payment ("I know what the bull's-eye is you're shooting at with all those proverbs of yours." [II, 7].), Don Quixote is quite unconscious of his own verbal tricks and the way his convictions so keenly serve his own interests. If he had material wealth or some actual province of power, this naïve duplicity would make him more dangerous than any conscious opportunist. Fortunately, he has nothing except his good conscience and his blindness, so he is effectively harmless.

Don Quixote's attitude toward money matters obliges us to revise our ideas about his madness. Generally, his aberrant behavior is interpreted as a form of detachment (sublime or ridiculous, depending on one's point of view). But Don Quixote is not as indifferent to contingencies as one might think and even exhibits, on occasion, a surprisingly pragmatic intelligence, for instance in his bargaining with Sancho, in the arrangements he makes before his death, and in the unexpected evidence he offers of his various skills (he says to his niece on this subject: ". . . if my mind were not wholly occupied with thoughts of chivalry, there is nothing that I could not do, no trinket that I could not turn out with my own hands, especially bird-cages and toothpicks . . ." [II, 7]). The Don is not a lost soul building castles in Spain. His madness is firmly directed toward a specific goal within a precise context, namely the framework of the ethical assumptions of his age. Don Quixote is mad only because he pushes to an unseemly degree the literal application of *right* principles and *fine* ideas that everyone mouths but avoids putting to any practical test. In this sense, his radical politics involve a critique of culture, and in so far as this is understood, he is not simply mad but importunate and even scandalous. Beyond the psychological motivations that Cervantes so admirably describes, quixotic estrangement is prompted by external causes that are related to the extraordinary prestige of literature in a world steeped in ideas and words, and to the mystery of a reality that had become largely opaque.

Books had imagined and predicted all there was to say on the subject of life and its right conduct, even as the real world had lost its clear and reassuring forms. Reality's multiple aspects and its complex nuances were disconcerting; it had become fleeting, unpredictable. Things had become imperceptibly reversed: as books were illuminated by the knowledge of the centuries, reality became a hermetically sealed book. Don Quixote does nothing more than articulate the logical consequence of this abnormal situation. He demands that books help him to decipher life. Before changing the world that he sees before him like an immense unexplored continent, he is forced to interpret the phenomena that come to his attention and literally leave him speechless. It is hardly astonishing if he wastes his strength on these matters and if this ongoing interpretation is his only claim to success.[21]

All of Don Quixote's adventures spring from this need to make interpretations. The others believe in their perceptions and never question the solidity of the world. Don Quixote, on the contrary, sees everything askew, and when he perceives objects correctly—this happens to him more frequently than one would think—he at once draws conclusions that are perfectly bizarre, at least from the point of view of common sense. In the case of the windmills, he seems to be the victim of an optical illusion; and in the affair of the monks from Saint Benoit, he perceives only their evil and otherworldly darkness. At other times, he recognizes things perfectly well, but he interprets the situation according to his needs, automatically modifying what he sees. Most of the time, however, his mistake is not really a perceptual illusion or hallucination; it is simply that his chivalric code suggests analogues to him without which he would, literally, not know what to do or how to think. He may suddenly see a mule, for instance and not know what it is, for an animal that is not defined by his code has, as far as he is concerned, no form or name. If the mule can become part of a conventional epic situation, it is a dromedary or a palfrey; otherwise it is a mule, and Don Quixote recognizes it without difficulty, to everyone's great surprise. He can see quite clearly when his code is silent about something he experiences, or when the material he is working with is patently much too base to be transmuted. He can make a helmet out of a barber's basin, but not a Dulcinea out of a fat peasant woman. So Sancho is simply wasting his time when

---

[21]If we accept Marx's definition of the intellectual as a person who interprets the world without the power to change it, then Don Quixote is truly one of the first intellectuals of our time.

he tries to offer Don Quixote a glimpse of his beloved at long last. What the Don sees quite clearly is a peasant woman mounted on an ordinary colt, and nothing can make him yield an inch (he hesitates only over the sex of the animal).

We would be wrong, however, to imagine that Don Quixote is actually mistaken in his desires, as he often gives the impression of being. He is mistaken when he must recall or invent a situation that conforms to his code. Otherwise, real objects don't interest him, and without any embarrassment to him they can maintain their usual appearance, be they highwaymen or police, curate or barber. Actor as he is, he never fabricates only for his pleasure. Rather he does it out of necessity, since he can puzzle things out only with the tools of literature. Take for example the situation where a distinctly violent act is witnessed: a man mistreats a child before his eyes and he is naturally revolted. What is he going to do? If he wished to intervene effectively and to act, moreover, as an impartial judge, he would have to be acquainted with the particulars of the case, hear the testimony of the interested parties, weigh their arguments, and, above all, oversee the execution of the sentence. But from the outset of the trial he is completely lost. The peasant gives a version of the facts that completely contradicts that of the boy, who is probably a parasite anyway and is just getting what he deserves. Here a literary precedent is a true gift from providence, for it provides the arbitrator with a simple, infallible rule: the peasant is required to pay, the child protected, and Don Quixote can boast of having accomplished an act of justice (this is true for a few moments, but he is wise enough not to demand more than that). For fifty years, Don Quixote has lived a contemplative life; now he wants to involve himself actively in the things of the world. But on his own he is helpless, indecisive, and unsure of his judgment, and that is why he has recourse to books.

Guided by his holy book, the righter of wrongs can calmly apply himself to his chief task, which is to reestablish the interrupted relationship between the elevated ideas, professed or recognized by the custodians of order, and reality such as it is, which is neither good nor bad, but chaotic and, in a sense, beyond the law. The first thing to do to eliminate evil is not to make distinctions between good and evil under the pressure of circumstance, but to find a constant measure for both, preferably fixed in some other realm. The problem is an arduous one. If it is true that Don Quixote rejects the theologians' conception of things (the mistake he makes over the statue of the Virgin seems to imply that the Catholic notion of the supernatural is not to his taste), then he must invent his own. He overcomes the difficulty however by creating the "enchanters," energetic, bustling characters whom he presses into service to cement the bond between the prosaic and the marvelous that has been so disastrously broken.

Naturally, the enchanters do not command a hierarchical order comparable to Olympos; they are closer to the "celestial" and mysterious realm of the Grail. Beyond these enchanters there is absolutely no one, no specialized gods collaborating in the progress of worldly affairs, no divine assemblies whose decrees dictate human law. Alone, free to act on their own whim, abandoned to their caprice, and probably their despotism, the enchanters are openly unfettered by any obedience to the higher authority that must once have created them, but from which they have somehow broken away. They are asocial beings, fierce individualists bent upon destroying rather than ordering in the image of their inventor, who experiences on their behalf a special mixture of sympathy and fear. Their mischievous and seemingly arbitrary intervention in the daily flow of events is malicious or beneficent according to a law that Don Quixote himself has not been able to fathom. In conformity with the iron age that has called forth their appearance, they scarcely illuminate the invisible world of their origin. But if they have lost all affinity with the supernatural, they are notably in sympathy with the natural world where they surface; indeed, their name, by a properly mythological euphemism, simply designates an incurable and not very beguiling disorder. The only enchantments reality has still left to undergo are those that are generated by its own hidden dissolution.

The supernatural world that Don Quixote invents for his consolation is thus in the image of the natural world that he tries to escape. This is his magic and the curse that follows him throughout his adventures where, in fact, enchantment and bungling are strictly synonymous. Instead of the supernatural guiding reality, offering it vivid models, it is rather a source of trouble. It becomes the very symbol of disequilibrium, the symptom of the mysterious malady affecting a disordered community and an individual disappointed by the marvelous. Don Quixote's phantasmagoria cannot re-create the primary unity of the ideal world and reality, or, to put crudely what Cervantes expresses with consummate tact and humor, the mind and the spirit. Even so, the effort is not utterly useless, since Don Quixote draws from it the only explanation of the world that after a fashion satisfies his curiosity as well as his benevolence and his insatiable pride. The notion of enchantment doesn't offer a key to the great cosmic mysteries in which the epic heroes participate, but it does explain the latent ephemerality of the ordinary world. Don Quixote is astonished by the simplest things in this world that everyone else takes as a matter of course. The fact that a book, for example, conceived in the hidden realm of imagination, suddenly becomes a tangible object, duly compiled, printed, sold and read, is so much beyond his understanding that he can explain it only by the intervention of sorcery. Books do not issue from their authors, but from wise enchanters who have at their command the entire corpus of the imagination, limitless archives containing all of literature. It is because of this occult origin that books have the remarkable power to *enchant* or to *deceive* their public.

The theory of enchanters is above all a useful support for Don Quixote's benevolence (this he finally recognizes as his chief virtue, calling himself, like a king, *don Quijano the Good*). Sorcery provides an adequate explanation of spite, cruelty, the perverse joy in destruction, all the things that the Don cannot impute to men of flesh and blood ("'for,' he says to Sancho, 'those who have so cruelly amused themselves at your expense, who could they be if not phantoms and beings from the other world?'"). Sancho protests in vain that he recognizes these phantoms and knows their names quite well, but Don Quixote will not allow himself to be convinced, he will not admit that there is enough evil here below to justify the way he is mistreated. Evil comes from elsewhere; this is a fact that he cannot question without losing his infinite benevolence and also—significantly—his self-respect and his sense of dignity. How would he keep these qualities otherwise when he is often forced to behave in such a cowardly way? Sancho must be convinced that if his master stood by without saying a word as his squire was so rudely tossed around (in a blanket), it was not from fear or impotence, but from the effect of a spell. Don Quixote is the chosen victim of the enchanters, who, in some sense, allow him not only to accept the incongruities, absurdities, and wickedness of life, but also to accept himself as he is, without dissembling the weakness and the childish fears that cannot be dispelled by any book, however heroic.

Failing at everything, Don Quixote finally disavows his former self and sinks into melancholy. The questions that have preoccupied him all his life are ultimately insoluble, just as his book has no conclusion. One thing, however, is certain: the pure epic has become impossible. Epic order, which was formerly tied to an actual world order, is stitched to the present by only the most tenuous, half-broken threads. There is no more "immortal" literature, only the temporal disguised as immortal, the relative passed off as the absolute, the particular disguised as the universal—it is all a lie, the more dangerous because it can be so adroitly dissimulated. In itself, the longing for the eternal is abiding and perfectly human, but it becomes suspect if it is not backed by the courage to admit frankly one's confusion and impotence, one's fears and childish regrets. The true reconciliation of the old and the new, which is in a sense the reconciliation of the heart's desire and the lucidity of the mind, of childhood and maturity, Don Quixote pursues with a comic grandeur through the twists and turns of his odyssey, knowing quite well that he will die before it has been accomplished.

Besides, is it truly a question of reconciliation? The two sides are not so inimical as Don Quixote would like to believe. In their rather special relationship, one can intuit a kind of mutual tolerance, indeed a complicity. One of the most profound lessons of *Don Quixote* is that thanks to books, objects no longer appear simply as they are, stripped bare, but always seem to be flatteringly and very discreetly embellished, so that beneath their borrowed nobility and sublimity their true value is found to be seriously compromised. Reality simply accedes to the extraordinary seduction of literature, exploiting it in order to enhance itself and veil its banality or its cruelty with a tissue of words. Literature fascinates the writer, and enchants the reader. The deceit does not lie in the pose of fiction as reality, but rather in this carefully hidden complicity by which the fictional and the real offer each other mutual support. Cervantes' sad knight is ravaged by this malady, not by an internal defect or a mistake of literary creation.

By posing the crucial question of art, Cervantes revealed what we take to be above all a sickness of his age. One begins to suspect, however, that this is perhaps only an illusion, one of those mistaken constructions so attractive to subsequent generations and to his own protagonist. Certainly the great epic works seem to realize this union of dream and reality that is the highest justification of literature. But what about epic truth? Is it so absolute and immutable? Do these works speak of the good of man in general, or of the Greeks contemporary with Homer, or even more specifically of the Greek aristocrat who seems to be the bard's real subject? By taking the epic's significant omissions as a rule of conduct, Don Quixote implies that Homer did not render perhaps the entire reality of his time, but only that elevated aspect of reality that was the lot of a privileged class. In fact, as colorful as it is, Homeric realism is notoriously remiss. Homer says nothing, for example, about the way the heroes support their subsistence, scrap for daily life, fashion their arms, raise their children, or build their palaces. In this respect, he is no more comprehensive than the obscure author of *Amadis*. And he falls well short of the book in Don Quixote's library that, according to the curate, is the best romance in the world because "Here the knights eat and sleep, and die in their beds, and make out wills before they die, and do other things that are never heard of in books of this kind" (I, 6).[22] These "other things," which are so important to the curate, are scarcely mentioned by the two principal sources of European literature. If their heroes eat and drink, suffer and die, they are never needy for long. Destiny weighs them down, but epic law protects them against the worst things—work, unhappiness, exhaustion, and the slow erosion of life. Their *attractive* nobility seems to be very much in proportion to the *unattractive* qualities that they lack, and by imitating them on this point, Don Quixote reveals what they owe to the secular complicity of life and literature whose misdeeds he denounces in spite of himself.

Is this to say that on the strength of quixotic proof literature must be definitively condemned? Certainly not. A formal condemnation of this kind would be as foolish and futile as the sentence pronounced by Don Quixote's niece (who in a way, however, has the last word, at least within the limits of the domestic sphere). What is evoked by the stupid young girl who wants to destroy all the books without even looking at their titles is clearly more the ignorance and ill-will of a limited mind than the passion of Cervantes, who was torn between the irrepressible need to write and the equally absolute claim of truth. *Don Quixote* is neither an apology nor an indictment; it is the unforgettable proof that literature can only endlessly repeat its dreams, and if the writer is wrong to mistake this repetition for immortality,

[22]This passage referring to *Tirant lo Blanch* has been much discussed. In general, critics do not understand why Cervantes, after praising a modern romance that is both poetic and realistic—in the sense he describes—hastens to have it thrown into the fire. The meaning of the passage is nevertheless quite clear: the best book in the world still contains a kind of sorcery, and as such it concerns the butcher. All the same it must be written, and loved.

at least he has the unique privilege of catching himself
openly in his own error. We cannot doubt that for Cervantes, the best book in the world is the one that is forever in
quest of the truth, yet always conscious of its own powers of
deception. We mustn't forget, of course, that this very act of
self-discovery is highly seductive. And in the eyes of a truly
rigorous censor, a book capable of this final seduction might
deserve to be tossed into the fire all the same.

THE LAST MESSENGER

He is undoubtedly afraid
of setting out as Abraham accompanied by his son,
and of changing along the way
into Don Quixote.

FRANZ KAFKA
Letter to Robert Klopstock

A Web of Fictions

"The impression this makes on me," K. said,
"is that there must be things there that I could
refute." *The Castle*
Appendix, p. 447

I. INTERPRETATIONS

IF DON QUIXOTE seems misplaced among the great figures of
Western literature, Kafka's hero seems very much at ease.
To find his equal we would certainly have to invoke Faust or
Hamlet, perhaps even the imposing character of Job or the
half-sacred figure of Abraham. Indeed, Don Quixote is
misunderstood because the pressing seriousness of his concerns is not immediately recognized. K. the Land-Surveyor
is no less so because the gravity of his is only too familiar.

K., of course, who has become a kind of symbol of Kafka
himself, does not bear the usual signs of election. He is quite
ordinary and has no power or authority. Sometimes he is
comfortably off (as in *The Trial*), sometimes poor and completely marginal (in *The Castle*). Nevertheless, he is distinguished by the seriousness of his acts, the weight of his
words, the tenacity with which he pursues a mysterious
goal. And reaching this goal, or at least approaching it,
seems to be more precious to him than life itself. Yet for all
his determination, his patience, his extraordinary powers of

171

concentration, he has none of the dramatic force of his classical predecessors. Paradoxically, he is significant in a sense *because* he is ordinary: his very lack of presence prevents him from pursuing any historical ambition and at the same time convinces us that he would fight only for a great spiritual cause.

Glancing at the first lines of the novel, the most inexperienced reader has the same impression as the critic or commentator: *The Castle* appears to be fertile ground for the kind of "superstitious" and, as we have seen, primarily theological interpretation so frequently encountered in the commentary on *Don Quixote*. There is the great Castle appearing on the crest of the hill, veiled in mist and darkness (when K. arrives it is hidden, "invisible"); the snow-covered village, wretched and inhospitable, held within the Castle's mysterious jurisdiction; the solitary traveler, distressed by the dreary life of the village, who tries to escape it by forcing the gates of the Castle. We are immediately reminded of a spiritual topography that is made familiar by an abundance of traditions and that cannot be entirely foreign to Kafka's intentions, since it organizes all the space in the novel. If they have a meaning, one would think, the impenetrable Castle and its elusive officials can only represent the "beyond"—heaven or some other inaccessible realm. Similarly, the situation of the village, its cold and dismal atmosphere, must signify the desolation and suffering here below.

The remarkable topography of the action, the relations between the Castle and the village, the tone of fearful respect in which everyone, even K. himself, speaks of the Castle, the aura of sanctity surrounding the persons and activities of the "gentlemen," finally the vague but persistent feeling inspired by K.'s particular enterprise—all this tends to situate the novel in a higher spiritual realm and to justify the theological and metaphysical interpretations that treat the novel as an allegory. Max Brod, who for so long seemed not only the first but the final authority on Kafka, particularly because of their long friendship, writes in his Afterword to the first edition of *The Castle:* "This Castle, to which K. has no access and may not even approach, is precisely what the theologians call Grace: the divine direction of human destiny (the village), the efficacy of chance, the mysterious decisions . . . that hold sway over us. *The Trial* and *The Castle,* then, depict both forms of divinity (in the sense of the Kabbalah)—Justice and Grace . . . ."[1] Brod completes this mystical translation of the novel by proposing an explanation of certain elements that seem in sharp contrast to his theory, namely the prismatic and complicated relations that women in the novel seem to have with the Castle and its officials—the eroticism that plays an absolutely decisive role in the novel, but whose theological significance is certainly far from obvious. In Brod's attempt to mitigate this dissonance, however, he seems to protest too much:

If one should find enigmatic the relations that K. experiences or suspects between women and the Castle . . . and if the Sortini episode above all seems inexplicable, in which the official demands something apparently immoral and obscene from a young girl, one should refer to Kierkegaard's *Fear and Trembling,* a work that Kafka loved very much, read frequently, and commented upon in great depth in many of his letters.[2] The Sortini episode is actually a parallel piece to Kierkegaard's book, which begins with the proposition that God demands a crime of Abraham, the sacrifice of his

[1] Cf. "Nachwort," Max Brod, in *Gesammelte Schriften,* Vol. IV, Schocken Books, New York, 1946. p. 417–18.

[2] Ibid., p. 421. Brod depends here on Kafka's letters, chiefly from 1918, dealing with Kierkegaard. Unfortunately, these letters do not display the attitude of a disciple but contain rather a violent refutation of Kierkegaard's ideas, expressed in a tone that is a mixture of admiration and distaste. If the Sortini episode is related to *Fear and Trembling,* and this is not at all certain, it can be only in terms of a critique. See the *Briefe,* S. Fischer Verlag.

child; and this paradox leads Kierkegaard to the triumphant conclusion that the categories of morality and religion can in no way
be regarded as parallel . . . .

Beginning with a simple analogy based on an inherited
body of religious assumptions, Brod arrives at an essentially
theological construction that is supposed to conform at least
to the broad outlines of the text.

Brod's thesis has been accepted and elaborated by most of
the "theological" commentators who take it as a working
assumption that the Castle is Grace, the divine gift, and K.'s
adventures then purely symbolic rites of passage. At this
juncture, however, interpretations diverge sharply, for if
this idea of Grace is not merely to float about in an atmosphere of vague religiosity, it must be firmly anchored to
some doctrine. But which one? Brod invokes both Kierkegaard and the Kabbalah, two forms of religious thought
that do not display any obvious historical or spiritual
affinities. There are commentators[3] who insist that Kafka's
spiritual thought is not bound to any religious authority or
dogma, whereas some understand *The Castle* as a modern
counterpart of Bunyan's *Pilgrim's Progress*.[4] Still others conceive of Kafka as a neo-Calvinist, indeed as a direct disciple
of Karl Barth.[5] Yet it is difficult to locate just where one or
the other of these doctrinal positions appears in the novel
itself. One commentator,[6] who firmly believes that a
theological concept alone could not sufficiently motivate
the novelistic action or justify the attention that K. and all
the villagers invest in the *social* organization of the Castle,
proposes a "clerical" reading of the novel. The Castle is,

[3]Herbert Tauber, *Franz Kafka, Eine Deutung seiner Werke,* Zurich, 1941.
[4]Edwin Muir, Note of Introduction to *The Castle,* Alfred A. Knopf,
N.Y., 1930–41.
[5]John Kelly, "The Trial and the Theology of Crisis," *The Kafka Problem,*
N.Y., 1946.
[6]Norbert Fürst, *Die offenen Geheimtüren Franz Kafkas,* Heidelberg, 1956.

of course, still heaven. The music that K. hears on the Castle telephone (as a strange cacaphony) is religion. The village does not represent just any sphere of earthly life, but, being at the foot of the Castle, the human city sanctified by its nearness to heaven, something like the City of God. The large inn, called the Bridge Inn, that is situated at the entrance to the village, clearly embodies the Protestant church; on the way out of the village, bordering on the domain of the Castle, is the Catholic church in the guise of the Herrenhof. Between the two, in a secluded back street, the house of the Barnabas family is of course identified with Judaism. The landlady of the Herrenhof who owns a great number of dresses, nearly all of them dark—grey, brown, or black— must be a nun, like Pepi, the young servant girl who lives as a recluse among the other young girls in a room (a cell) to which men have no access. The function of the secretaries, who are evidently the priests, consists of implementing the decrees of the Castle, or rather of Providence. The social and moral "ghetto" to which Amalia condemns her family by refusing the obscene proposition of a Castle functionary has nothing to do with the sacrifice of Abraham; it must be understood as punishment for the stubbornness of the Jews, who for centuries obstinately refused the new dispensation. As for K.'s activities, these signify the spiritual comings and goings of a Western intellectual impelled more by curiosity than faith to follow the path of one of the three churches. K. bustles uselessly between the Bridge Inn, the Herrenhof, and the Barnabas house, the three places that delimit his action. Yet he reveals the inner cause of his failure to the mayor of the village: "I don't want any act of favor from the Castle, but my rights" (5th Ch.). This is his mistake. Only the man who desires Grace and justice together can succeed.[7]

[7]Fürst says precisely: "He should want both . . .," op. cit.

If K. were indeed a seeker after Grace he would hardly refuse it, as he so categorically does. Hence the view of other exegetes that the religious allegory of *The Castle* is, like many of Kafka's narratives, a "negative theology"[8] representing in fictional form the Nietzschean idea of the *death of God*. Alternatively, the Castle is seen as an expression of Kafka's rationalism,[9] indeed of his militant atheism. Viewed as a negative theology, the value of faith is by implication restored to the sense of absence, of loss and helplessness, which determines the desperate and futile nature of K.'s enterprise. The rationalist interpretation, however, adheres strictly to K.'s actual remarks about the Castle that belie his piety and are, besides, entirely unorthodox. The Land-Surveyor's obsession with the Castle and his desire to penetrate its mysteries move him from the outset more powerfully than anything else. Yet he has scarcely arrived when he rejects outright (and quite gratuitously) the idea that he might settle permanently within the Castle's sacred precinct where we imagine he has been drawn by some irresistible vocation. K. says to the landlord of the Bridge Inn: "If I have to work down here, for instance, it would be more sensible for me to lodge down here. I'm afraid too that the life in the Castle wouldn't suit me. I like to be my own master" (1st Ch.). Here is a knight of the faith who is afraid of being duped by Grace and above all wants to preserve his freedom. His reaction is equally peculiar when

[8]The idea that Kafka's work has the features of a "negative theology" is supported notably by Jean Carrive. Cf. Notes to *La Muraille de Chine,* Gallimard.

[9]Theodor W. Adorno, "Aufzeichnungen zu Kafka," in *Die Neue Rundschau,* 1953. Adorno considers Kafka an "Aufklärer," an idea he develops taking off from a parable by Lessing, "in which," he says, "a certain shift of emphasis would be enough to turn it into . . . a story by Kafka . . . ."

the Castle takes up his prospects and recognizes him as the Land-Surveyor, a title that for all we know he has conferred upon himself. Ordinarily, he ought to be delighted. But no, he is suspicious, as if the confirmation of his title were simply a devious way of getting rid of him, of sapping his strength. "So the Castle had recognized him as the Land-Surveyor. *That was unpropitious for him, on the one hand,* [10] for it meant that the Castle was well informed about him, had estimated all the probable chances, and was taking up the challenge with a smile . . ." (1st Ch.).

How can we believe that K. has come to the Castle to bask in eternal beatitude (he says later that he has not come "to lead an honored and comfortable life" [13th Ch.]) when he has declared his intention to wage a struggle? We cannot, even if we invoke the prophets who traditionally struggled against their awesome fate. In K.'s case, there is no pathos in the conflict; it is a cunning guerilla operation conducted by dint of subtle quibbling, something more like the struggle of a nonbeliever than one of the elect. It is true that in general K. shows a quasi-religious respect for the beliefs of the community. But beneath the facade of veneration he never stops questioning, cavilling, digging at the villagers and even hurting them by pointing out their faith in extravagant tales or vulgar gossip. And from their point of view, his actions are decidedly sacrilegious. K. impulsively vents his rage against persons and objects held sacred by everyone around him. The whole village fears and respects Klamm (who according to the various theological interpretations is a divine avatar, an angel, an arm of Providence, or more modestly, a highly placed ecclesiastic). K. steals Klamm's mistress, maliciously spies on him through a peekhole, secretly enters his sleigh and drinks his cognac (a potion that

[10]My italics.

must, of course, be divine or at least blessed). Besides, K. intends to speak with Klamm in person, *man to man,* which as everyone understands is an assertion of the right to free inquiry. And every faith has strong reasons to be suspicious of such an assertion. "So what are you afraid of?" K. asks the landlady of the Bridge Inn, who is scandalized by his project, "Surely you're not afraid for Klamm?" His remark hits home. The people of the village do fear for Klamm and their fear is understandable, for K.'s questions and arguments threaten to destroy their faith. "That seems quite unlikely to me," he says, this time referring to a belief held by the same landlady, who is the most fanatic of Klamm's devotees and K.'s worst enemy, "and secondly it is undemonstrable, obviously nothing more than a legend . . . ." Then, having characterized an age-old belief as a legend, he simply discounts the common experience on which it is based: "I see, a thing then to be refuted by further experience" (6th Ch.). There they have it. K., whom they all believe so reticent, frankly displays his true intentions: he has not come to the village to share its spiritual servitude but on the contrary to proclaim the need for doubt, to supplant tradition with immediate experience, to free individual thought from the fetters of obscure collective beliefs. Indeed, K. acts exactly like a true descendant of Enlightenment philosophy whose first task is always to deliver the "village" from the archaic shadow of the "castle."

Armed with this method of interpretation, the proponents of religious exegesis find themselves confronted with an insoluble dilemma (the same dilemma that prompts the disagreements over *Don Quixote*). This is all the more awkward since each thesis derived from this method accounts for certain selected elements but none for the novel as a whole. Of course the theory of K.'s "positive" faith is supported by impressive evidence: the general atmosphere of the work, the "mystery" of the Castle, the apparently nonempirical narrative events. But this view can be made convincing only by a sleight of hand, for either it ignores the elements that contradict it or colors them with a positive meaning for which the text clearly offers no proof. In this way, K.'s dramatic atheism is explained by the "vicissitudes of faith," his failure by the immeasurable distance between the human and the divine. This explanation, however, remains vague and unfounded and has no more basis than the argument of "negative" theology that transforms K.'s doubts into a critique of modern spiritual exhaustion. Here K.'s despair, his loneliness, his nostalgia, reintroduce a positive religious substance through the entirely negative idea of the "death of god." Equally inadequate is the rationalist theory that pulls all the fragments together to create a simplified character having little in common with Kafka's hero, who derives his most powerful singularity precisely from his dreams of the absolute, his illusory hopes and desires. As a spiritual model, however, it must be admitted that Kafka's Land-Surveyor is a bit too cleverly disguised. He is cunning and disputatious and so proud that he pretends to rival the supreme authority. He has none of the qualities we would expect in a saint, a prophet, or even a modern "defender of the faith." But with his dreams of the absolute, his nearly abject attitude toward authority, and the indecision that paralyzes him, he is not much better suited to play the role of a militant free-thinker. Whatever the cause, his example would be corrupted by jarring contradictions. Yet he is also seductive and perhaps for this very reason, dangerous.[11]

[11]Just as the view of "negative theology" attempts to reconcile the irreconcilable by presenting K. not as a kind of saint or prophet but as the *witness* of a Godless age (a witness who criticizes, suffers, and regrets), so

Is it certain, in any case, that the narrative is really constructed around a religious debate? Is there sufficient proof that the village is indeed the mundane world, the Castle heaven, and Count West-West the divine landlord whose decrees are equally mysterious and perfect? Not at all, answer the opponents of theology. In the whole of the novel there isn't a single indication, even an ambiguous or elusive one, that could readily support such a conclusion. Furthermore, everything that has immediate bearing on the Castle and the Count points to a precisely contrary view; this not merely after studied reflection, but from the first pages, indeed the first lines, of the novel. How does Kafka actually present the reputedly celestial Castle and its invisible master? How does he describe them, with what specific features are they embodied for us and placed in their particular context? Nothing very much, in fact, is said about the Count, whose "absence" itself provokes rampant speculation. But Kafka does mention him twice, in extremely dramatic circumstances that are underscored by their novelty. The first is the day after K.'s arrival in the village, when he prepares to leave the Bridge Inn after an extremely eventful night. On the way out he notices a picture on the wall, so blackened and deteriorated that at first he cannot make out the subject. Then he realizes that it is a portrait and is gradually able to distinguish a face. He immediately assumes that this

---

Günther Anders (*Kafka, Pro und Contra,* Munich, 1951) tries to explain these contrary tendencies—mysticism and negation—by the theory of *shameful atheism.* Not satisfied with this obviously pejorative label, however, Anders adds another one of heresy (seeing Kafka not as an unbeliever but as a believer in an evil god), and for good measure he throws in the charge of fascism (in spite of the extraordinary lucidity and honesty of his art, Kafka would seem to be, deep down, a worshipper of the worst brand of social authority, something like an unwitting proto-fascist and all the more dangerous because of the fascination of his art).

is Count West-West, whose name and rank he has learned the previous evening. Of course, he is soon disabused of this notion; it is not the Count but the castellan. K., untroubled by such a major error, comments only that this is "A handsome castellan, indeed"[12] (1st Ch.). A little later he meets the teacher with his students and, as this is the first person K. can freely approach, he greets him eagerly. The teacher declares point-blank that strangers never like the Castle, and K., taken aback, asks him if he knows the Count. At this, the young man is apparently seized with panic and tries to leave, but K. insists: "'What, you don't know the Count?' 'Why should I?' replied the teacher in a low tone, and added aloud in French: *'Please remember that there are innocent children present'*"[13] (1st Ch.). These two brief references seem to imply that if the Count is God, K. himself knows nothing about it, otherwise he would not confuse his image with a common castellan, handsome or not, nor would he be so naïve as to ask the first person he meets if he knows the Count and be so surprised by a negative response.

But if K. is quite ignorant of the Count's divine character, the teacher himself, who clearly shares the common beliefs of the village, seems to have a notion that is at least somewhat strange. One can understand the fact that he might resent K.'s question as a tactless invasion of his religious privacy, but not that he finds it threatening to the children (we should note that he expresses this in French—that is, in a language that students do not understand and that has the reputation for being particularly suited to licentiousness or equivocality). This is liable to perplex educators and

[12]Kafka is playing here on the double meaning of the word *Kastellan*, which, depending on the context, can mean either lord of the manor or porter.

[13]My italics.

moralists of every persuasion. With the authority that one must grant him in the matter, given his functions, the teacher in fact intimates that Count West-West is a subject of immoral conversation, someone or something that adults can discuss in veiled language (he himself does this, so far as we can see, only reluctantly), but never in front of innocent children. K., who understands nothing about the customs of the village and pays dearly for his blunders, takes this one to heart. He never speaks about the Count again, whether he actually decides not to shock people any more or simply forgets about this obscure personage who figures so little in the rest of the novel that he might never have existed. With all of K.'s avid, insatiable interest in everything concerning the Castle itself, its fantastical bureaucracy and the character of the "gentlemen," we must acknowledge that in this instance he displays a remarkable indifference. Should we deduce from this that he already knows the meaning of this hidden, ambiguous, possibly obscene figure who is the source of unspeakable thoughts? Possibly. In any case, he stops asking his questions, as if on this single point he shared the fear or the prejudices that account for the general silence.

Such a God of the Castle would be an embarrassment to any theology. But the Castle itself would be even more so, judging from its appearance. We know that on the evening of his arrival K. can scarcely make it out in the mist and darkness. The following morning, rising early, he takes the road leading to the Castle at once, impatient to become acquainted with this building that occupies all his thoughts. He glimpses it at first at a distance and observes that from this vantage point it nearly satisfies his expectations: "It was neither an old stronghold nor a new mansion, but a rambling pile consisting of innumerable small buildings closely packed together. *If K. had not known it was a castle he might have taken it for a little town . . . ."*[14] K. hopes to see more of it and continues on his way: ". . . But on approaching it he was disappointed in the Castle; it was after all only a wretched-looking town, a huddle of village houses, whose sole merit, if any, lay in being built of stone; but the plaster had long since flaked off and the stone seemed to be crumbling away . . ." (1st Ch.). From this moment, K.'s judgment of the Castle, which shifts with astonishing rapidity but never in a favorable direction, puts the reader on guard against the ideas, images, and value judgments associated with the very word "castle." Externally, then, this "castle" exhibits none of the superlative qualities proper to structures of this kind: no beauty, elegance, aesthetic merit—not even simple symmetry. It is a little town which at first K. is reluctant to characterize, only to find it quite dilapidated and wretched. Furthermore, the huddle of village houses has something dull and commonplace about it that disturbs him and reminds him, by contrast, of his native town: ". . . *It was hardly inferior to this so-called Castle,*[15] and if it was merely a question of enjoying the view, it was a pity to have come so far; K. would have done better to revisit his native town, which he had not seen for such a long time. And in his mind he compared the church tower at home with the tower above him. The church tower, firm in line, soaring unfalteringly to its tapering point, topped with red tiles and broad in the roof, *an earthly building—what else can men build?—but with a loftier goal than the humble dwelling-houses and a clearer meaning than the muddle of everyday life"*[16] (1st Ch.).

After this description by the single character whose judgment has meaning—the villagers live in the neighborhood of the Castle and don't seem to be aware of its aspect—there can be no more doubt about the nature of this

[14]My italics.   [15]My italics.   [16]My italics.

mysterious structure. It is an *earthly* building ("What else can men build?" says Kafka, in order to avoid any confusion over this place and the limits of his own symbols) and not even one of the most imposing. On the contrary, it is such a dull and dreary structure that even a simple village church might easily surpass it in grace and spirit. If K. had come there to seek the divine, he should logically renounce his project. But he does not do this, for contrary to what the commentators say, he expected something of this sort and simply continues on his way. It is not the *earthly* nature of the place that disappoints him, but the air of misery, ugliness, and monotony it so uselessly casts over the objects of daily life.

An earthly building whose bearing and appearance (with the exception of a few disagreeable details) K. had foreseen: such is the Castle in the eyes of the most interested party, who is a reliable witness, since presumably he, at least, knows where he is going and what he is looking for. Built in a human way, not in some ethereal space but on earth, out of the crude and perishable materials at man's disposal, this Castle violates its very name; for it is neither ancient, majestic, nor graceful—absolutely unsuited for idealization. It even lacks that imperfect ephemeral beauty of earthly things where one can sometimes read a divine message in distorted form. What distinguishes the Castle, then, from the anonymous village over which it holds sway? Surely nothing essential, for in its wretched state, with its forsaken and forbidding air, it is itself only a village, and the poorest sort at that.

But what about the authority that resides in the Castle? Must we infer its nature from the strictly temporal character of the building? Certainly it is just as logical that the building may be neutral in itself and need not correspond in any way to the substance of the Castle. Yet Kafka dwells on its external aspect, as if to warn the reader against overestimating the kind of power sheltered within the Castle walls and so against grossly misconceiving the text (which is precisely the blunder of his major interpreters). The structure of the Castle is the image of what it contains. Its ugliness, its banality, its monotony, provide an appropriate material envelope for a crushing earthly power that is indeed exclusively temporal. Its arbitrary and fantastically absurd transgressions require no supernatural explanations; they have more than enough human cause.

In order to forestall any mistake on this subject, Kafka has the teacher inform K. that "there is no difference between the peasantry and the Castle" (1st Ch.). Even if the peasantry could be construed as the "elect," this statement would be puzzling if not simply monstrous. The peasantry are not citizens of heaven but rather dull, brutal creatures, inhospitable, suspicious, and infantile. They are even more earthbound than their condition would warrant. K. is bewildered by their blunted skulls, that look "as if they had been beaten flat on top," their faces and features which seem "as if the pain of the beating had twisted them into the present shape" and express nothing but fear, vague curiosity, malice, and brutelike patience (2nd Ch.). Yet although K. perceives the Castle as it is, he, too, holds it in special regard, for he never recognizes the Castle's resemblance to its disinherited subjects, who are almost inhuman in their stupidity and destitution.

According to the sociological reading, then, nothing about the Castle is hidden or mysterious. It is a precise mirror of modern society with its singular combination of anonymity and rigid stratification—it is surely not an accident that the Castle is structured like an enormous industrial or commercial enterprise. It represents something like the cosmic version of an anonymous society responsible for the management of the world. This is the force that establishes the rules, regulates and maintains all collective life, and is for the individual always to some extent opaque—a ubiquitous and imposing presence with no visible head or specific authority. As the village lives under the sway of this authority without questioning its legitimacy, the Castle has an aura of permanence and omnipotence about it that disguises its true nature. In fact, it represents only that undefined force pervading every highly developed society that thinks, plans, acts, decrees, and organizes in the name of individuals and has therefore a formidable influence on the actual course of daily life. To be sure, such a force cannot be grasped in its entirety and eludes human judgment. We can never take full account of its effect, for if specific events often seem unjust and problematic when scrutinized in detail, presumably they are not negative, all things considered, since for good or ill life goes on. In the face of this limitless organism that in itself is neither intelligent nor stupid, just nor unjust, good nor evil, but is moved by pure necessity, the vision of the individual wavers and grows dim.

This, at least, is what happens to K., but not to the majority of the villagers, who find no cause for reflection or disturbance. The Castle is not an accommodating master, of course; it pesters and bullies the individual gratuitously, complicating his already difficult existence. Its machinery is heavy-handed, its decrees are irrational, its laws arbitrary, its functionaries deceitful, decadent, jealous of their power, bungling, and all told, quite inefficient. But it is the "world as it is," "things as they are," immediate necessity, which no sensible person would defy or challenge. The villagers would rather not think of the Castle at all, if they don't have to; they submit to its rule, try to profit from it (namely, to obtain better positions) when they can, and otherwise simply withdraw, do their work, and keep their mouths shut.

Understandably, K.'s intrusion into the village provokes almost unanimous hostility. In his role as stranger, he is impelled to break the law of silence, to defy the quiescence of the common people who are by definition more committed to peace than to truth. Astonished by what he sees and hears of the Castle, which he finds an inexhaustible subject for reflection, K. makes inquiries, poses questions, and endlessly speculates about it. Yet nothing could make him more suspect, for each of his questions constitutes an attack upon the status quo—manners, the basis of social relationships, customs—whose necessity neither the natives nor their rulers feel any need to demonstrate. A man who wants to know the precise connections between the Castle and his particular existence, who is not prepared to grant automatically that these connections are real and humane, who wants to see Klamm face to face, in other words, who wants to pierce the veil of anonymity that allows these obscure collective powers to work their dangerous influence—this man is a subversive spirit, though he might give the impression of bowing to convention. And from the beginning, the village, instead of welcoming K. as a liberator which in fact he is, leagues itself against him, almost to a man, in order to silence him or force him out. According to this interpretation, which is supported by so many critics,[17] and a large part of the read-

[17] Among them most important, Pavel Eisner *(Franz Kafka and Prague,* N.Y., 1950), who relates Kafka's acute and tormented social consciousness to the very special situation of Prague under the old Austro-Hungarian monarchy (cf. also "Analyse de Kafka" in *La Nouvelle Critique,* Jan. and Feb., 1958); Theodor W. Adorno, "Aufzeichnungen zu Kafka," in *Die Neue Rundschau,* vol. 3, 1953; Peter Demetz, Heinz Politzer, Günther Anders, Hannah Arendt, etc.

ing public as well, the Castle, in its absurd aspect, represents the revolting absurdity of an iniquitous collective system, and K. is the free man whose motives become one with the cause of reason and justice. This man, alone, armed with his lucidity and compassion, supported only by the powerless (women, young people, children, all the victims singled out by the social order), confronts this anonymous power that is highly organized and at the same time profoundly archaic. Exhausted by the struggle (and who would not be?), he is apparently crushed by a nameless, faceless monster who doesn't devour him, of course, but simply throws away his file. Nevertheless, K.'s effort is not in vain. Before succumbing, he has time to unmask the fallacy of the Castle and to prove by his example that if no individual can bear to confront Klamm's gaze, Klamm on his side can be seriously threatened by the penetrating vision, the tireless intelligence, the reason of a single man.

As we have seen, the theological interpretation of *The Castle* draws some support from certain features of Kafka's life and relies heavily on his autobiographical writings (the *Diaries* and a number of posthumous notebooks that attest to Kafka's penchant for metaphysics, his asceticism, his fascination with theological speculation and even certain doctrinaire sects).[18] In the same way, the realistic and sociological version cites the particular circumstances of Kafka's life that might logically have played a decisive role in the genesis of his work. Kafka was rootless, isolated in the midst of a society that treated him sometimes as an intruder, occasionally as a tolerated guest, at other times as an undesirable alien, and that was itself only a grotesque conglomera-

[18]Cf. "Reflections on Sin, Suffering, Hope and the True Path," in *Wedding Preparations in the Country,* and also the *Diaries* (the story of the visit to Dr. Steiner, the founder of anthroposophy, for example).

tion of races, peoples, classes and disparate interests.[19] As a writer dispossessed of his own language ("I am," he said, "a guest of the German language"), deprived of a public, and condemned to write in abstractions, Kafka composed his work in the image of this untenable situation. Indeed, it seems that he searched in vain all his life if not for a personal remedy—there was none—at least for some compensation or escape. In each of his stories and novels, he proposes—in a sense to himself—a solution or possible expedient. *Amerika* is a dream of emigration that cannot be realized because of the youth and candor of its hero. *The Trial* is a serious attempt at accommodation to the life of the Prague bourgeoisie, a life that looks normal on the surface but is riddled with inequities and absurd contradictions. *The Castle,* the last of the three novels and contemporaneous with certain historical upheavals,[20] is seen as the hero's final attempt to mingle more intimately with the life of the country and the people, to put down roots in a community rich in warmth and meaning. Yet no matter how he goes about it, the stranger is rejected by everyone, brutally cast out, killed by prejudice and indifference. But this failure is also his dubious luck. Certainly he suffers from living outside the life of the community, but he also sees more—and more profoundly—than the others, and because of this unobstructed view, his impartial position as a witness assumes the value of a decisive act.

[19]Cf. Pavel Eisner, op. cit., and Marthe Robert, Preface to the *Journal*.

[20]Kafka's posthumous papers, his letters, his diaries, indicate that he began to think about *The Castle* in 1920 and worked on it chiefly during the year of 1922, immediately after the formation of the Czechoslovakian Republic. Normally, he could have expected an improvement in his psychic situation as well as his objective status, but in fact this event had no effect on his isolation. See also, on this subject, the years 1920–1922 in his *Diaries,* the *Letters to Milena* and the *Letters* (*Briefe,* S. Fischer Verlag).

All this seems simple and reasonable enough, but this realistic sociological theory does not exhaust the problematic of the novel, which involves precisely K.'s equivocal attitude and the subtle contradictions of his activities. It is true that the Castle represents a social reality that Kafka experienced, unhappily, and that on the whole K. behaves as an enemy of the Castle and provokes its wrath. But how do we account for his tone of veneration, acquiescent respect, and humility, which tends to confirm the notion that the Castle embodies, after all, a superior reality to which the individual must bow? How is it that K. can say to the landlord of the Bridge Inn, one of the most timid men in the village: "You're a keen observer, for between you and me I'm not really powerful. *And consequently I have no less respect for the powerful than you have, only I am not so honest as you and am not always willing to acknowledge it"* (1st Ch.)?[21] Why, after stating that the Castle is nothing but a common huddle of village houses, is he so moved by the ringing of the Castle bell: ". . . as if to give him a parting sign until their next encounter, a bell began to ring merrily up there, a bell that for at least a second made his heart palpitate, for its tone was menacing, too, as if it threatened him with the fulfillment of his vague desire" (1st Ch.)? This is a rather unusual emotion for a self-appointed adversary of the social myth, yet K. has this experience more than once. The Castle not only attracts him but moves him, this is quite clear. We might even imagine that precisely in its ambiguous and fascinating image K. will seek the strength to fight, since he imagines that "everything"—the most forbidding tasks—"must be easy when one can keep the Castle in view." His ambivalence explains his lack of sympathy for the village malcontents who logically ought to become his allies. He has only

[21]My italics.

contempt for Pepi, the humiliated servant girl who constantly rails against her condition, and he is inspired with something close to hatred for Amalia, the young woman who has become a pariah because she has radically challenged the Castle's authority, though it is said that she lives "face to face with truth." On the other hand, he tries to win the good graces of the worst conformists. He loves Frieda, who has been Klamm's mistress and remains to the end a creature of the Castle, submitting to its bureaucracy as she does to the virility of the "gentlemen." What inconsistencies appear when we have to wrench the novel round to a single critical view! We must always distort the text—and what we know about Kafka—to make it congruent with a predetermined political and social attitude. Whatever the functional worth of his perceptions, K. in fact does not choose. He remains torn between love and hatred for the Castle, between the contradictory needs for submission and revolt, between the necessity of choice and what Kafka has called in *The Trial* "indefinite postponement."* No doubt K. observes the social phenomenon of the Castle with a unique lucidity and a fierce honesty. But after all, for what purpose? In order to state objectively what is? To transform pure observation into a critique or, on the contrary, to give tacit approval to reality? The art of Kafka, says Günther Anders,[22] must not be so profound if he chooses not to

---

*The Trial, p. 196 (Modern Library, New York: Alfred A. Knopf, 1937, 1956).

[22]Cf. op. cit. Anders considers the Kafka vogue as a "bad omen," he invites the reader to understand Kafka *to the death (Man soli ihn zu Tode verstehen).* Georg Lukacs doesn't go to such extremes; he condemns Kafka as a belated representative of the naturalist tendencies of the nineteenth century *(Studies in European Realism).* In general, the Marxist critics consider Kafka to be reactionary and corrupt. An inquiry on this subject not so long ago comes to mind that caused quite an uproar ("Faut-il bruler Kafka?" *Action,* 1948). We should note, however, that the Czech Marxists

answer such a banal but essential question. Among all the possibilities offered by the Castle, Kafka does not know, any more than K., which he prefers; his judgment remains suspended, and he, as clear-sighted as he is irresolute, seems condemned to understand everything without ever taking sides. This is the source of the beguiling beauty of his work but also of its reactionary, perhaps even politically dangerous message.

We can see that it is not enough simply to attach a label to the Castle to generate a coherent interpretation of the novel. Any such "translation" still leaves the hero's fundamental attitude toward the Castle's authority ambiguous and so, too, the general direction of his efforts and thoughts. Is K. for or against the Castle? Does he play the role of novice, iconoclast, witness, or victim? The meaning of the book evidently hinges on this question. But it is now quite clear, after some thirty years of exegesis, that if we assume in advance that the question must be resolved, we simply translate Kafka into another language—religious, sociological, psychological, philosophical, etc., depending on our intuition, personal preferences, or the vogue of certain dominant ideas. It is wasted effort to look for new keys, for all finally amount either to passing off hypotheses as established facts or demonstrating that all positions are equally plausible and equally unconvincing. No choice can honestly be justified, and since the most ingenious explanations are false and the most honest are simply useless, we shall lose nothing and perhaps gain something by discarding them all.

---

around 1920 had an entirely different opinion of Kafka. Neumann's socialist review, "Cerven," had published the whole of "The Stoker," the first chapter of *Amerika* (which obliged them to omit the other articles planned for the issue), emphasizing Kafka's extremely accurate knowledge of the organization of the capitalist world and his acute analysis of it.

Kafka and literature will surely benefit from such a clean sweep, say the philologists, who for some time have attempted to replace exegetical commentary with a more classical analysis that is not committed to some external discipline but exclusively to the text.[23] This about-face is so valid, so obviously full of good sense, that one wonders only why it was so long in coming; for Kafka is above all an artist and art is his only *idea*. Furthermore, by treating his work as some kind of science, religion, or applied philosophy, we seriously damage the poetic creation that is betrayed as soon as it is translated, for it cannot be converted into any other form of expression. And by conceiving of him as a thinker who had to clothe his ideas in novelistic garb, we shatter the unity of form and content that is the beauty and, more importantly, the truth of his fiction.[24]

This said (and it cannot be repeated too often), it is unthinkable that the commentary that has developed and flourished in all the countries where Kafka's work is read can be explained by the arbitrary influence of fashion or a kind of widespread intellectual malaise. The finest writers and most informed critics of our time have written on Kafka, and if they have occasionally fallen into this trap of "meanings," which we now justifiably try to discourage, they were led on by Kafka himself, who, in the final analysis, offers the reader not so much a novel as the record of an extended inquiry. Indeed, the hunger for knowledge is necessarily stimulated by a work in which everything is questioned and action is finally reduced to a systematic examination of opinions, solutions, or possible truths. By searching for the meaning of the Castle, the Trial, the Law, the Great Wall of China, the Penal Colony, etc., the critic actually applies

[23]Friedrich Beissner, *Der Erzähler Franz Kafka,* Stuttgart, 1952.
[24]Marthe Robert, *Franz Kafka,* Gallimard, 1960.

Kafka's own method and then follows the seductive movement of his thought.

The fact is that Kafka's three novels and his principal stories have as their theme a difficult quest whose object is always obscure, and for this reason all the more fascinating. Yet, what distinguishes this search from analogous quests described in the allegories, parables, and symbolic tales to which Kafka's work seems related? Certainly not its difficulty; all quests of this kind are difficult and dangerous, frequently undertaken but rarely completed. Unique to Kafka is the fact that the prized object or goal has itself no fixed value. The hero has no measure of its worth, no notion of whether what he is seeking is useful or necessary, and consequently no assurance that his success will bring him some benefit or salvation. Kafka's hero is the inverse of the traditional quest hero who may be overwhelmed by the trials he must undergo but knows at least the value of the Golden Fleece or the Grail or any other symbolic object worthy of his efforts. K. the Land-Surveyor knows nothing at all about the Castle save that it exists and that apart from himself no one seems much concerned with it. Therefore he must postpone his quest and meanwhile carry on his patient investigation, which is the only way he will acquire the tools to act. Any interpretation can only deal legitimately with the fruits of this investigation, which indeed constitutes the entire substance of the novel.

In the beginning, K. conducts this inquiry in a rather banal way: he asks questions, seeks information from important people, compares their answers, and endlessly collects testimony in the form of legends and even commonplace memories. In the process of doing this, of course, he encounters numerous obstacles. His informers are suspicious, ill-disposed, capricious; either he can't get a word out of them or, on the contrary, they besiege him with their interminable chatter. Besides, his position as a foreigner prevents him from discerning their actual connections with the Castle. He prefers to address himself to the notables, the Mayor, the teacher, the landlady of the Bridge Inn, who is a respectable and prosperous business woman. But even here he is mistaken. The Mayor has no power, his wife does all the work. The teacher is nothing, while in fact his colleague, Mlle Gisa, rules the school with an iron hand. As for the landlady, Klamm's ex-mistress, she is an old woman lost in her memories, for whom the whole of the Castle is reduced to a love affair. The information collected in this way— namely by means of public opinion—is so contradictory and vague that nothing much can be done with it. But what K. learns from his own experience is even more deceptive. Each time he believes he has understood something, facts soon destroy his illusions. For example, he is told that he cannot remain in the village without the Castle's authorization, yet he remains there and no one forces him to leave. After denying that he has been summoned to the village as Land-Surveyor, the Castle recognizes his functions and everyone calls him "Land-Surveyor." But as he has nothing to survey, they offer him a post as janitor at the school. Yet he can trust neither his assistants, nor his so-called messenger, nor the women in whom he seems to place so much hope. In the end, he knows scarcely more about the Castle than the day he arrived, or, if he has learned something, it is too late and has been obtained at the price of such exhaustion that it no longer does him any good.

From the outset, however, K. seems to discern the real reason his search is thwarted: the people of the village call "Castle" something that in the light of his own experience he would never think to designate by that name (. . . "if K.

had not known that it was a castle he might have taken it for a little town"). This is the enigma. The word "castle" suggests fine and beautiful images, magnificent festivals, or heroic battles—precisely the contrary of what K. finds, which judged objectively is only a little town, quite ordinary and shabby. Yet the word has an infinitely more convincing force than the thing itself. It does K. no good to know that the Castle is not what the villagers think, that it is incorrectly named, embellished with false titles and borrowed qualities. He cannot help identifying it with the castles of legend, which at least have the merit of being coherent phenomena. The actual castle he encounters is impenetrable because of its name and always tends to disappear behind its literary analogues—ancient, feudal, magical, haunted, fairy, invisible, mystical castles, not to speak of castles in Spain,[25] which are purely illusory, and castles of Bohemia, which are historical constructions reconstructed by legend. Each time he strains to understand his own situation, to unravel the precise connections between the Castle and the village and deduce a rational plan of action, he is flooded by a wave of images—half historical memories, half literary remnants—that are more seductive than flat daily reality. These images continually divert him, and indeed inspire him with disgust for the real castle. As K. has only very fragmentary notions of the Castle and little credible information, nothing protects him against the insidious influence of all kinds of books that deal with analogous quests and hence lead him down previously charted paths

[25]Castles in Spain are called in German *Luftschlösser,* castles in space or in the air. K.'s is built in air (on high ground that seems like empty space). It is in Spain as much as in Bohemia, where Kafka frequently stayed beginning in 1917 (the year when his tuberculosis was medically confirmed) and where he lived for the first time among peasants.

where he is only too inclined to go. As a result, he is in great danger of confusing himself with one of those famous heroes who also pursued castles with the expectation of winning power, happiness, knowledge or salvation. Since he shares with them his faith in a particular goal, the obsession to pursue it, and a certain visionary inclination, he especially risks drawing premature conclusions about the meaning of his own "mission."

But he is on guard. Knowing what errors he is prey to simply by hearing the magic word, he does not try to avoid them—this would be futile; rather he commits his errors with a certain purpose, in order to control them and possibly turn them to some advantage. Among the litany of ideas and associations called up by the word "castle," the most elevated symbols exist side by side with the most vulgar dreams of power, epic splendor with the worst trivia. Taken in the absolute sense, as it is always done in the novel, this word inevitably conjures up for K. (and for the reader, who is, of course, subject to the same mechanism) a fortress, a palace, a tyrant's stronghold or brigand's refuge, a haunted house, a sacred place, a promise of love or madness, a chimerical plan. And this, even though he states that his castle is neither "an old stronghold nor a new mansion." K. is aware of this, he knows that he will not plumb the meaning of the Castle until he has eliminated one by one the old meanings, the literary fragments and symbolic leftovers that clutter his path and prevent him from approaching the actual Castle. Obviously, such an elimination of meanings could not be achieved by a purely linguistic analysis, for this is not a rational matter but a dream, into which K. lapses again and again at unguarded moments, a dream that fascinates him and cannot be resisted with the weapon of logic. K. takes, therefore, the opposite tack and achieves his dream by re-creating one by one the literary situations generated by the magic of the word. He reenacts for objective scrutiny the adventurous careers of the seekers after castles, who, in their exemplary way, succeeded or failed and are hence his models. Caught up in this exploration, which should be only a preliminary task but proves exhausting and endless, K. not surprisingly has no more time or energy to go further and to act on his findings.

K. resolves to explore not imaginary lands but familiar books filled with marvels. He deserves more than we think his title of Land-Surveyor, which is honorific (everyone in the village calls him by this name) and semi-official (the Castle does not confirm it). Officially, he does not have and will never have any real earth to measure, but privately nothing prevents him from surveying the enormous literary space that is part of the public domain. The Castle, though we often suspect its malicious intentions, is quite loyal to K. on this point. It cannot encourage his "vocation"—this is an entirely personal matter—but it leaves him free to follow it and even supports his efforts to survey the territory of literary imagination by sending him two qualified assistants (Arthur, the king of legend, and Jeremiah, the biblical prophet).

K. is thus the surveyor of books just as Don Quixote is the literary knight-errant. He has two assistants, however, instead of a squire, and has no real need of a horse or arms. On the whole, he is hardly noteworthy, except for his extreme penury, which is the inverse of his function.[26] With no other instruments than those his memory provides (his "equipment" remains problematic and, in any case, never

[26]At the beginning of the novel, Kafka openly plays with the word *Landvermesser,* close in sound and meaning to *Landstreicher,* vagabond. Besides, K. has the attributes of a tramp: a stick and a pack.

arrives), he is more impoverished, more alone, and freer than his illustrious predecessor, but also committed to a more difficult task. Don Quixote only had to imitate a single book, an ideal book, which, sublime or absurd, embodied all the virtues and vices of the others. It was a model, at any rate, and K. cannot allow himself such easy terms. In an era when literary models are scattered, nuanced, confused, and attenuated, when the new values are not so much opposed to the old as they are scrambled, lost in infinity, or, on the contrary, become highly specialized, when books and life no longer illuminate and mutually support each other but come to mirror each other's confusion and fragility, the quixotic imitator must evidently modify his technique if he wants to preserve his principles. Degraded as it was when Cervantes took up its cause, the single genre of chivalric romance—a single title, a single hero (Amadis)—could still powerfully suggest this unity of literature and life, or at least the epic dream of unity. Around 1920, the period when Kafka wrote *The Castle*, [27] the genre was dead, the titles were legion; the hero still had a good deal to say, but there was no one to listen. In the midst of perpetual flux, books disappeared with a burden of news that they had not had time to deliver. Each day the old was condemned to death (by naturalism, symbolism, expressionism, etc.), but it did not die. It defied its sentence by surviving in minor

[27]The sketches and fragments in *Wedding Preparations in the Country* seem to support the notion that Kafka began to think about *The Castle* around 1920. But he refers to it in his letters only beginning in the spring of 1922. On July 20, 1922, he recalls that he gave Max Brod a notebook "that existed only to be written, not read." And on September 9, 1922: "I have not spent a very agreeable week, for I have abandoned the Castle probably for ever, although what I wrote at Plana was not as bad as what you've seen." We do not know if, at this date, the novel was in its present form or if Kafka, in spite of what he said, continued to work on it.

genres so flabby and stupid that even Don Quixote would have refused them. Epic truth, which three centuries earlier was already as feeble and pathetic as Rocinante, had retreated entirely into popular fiction—into the serial novel, the detective story, novels about Indians and espionage—where it led a stunted life underground. The quarrel of the ancients and the moderns was not over at all, only muffled by a deafening uproar that was not caused by books but by an excess of reality in which nothing was certain, stable, or clear. So we find the new aspect of the old quixotic mission that must in these times mediate the dispute between the moldering but tenacious truths of the past and an anguished modern consciousness aware of its own mortality.

K. himself reflects the image of this impatient era. Although he has lost nothing of the quixotic passion, he has read too much by now to be a man of a single book or the hero of a single epic. K. is perplexed before he begins, hesitating between nonsensical models and the great examples whose voices he can no longer hear. Don Quixote's heroic imitation is closed to him: he must transpose it into a more discreet mode, equally stubborn and self-sacrificing, but more modest, and, at least on the surface, more rational.

II. THE QUEST

> "What village is this I have wandered into? Is there a castle here?"
>
> THE LAND-SURVEYOR
> *The Castle,* The First Chapter

Like Cervantes, Franz Kafka was a practitioner of imitation and for similar reasons, which were perhaps aggravated by the precariousness of his time and the unhappy peculiarities of his own situation. Kafka's enterprise was also one that had to be conducted with discretion, indeed with the utmost secrecy. Unlike Cervantes, however, Kafka does not deal with a particular book or books, specified by title, author, and reputation. Rather he takes up a number of genres or prototypes—in a sense, books in the abstract. He evokes these literary categories sometimes one by one, at other times jumbled together, as they probably were in his memory and the minds of contemporary readers. Most often his imitation comprises many modes simultaneously reproduced and at the same time modified. Confused as this is, the separate literary strands of Kafka's work can be easily unraveled. *Amerika,* for example, is a myth of paradise lost and a utopian vision with the natural world of Oklahoma as paradise found; it is a fairy tale, the fairy being Karl's uncle who punishes him like Cinderella at the stroke of midnight, as well as a romance of adventure—the New World, the uncle from America; and finally it is a serial novel concerning a young man who has gone astray and is pursued by his family.[1] The same mixture, in different doses and with perhaps some additional ingredients, determines the composition of *The Trial,* which is a detective story (where the mystery does not lie in the identity of the criminal but in his crime) as well as a commentary on a juridical or religious document (the exegesis of the parable). All of the stories that have talking animals as their protagonists ("Josephine the Singer," "Investigations of a Dog," "The Burrow," etc.) are clearly fables, but the *Metamorphosis* is also a fairy tale ("Beauty and the Beast"), and "The Giant Mole" ("The Master of the Village School") is related simultaneously to

[1]*Amerika* is the only one of his works whose model Kafka has openly revealed. "It is," he says in his *Diaries,* "Dickens' *David Copperfield,* but enriched with the liveliest hues I could borrow from my epoch and the dullest I could take from my own invention . . . ."

the myth and the scientific report. One by one, Kafka re-creates the ancient myths ("Prometheus," "The Silence of the Sirens," "Poseidon"), Indian tales and old chronicles ("The Great Wall of China"), and the fables, apologues and parables that are in some sense his first literary models, as opposed to the more recent fiction from which he borrows a scholarly vocabulary or a trivial mystery (the detective plot). This is the unique and protean originality of his work, which is laden with so many resemblances and is precisely what it least resembles—namely, an endless journey through centuries and books.[2]

The Castle is the most perfect example (though the novel itself was unfinished) of this imitation by which Kafka sought to reconstitute a kind of universal library, a reposi-tory of age-old wisdom. In it we find many layers of stories whose origins, chronology, and style are highly disparate; these stories, which are sometimes superimposed, some-times interwoven, and sometimes developed along parallel lines, contribute jointly to the development of the novel. K. is the hero of each of these component works and follows them out as far as he can to cull their secrets, since all have equal value for him as precedents. His first role[3]—literally

[2]Of course, these brief remarks by no means exhaust all of Kafka's models (cf. Marthe Robert, op. cit.). One can also find in his work an obsession with *Robinson Crusoe* and many other literary souvenirs that are treated quite consciously. There is proof in Kafka's *Diaries* that he valued imitation as a form of knowledge and that it always guided his art: "All that literature is an assault against the frontiers, and if Zionism had not inter-vened, it could easily have resulted in a new secret doctrine, a kabbalah. The possibilities for this still remain. It is true that such a task demands genius, *an impenetrable genius that would take root once again in older centuries or recreate them . . .*" (my italics). January 16, 1922.

[3]It is not absolutely the first. Kafka actually had conceived the opening of *The Castle* in the style of a detective story or spy novel, we cannot be more specific about it given the brevity of the manuscript. In this fragment K. behaves as if he were persecuted by the police or a secret organization, and

the most contemporary, least spectacular, and also least complimentary, and therefore least obvious—is the role he plays in a novel of manners in which his entire ambition is simply to "arrive." In this version, which is continuous throughout the novel, the hero is a man between thirty and forty years old, a vagabond who comes from an unknown place and throws the village into a turmoil over a summons he may have received from the Count, no trace of which, however, can be found. He makes a bad first impression, and while his penury makes him mistrusted in the beginning, his indiscretion, his insatiable curiosity, his penchant for speculation soon make him utterly suspect. On the second night of his stay, he seduces a barmaid at the Herrenhof who is intimate with Klamm, a powerful "gentleman" who is one of the most visible officials of the Castle. Frieda has the misfortune to fall promptly in love with K., a transgression that causes her to lose her patronage and her position, which is an enviable one in the village hierarchy. Nevertheless, she has no regrets and bravely accepts the consequences of her choice. Scarcely is K. certain of the girl's love than he tries to extort from her all kinds of information about the Castle and the "gentlemen," about his rival Klamm in particular, for he expects Klamm to support his enterprise (which is, quite simply, to *arrive*). Enlightened by her friend the landlady of the Bridge Inn, an older experienced woman who instantly perceives the adventurer's real intentions, Frieda understands that K. does not love her but only wants to use her, since she was born in the village and has many connections there. (". . . Providing that you reach your end, you're ready to do anything; should Klamm want

seems to have come to the village—they call him simply the traveler or the guest (der Gast)—in order to foil the plans of his enemies. (See "Another Version of the Opening Paragraph," Knopf, pp. 418–21.)

me, you are prepared to give me to him; should he want you
to stick to me, you'll stick to me; should he want you to fling
me out, you'll fling me out . . ." [13th Ch.].) In fact, K. is
indifferent to the plight of his future wife and is interested
only in his own pursuits. He uses all the means available to
him to achieve success. He tries to exploit his "assistants,"
the messenger sent by the Castle, and above all every
woman he meets, even clandestinely, for of course women
play a crucial role in his plans. When Frieda learns of his
relations with Olga and Amalia, the two sisters whose family are the outcasts of the village and particularly obnoxious
to her, she leaves him once and for all and resumes her old
position at the Herrenhof. When the novel ends, K. is as
ragged and disreputable as ever, his eyes still fixed on the
lofty reaches of the Castle to which he will never gain access.[4]

A good-for-nothing who manipulates women, an adventurer with no taste for risk or even the virtues of the *parvenu,*
a somewhat aging Rastignac, a small-time Julien Sorel—
this is K. in the sordid novel that is not merely a brief digres-
sion but a fragment developed at length in which his situation takes on a coherent meaning. And this is precisely how
he is viewed by most of the villagers and, unfortunately for
him, by the authorities of the Castle themselves. In one of
the passages Kafka deleted, K. is shown a page from an
official report describing his activities and his motives: "So
he roamed about in a seemingly aimless way, doing nothing
but disturbing the peace of the place. In reality, however, he
was very busy; he was on the lookout for an opportunity to

---

[4]Kafka represents here the condition of the Western Jew who is never
entirely assimilated and who is left to choose between the status of *pariah*
and that of *parvenu.* Cf. on this subject, Hannah Arendt, "The Jew as
Pariah," in *Jewish Social Studies,* N.Y., 1944.

get a foothold, and soon he found one. Frieda, the young barmaid in the taproom at the Herrenhof, believed in his promises and let herself be seduced by him . . . . In the margin of the page was a childishly scrawled drawing of a man with a girl in his arms. The girl's face was buried in the man's chest, but the man, who was much the taller, was looking over the girl's shoulder at a sheet of paper he had in his hands on which he was joyfully inscribing some figures . . ." (Appendix, p. 453–454). In the most contemporary and sustained version of his story, the Land-Surveyor is very much the sorry individual his enemies make him out to be.[5]

He cuts a rather better figure in the serial novel, and although this second role is more fragmentary, it nonetheless extends over several important episodes. In this version, he appears as a reformer, a champion of justice, and a defender of the weak and helpless against the abuses of power wielded by a privileged caste. The villagers quietly submit to the tyranny of their lords[6] who hold them in a state of bondage that is positively feudal. Customs that were abolished elsewhere long ago survive here, to the unhappiness of all, particularly the women, who are usually the chosen vic-

[5]In a fragment dated 1920 that seems to be a brief sketch of *The Castle,* the same interpretation of K.'s goal is suggested with some variation: "All this is obvious. It is not only that K. doesn't understand it. Recently, he took it into his head to find his way into the family of our castellan; but he doesn't try his luck through ordinary connections, he wants to go straight to the goal. Perhaps the usual way seems too long to him; actually, it is, but the road he tries to take is obviously impossible. Not, of course, that I exaggerate the importance of our castellan. He is a sensible, hard-working, respectable man, but nothing more. What does K. want from him, then? Does he want to find a position in the realm? No, it's not that. He himself is well-off and leads a carefree life. Does he love the castellan's daughter? No, no, he is above this suspicion . . . ."

[6]The word *Herr* can be translated equally as gentleman, lord, or master.

tims. Indeed, the lords exercise a kind of right of the first night from which no one can escape. The landlady of the Bridge Inn in her youth and Frieda, K.'s fiancée, have known the summons of the imperious "gentlemen" who raise the women momentarily above their station and then leave them forever embittered. The only girl in the village who has rebelled against the custom, Amalia, has brought about the disgrace of her family, the humiliation of her old parents, her sister's fall—Olga has become a prostitute to support the others—and the despair of her young brother, who tries in vain to promote a reconciliation between his family and the Castle by becoming its messenger. Beyond its degrading servitude, the village must also put up with the violence of the "gentlemen's" domestic servants (Klamm's are the worst), a horde of alcoholic brutes whom no one can control except Frieda, who cows them with her whip. The entire village is corrupted by the ways of the Castle, but the evil lies strictly in the upper levels of society. The lower classes keep themselves honest: the peasants are the victims, not the accomplices of the Castle, the girls are skillful workers (Amalia, before the scandal, was a distinguished dressmaker patronized by the best people), the servants display a nearly heroic courage (Frieda, Pepi), or, like Olga, they are good-hearted and self-sacrificing. Is it so surprising that all of these humiliated women welcome K. as an unforeseen savior? He is a foreigner, and consequently free of the prejudices and fears that create a reign of terror among the natives; he in intrepid, intelligent, just, well-qualified in all respects to bring some happiness and dignity to the village. Frieda has scarcely laid eyes on him when she gives herself to him and has the courage to defy Klamm; Pepi falls in love with him before she has even met him, defining him in advance as a "*hero,* a rescuer of maidens in distress"; Olga and Barnabas greet him as their savior (Olga says to him: "What happiness for us that you've come!"). Even little Hans, a small boy, comes to ask him to take care of his mother, and K. consents, boasting of his gifts as a healer ("At home they called him 'the bitter herb' on account of his healing powers" [13th Ch.]). On all sides, the weak and oppressed, the disabled and abused seek his support and perhaps regard him as their last hope.

The four chapters that tell the story of the Barnabas family, the only chapters in the whole novel with specific titles—"Amalia's Secret," "Amalia's Punishment," "Petitions," "Olga's Plans"—fall into the realm of this complicated serial novel in which, predictably, mistakes and unforeseen reversals are rife (as in the story told by Gardena, the Landlady of the Bridge Inn, who was seduced as a young girl). The chapter titles are in the style of this genre, as are the familiar motifs: the old parents racked with grief, the shame of one person that is reflected on a whole family, social barriers, the danger of improper alliances, the imminent punishment for anyone who violates an unspoken law or fails to observe a custom. It doesn't matter that Amalia is innocent and that, seen objectively, the entire business seems immoral or absurd. The criterion here is not the validity or error of the community's moral judgment, but, as always in the popular novel, the coercive power of convention.

Neither of these hypothetical Castles, however, is completely satisfactory. The first represents only the most trivial aspect of K.'s ambitions; he does want to "arrive," certainly, but not only in the way his enemies imagine. Moreover, this first version, the novel of manners, explains nothing about the phenomenon of the aberrant bureaucracy that is his chief obsession. And the second, the serial novel, answers only very imperfectly his deepest impulses, which on the one hand lead him to play the role of liberator, healer, even savior, but on the other prevent him, justifiably, from giving in to what he considers a temptation ("He had not come to bring luck to anyone; he was at liberty to help of his own free will, if things turned out that way, but nobody was to hail him as a bringer of luck; anyone who did that was confusing his paths, claiming him for matters for which he, being thus compelled, was never at their disposal . . ."[7] [Appendix, p. 472]). As *arriviste* or con man, his ambitions are too restricted; as reformer or savior, he is afraid of losing his freedom. In both cases, all he gains from his inquiries into the nature of the Castle, and hence the nature of his own ambitions, are schematic and partial explanations that he must take into consideration, of course, but which have only a relative and provisional value. So he goes on with his inquiry and consciously tries out other literary roles, going farther and farther back in time.

We discover him next tricked out as a folk hero, prepared to act in a real fairy tale. Like every character in a tale, he has no definite origin or identity; all we know is that he comes from "far away"—and is utterly absorbed in his mission. Solitude is part of his role, but he can escape it through a happy marriage, on the condition that he has properly come through his fantastic adventure. This involves delivering the village from the malevolent powers that govern the Castle and bring sickness and disaster to the land (the inhabitants of the village are sad and sickly, some are invalids; they know neither summer nor spring; in their world winter lasts nearly all year round). K. has scarcely arrived when he is exposed to these mysterious and malign forces that challenge him, lay traps for him all along the way, and work

[7]Deleted passage.

their magic before his very eyes. When he believes he is approaching the Castle, he is actually turning around in a circle or running in place; in any case, he gets nowhere, for the enchanted way keeps him *prisoner*. Although the young people of the village walk easily through the snow, he sinks in it up to his knees and would be swallowed up if his messenger did not come and carry him on. Is he away one hour or two? When he returns to the village, night has suddenly fallen ("And it had been morning when he left. And he had not felt any need of food. And just a short time ago it had been uniform daylight . . . 'short days, short days,' he said to himself . . ." [2nd Ch.]). Time, space, and beings are enchanted. Barnabas, his messenger, charms him with his agility, his luminous features, his smile, and his gleaming silken tunic, which lends him a hint of divinity. But a bit later, K. perceives that the boy has the muscular chest of a laborer, and underneath his angelic tunic he wears a "coarse, dirty gray shirt patched all over" (2nd Ch.). Later, K. understands that Barnabas is "a will-o-the-wisp," just like his so-called "assistants," who materialize as if by the wave of a magic wand and are only monstrous elves sent purposely, it seems, to torment him. So it goes with everything: the villagers are deaf to his presence, but he cannot comprehend them either; what he thinks is far away is near, and vice versa. In order to fortify his strength and finally break the enchantment, he drinks a few drops of a magic potion (Klamm's cognac, whose odor is "so sweet, so caressing"), but this elixir of youth or love potion is transformed in his mouth into a "drink fit for a coachman." Furthermore, he doesn't know what he has to do or what he ought to avoid; he is versed neither in the prohibitions he must observe nor in the ritual acts necessary for his success. He hasn't been taught the strict assumptions that operate in the tale and he tries in vain to reinvent them. Alone in the face of hidden forces that paralyze him, he meets no animals gifted with speech, no bird or good fairy who in other contexts generally comes to the aid of characters like him. He recognizes the only fairy he may have found—the landlady with the luxurious, old-fashioned gowns—only at the end, and she is not a guardian angel but perhaps death itself, which marks the completion of his quest.

K., however, does not admit that he is beaten. He has failed in his assault upon the castle of fairy tales, but he tries his luck one last time with the most celebrated of castles, the castle of the Holy Grail, which requires a triumphant and ascetic quest and reveals its mysteries only to its chosen hero. In this new view of his story (the only one, we should observe, which is preserved in the mystical commentary on *The Castle*), he follows in the footsteps of Perceval and Parzival, Peredur or Galahad—the Grail hero bears many names and frequently changes his appearance—in order to learn a secret that will be revealed to him and to him alone if he obeys the laws of the quest and fulfills its foreordained conditions. At first glance, of course, K. seems rather poorly equipped for such an heroic mission. But after all, the Grail quest does not refer to "earthly" chivalry, it is a wholly interior ordeal, demanding not so much material goods and physical strength as devotion, faith, and humility. K. does not know whether he possesses these special qualities, which are the indispensable signs of his election and success. Yet he intends to acquire or discover them by imitating the famous knights whose merit and purity are confirmed by tradition.

And so K. renounces Don Quixote's epic gear, which would not be of much use under the circumstances, since the central Grail adventure does not involve excursions on horseback or acts of knightly prowess, but a decisive and highly ritualized visit to the Castle Perilous. K. is quite ready to make this visit. The Castle stands before him, dominating the village where he has wandered by chance, as tradition dictates, after an exhausting and perilous journey. Once he has overcome the ordinary obstacles along the way that are preludes to the supreme test, he must finally gain access to the Castle and personally undergo the experience of the celebrated visit.

In general, his situation in the village has certain features that support an imitation of the Grail quest. The Castle has all the qualities needed to represent that other world whose magic enchants the human realm, bringing barrenness and desolation. It is the very image of silence and stasis ("K. had never yet seen there the least sign of life . . ."), and viewed from a distance it is bathed in a calm so absolute that the glances of the observer slip over it "without being able to catch hold of anything." The neighborhood surrounding the Castle is surely the place of death, the Ruined Land that the successful revelation of the Grail alone will restore to its original prosperity and health. And to complete the analogy, the way to the terrible Castle is no longer known; it is K.'s duty, he believes, to find it again.

From the first, K. is convinced of the importance of his task. If the knights of the Grail are characterized by fearlessness, unshakable resolution, renunciation, and the capacity to risk everything with no second thoughts in order to reach their goal, K. is second to none. His disinterestedness is even greater than theirs, since he cannot foresee the actual end of his quest and so doesn't anticipate any personal gain. Like Perceval and his more or less fortunate companions, who are both guided and detained by women, K. has many amorous adventures. But compared to the necessity that binds him to the Castle, his human ties are fragile and secondary ("if he were carried away by his hopes—he could not do otherwise—he had to focus all his strength on them, and not concern himself with anything else, with food, lodging, the authorities of the village, or even Frieda . . . ."). The love offered by Frieda, Olga, Amalia, and Pepi must only further the progress of his quest, not hinder it. And he is bound to neglect even the woman he has chosen as his companion ("it is unfortunately true, I have neglected her . . . . I would be happy if she would come back, but I would at once begin to neglect her again"). The Grail hero must remain free, completely disengaged, prepared at any moment to sever his earthly bonds.

The Land-Surveyor sees the Castle suddenly loom up before him and recognizes it, although he has never seen it before ("What village have I wandered into? Is there a castle here?" [1st Ch.]). Come to the village apparently by chance or error, but actually guided there by fate, he will leave it only when he has rediscovered the way to the other world (represented in a rather mediocre way by the wooden bridge and the Bridge Inn, both situated at the edge of the village) and cured the land of its scourge. According to the tradition, this restoration of general health and prosperity that accompanies his own apotheosis is tied to one or several questions related to the sacred object of the quest. These are, however, questions that he can pose only after he has discovered them for himself, since the formula is not given. This, we recall, is the cause of Perceval or Parzival's partial failure, for he was too timid or too immature to undergo the ordeal of the Grail and so refrained from asking the fateful questions that would have led to his initiation. Learning from his example, K., who does not contemplate the Grail but only its dwelling, spends the major part of his time questioning everyone to be certain that no stone is left unturned. This is his mistake: K. is too indiscreet and curious, he loses more through his liberty with language than Parzival did through his inhibition. Not only does K. fail to rediscover the way to the Castle, but the Grail never appears to him, even in enigmatic or veiled form.

His excess of words has such infuriating consequences only because it prevents him from posing the fateful questions at the proper time. But how could he keep silent when he is quite ignorant of all the conditions of the quest? He does not even know the name of the object he must seek. Is he summoned to cure Count West-West of a secret malady like that of the wounded Fisher-King? This is quite possible (he could do it, if we believe in his epithet, the "Bitter Herb"), but there is no indication that the Count is sick, except perhaps for the doleful appearance of the Castle (K. also finds the sun's glitter on the windows "somewhat maniacal") or the peculiar consumption suffered by little Hans' mother, the only woman in the village who is of higher birth. Is K. the man who will put an end to the plagues of snow and perpetual winter and bring light to this land of shadows whose ruler (West-West) is the last of the setting sun? No one tells him this, no one shows him his goal or even tells him its name. He seeks nothing but the Grail itself, and so with no visible goal and no path to follow, his quest must remain in the realm of speculation or dream.

The Grail, in fact, throughout the body of legend[8] and whatever its form or hero, always has a single consistent function that is more epic than magic. It does not tend to suspend natural laws but rather to reestablish the order and well-being of earthly things. Whether the Grail is a marvel-

[8]Cf. "Lumière du Graal," *Cahiers du Sud,* 1951, and especially "Le héros du Graal," by Jean Marx.

ous vessel, a precious stone, or a liturgical object, it always signifies the same correspondence between the visible world and the invisible realm from which earthly things derive their stable form and their tangible validity. When the Grail is lost or forgotten, the earth decays, the world falls sick, and time itself is out of joint—until the Grail hero restores to the lost object its communicative force and living power (whoever sees the Grail is also rejuvenated). Now, in K.'s time, the sick and aging world is more than ever in need of the healing powers of the quest, and certainly the new champion is prepared for anything. But his good will serves no purpose, for there is no longer any object called Grail or anything else that represents a goal or even a direction[9] for all men of the same period and culture. In the modern era, the loss of the Grail is no longer the loss of a precious object that has been withdrawn from the world or temporarily hidden from men's eyes. It signals the decline of the symbol itself. In a time when order and disorder, sickness and health, error and truth no longer stand in diametric opposition but tend to merge and simulate each other, all that symbols provide is the support for rather primitive superstitions or half-forgotten literary remnants. Therefore, K. is bound to fail; indeed, he never even sets out on his way. He only prepares to do it by trying to forge for himself the symbolic tools that have disappeared and must be reinvented.

As with all of Kafka's heroes, the Land-Surveyor's adventures are limited to these literary investigations that he pur-

[9]All of Kafka's work revolves around this absence of direction, which is indeed a disease of language that literature is naturally the first to contract. His work does not deal with the absurdity of things, as we would think, but with their disorientation in a mental universe where they are no longer represented with any certainty.

sues with the professional consciousness of the modern hero, a hero who, because he is prevented from acting by the uncertainty and confusion of the times, has become an intellectual—a reasoner and a calculator who is hopelessly abandoned to the exegesis of the past. In previous times, perhaps, he would have been capable of heroic things. But he is like Bucephalus,[10] Alexander's old charger, who has lost his master and his purpose and so has turned to the law:

Today, as no one can deny, there is no Alexander the Great. Many, of course, still know how to murder; nor is there any lack of skill at stabbing your friend over the banquet table with a lance; and for many Macedonia is too narrow, so that they curse Philip, the father—but no one, no one can lead us to India. Even in those days, India's gates were unattainable, but their direction was designated by the royal sword. Today, the gates have been shifted elsewhere and higher and farther away; nobody points out their direction; many hold swords, but only to flourish them, and the glance that tries to follow them becomes confused.

Under these difficult circumstances the hero's only field of battle is the study where he can take refuge: "under a quiet lamp, far from the din of Alexander's battles, he reads and turns the pages of our old books."

Absorbed by this activity, the Land-Surveyor doesn't have time to become familiar with the village and he doesn't find the entrance to the Castle. On the other hand, he scours the centuries in order to see if, finally, somewhere in the far reaches of time, these ancient books don't contain some message for him. So, after playing the hero of a novel of manners, a serial novel, a fairy tale, and a medieval *chanson de geste,* K. becomes at last the follower of Odysseus. To recover and restore order to the land, K. must become, like his model, a nomad and a true penitent.

[10]Cf. "The New Attorney," in *Parables and Paradoxes,* Schocken, 1961.

It is clear that K. is specially gifted for this last stage of his imitation. In any case, he is persevering and shrewd, and he is very much, in his own way, the man of a thousand ruses, capable of foiling even the intrigues of the gods. Particularly fortuitous, however, is the arrangement of the place where K. must enact his plan, for in general it is like a replica of Homeric topography. In K.'s world, even more than in its Homeric model, Olympia is inaccessible, nearly lost to human sight. Situated on a hill and usually veiled in mist, the Castle dominates the village and extends its influence from afar into every aspect of daily life. The Castle gathers its information and exercises its power by means of a complete network of agents. Like Olympos, the Castle is an administrative entity responsible for the maintenance and organization of life, and at the same time it determines the norms that generate the ways and customs of the village. It is a complex hierarchy governed by the numerous officials, who, like the gods, control and administrate the diverse sectors of nature and history. They at once rule and represent these realms, since in a sense they embody only what exists. With their functions distributed according to the Olympian model, the gods of the Castle exercise their "official" competence only within their strictly designated limits, while the bureaucracy as a whole is omnipotent (from which arises K.'s puzzlement over administrative departments). Everything that happens in the village comes to the attention of the officials, nothing escapes them; they are the source of laws, morals, and collective customs, of life and death, of individual happiness and misery.

The Jupiter of this new Olympos hardly has the power and terrible majesty of his celebrated colleague. He is a twilight god (the last of the setting sun) who has relinquished his thunder and lightning and withdrawn from mundane affairs quite as much as from the divine bureaucracy. A retired Jupiter, in short, who no longer presides over any assembly and delegates the care of his government to the gentlemen and secretaries who record, consign, classify, and judge the most minor thoughts and events in his name. Understandably, the village, that has made a cult of the gentlemen,[11] and worships particularly those who have the most immediate jurisdiction over their fate: Klamm, god of love and marriage—no union is possible without him; Momus, the Greek god of banter and mockery, the only one who has kept his name and his primitive functions; Sortini, god of destiny and chance, who provokes dissension; Sordini, god of work and silence; Erlanger, god of applicants; and Bürgel, god of safeguards, with whom K. has special dealings and whom he sees in a dream posing like a Greek god, or to be more precise, like the statue of a god.[12] All these divinities work together to determine what is thought, said, and done in the world. They dispense jobs in the village (K. knows something about this, for he obtains no *official* post), encourage or break up love affairs, cause the village grief as well as prosperity and ruin. Socially, the cult of the Olympian gentlemen, which has its rites, its myths, and even its temple (the Herrenhof), is at once a natural bond and a rigid law for the entire community. Foreigners

[11]All of Kafka's art, its humor and high seriousness, is based on words that have been emptied of meaning through use, but suddenly take on their most primitive significance. We will see further on how Kafka's epic imitation is reenforced by such locutions as "to make a cult of someone," "to worship power," "to observe something religiously," etc.

[12]We will see later in detail the role of etymology in K.'s epic. In general, the administrative "competence" of the gentlemen is revealed by the etymological meaning of their names.

usually have no place (K. learns at his expense), and whoever refuses to practice the cult (like Amalia) puts himself
outside the law.

The Castle, which is not only the master but the model of
the earthly village (it is a small town, similar to all human
settlements though situated on higher ground), is in constant communication with its subjects. In addition to the
emissaries committed to the service of individuals (K. has
three of them: Barnabas, officially his messenger, and the
two assistants who are agents of Klamm, as K. learns too
late), the Castle also has a telephone line to its human counterpart (of course the operation of this connection leaves
something to be desired) and a crowd of "village secretaries," essentially liaison agents whose work consists
chiefly of traveling back and forth between the Castle and
the village. Ruined and abandoned as it seems, the village
actually has a firm system of support, for it is solidly upheld
on all sides by the bureaucracy of the Castle.

With such a well-constructed epic setting, the novel of the
Castle can be easily transformed into an Odyssean drama
with K. as director, actor, and, when he can be, audience-
witness. At the moment the novel begins, of course, this
Odyssey is already well advanced. K., routed from his
home by some Trojan war,[13] speaks vaguely of the wife and
child he has probably abandoned. He mentions as well a
long journey, of many years perhaps, during which he has
probably encountered dangers and hardships. But we are
not told what happened to him along the way. His adventures, properly speaking, begin when those of Odysseus
end, at the moment of his return—in K.'s case, the moment
of his arrival. Appearing, as Odysseus did, in the guise of a
ragged and exhausted vagabond, he is not recognized; in-

[13]Cf. below, the letter of Max Brod on this subject.

deed, he could not expect to be, for he has never been to the village before and will always remain a stranger there. But this doesn't prevent him from playing his role faithfully, with a courage, a humility, and an inventiveness that the hero of antiquity or Don Quixote himself might envy.

The hero of an impossible arrival and not a triumphant return, K. necessarily shifts around the episodes, which in any case are rather badly arranged in his epic model. Hence his adventures are not part of his wanderings but occur afterward, in the very place where he wants to settle and where, consequently, he must confront all at once his monsters, his sirens, and all the subtle enchanters who will try to ensnare him. These enchanters, as their function traditionally requires, represent the different degrees of femininity through which he must pass, one by one, before he is mature enough for a true marriage. (Unlike Odysseus, he is not married but only engaged, though in reality he is married elsewhere, at least if his first wife is not a pure invention intended to make him seem respectable.) There is Olga, the brave girl who is involved in the most repulsive aspects of love; Amalia, the fierce virgin who lives "face to face with truth" in proud contempt for the intricate love affairs of the Castle; Pepi, the young girl who has given up the world of men and who, like a new Circe, wants to hide K. on her feminine island where she would make him king; the mysterious woman who calls herself a girl, though she is the mother of two children, and who, coming from the Castle, watches over him from afar; the landlady of the Bridge Inn, the experienced matron who endeavors to initiate him into the secrets of Klamm-Eros in order to prepare him for the trial of marriage; the hostess of the Herrenhof who half unveils for him the ambiguous face of fate; and finally Frieda, the free, strong woman who has a "striking look of conscious superiority" (she subdues the obscure forces of life, like Klamm's servants, with a flick of the whip) and whose name holds out the promise of inner peace *(Friede)*. Each of these female figures frustrates his plans by showing him a possible kind of love, an accomplishment, and a hope of freedom, realized either in perfect harmony with the Castle or in open revolt against it. From the oldest to the youngest, all attract him and delay him, all enter into his calculations and offer him inordinate hopes; but he remains on his guard, and they all, finally, provoke his suspicion. Not as happy as Odysseus, nor as wise, he goes from one woman to the other without approaching his goal. He is too impatient to grasp fully the opportunities they offer him, too distracted to allow himself to be touched by them, too jealous of his freedom to consent to any real attachment. Seduced by all the women and girls of the village but incapable of forming a full and free union with any of them, K. misses the Castle as Odysseus would have missed his return if his "sentimental education" had also lamentably failed.

Before he declares his own bankruptcy—which is incontestable, socially speaking, but not at all from the particular perspective of his quest—K. sees the vast epic field open before him where his active meditation takes on the compass of time itself. He is provided with exemplary partners who are raised to epic heights by their exceptional character and the importance of their functions (according to the norms of the Castle and the village, all are infinitely powerful), and who provide him in some sense with a qualified cast. He is surrounded by honored, respected women ready to fulfill the many tasks of the Homeric heroines. He is gifted with unflagging vigilance and penetrating powers of observation, as well as a protean capacity for metamorphosis. K. possesses, it seems, all of the indispensable elements for the theatrical compilation of literary texts to which he is prompted by the sight of the monstrous library, filled to overflowing with current paperwork and musty archives, and called, for want of a better name, the "Castle." The way in which he deploys and uses these elements and with what success, guile, and integrity, we will discover by following him patiently through the labyrinth of deceptive and seductive images that he himself evokes as he makes his way.

Momus or Mockery

"Here you have your Greek god! Go on, haul
him out of bed!"
THE LAND–SURVEYOR
The Castle, The Eighteenth Chapter

I. EPIC LAW

IN SPITE of, or rather because of, its long history, the epic
easily overrides the more recent genres that are woven into
the texture of *The Castle*. These, in fact, scarcely do more
than sketch out the stages of the epic's decline and are in
themselves too weak to support the internal organization of
the narrative (although certainly the novel of manners and
the serial novel, among others, contain a kind of validity).
Indeed, Kafka is imitating Homer even as he tells the stories
of K., the opportunist, the reformer, the adventurer and
skirt chaser. Not merely to pay homage to the first master,
but because the epic seemed truly able to harmonize books
and life, in other words, to articulate a universal truth, and
this task still remains the most vital subject of literature.

In the service of his Homeric imitation, Kafka appropriates the indispensable science of names and the method of
epic composition that even more than the Olympian subject
of *The Castle* allow him to suggest an encompassing world
order, the fixed relations between things, that provides a

legitimate support for life (and of course for literature as well). In short, he borrows all of the vanished certainties that he would like to have the luxury of accepting or rejecting for himself. Thanks to a language and a method of composition that perfectly correspond to the demands of an exemplary action, the Castle will be the site of extraordinary events, a place where unusual things and absolutely unparalleled characters will make their appearance.

Paradoxically, the enormously rich vocabulary of names in the novel, and K.'s anonymity, which would of course be unacceptable in a truly novelistic hero, support Kafka's epic plan and its avowed aims in the same way. K., in effect, enters the realm of the novel already stripped of everything that constitutes corporal reality but that also marks the limits of the ordinary man: physical qualities, features, a natural circle of friends, family, and civic status. He is rootless in every sense of the word, entirely dispossessed. The poorest, most disinherited men still retain a surname, obscure as it may be, and a first name that is associated with childhood and parental affection. K. is the quintessential outsider, with no country and no history, more naked and alone than any other creature, real or fictional.[1] In this, of course, he reflects the typical situation of the modern man thrown into an anarchic world, where rootlessness and disorientation are the law. But precisely the extremity of his

[1]Even the most impoverished protagonist we can imagine—let us say Jakob Wassermann's Kaspar Hauser—still has a name and a creed, and the Marchioness of O., whom Kleist stripped of her name, is otherwise too well endowed—she has beauty, family, children, wealth—to retain her anonymity. Once someone compared K. to Kaspar Hauser, the man with no past and no place of origin, and Kafka answered that his protagonist was only "like Franz Kafka." (Cf. Gustav Janouch: *Kafka m'a dit,* 1952.) In the same way, the solitude of his fictional character is unique in literature.

solitude and uncertainty makes his fate unparalleled, so that with all his negative qualities he also represents an unprecedented frontier of the human. Distinguished only by his rags and his initial, unencumbered by that heavy baggage of dates, facts, memories, and possessions, which in life and in books represents the triumph of having over being, K. is free. It is precisely the enormity of what he lacks that makes him unique, as the hero of the epic must be.[2]

If Odysseus is too gifted, too privileged, burdened with too many unusual misfortunes for any mortal to boast of knowing trials even remotely comparable to his, K. on his side is so utterly dispossessed, so abnormally stripped of goods and qualities, that he must be located beyond ordinary experience in a realm that may be negative but is also unparalleled and therefore inaccessible to statistical measurement or empirical observation. With nothing of his own but his naked humanity, K. is infinitely closer to Odysseus and the great Homeric figures than to the bourgeois hero who is always a representative of his kind. K.'s destitution, which so forcefully pushes him below the common level of humanity, is also what dignifies his condition, and, from a literary point of view at least, restores to him a kind of nobility.

Kafka's radical paring down of his chief character has the same effect as Homer's embellishment of Odysseus and the other epic heroes. Reduced to the lowest common human denominator, K. can immerse himself entirely in his vocation of land-surveying and take on the epithet that serves him as an identity. K. is not a land-surveyor, then, as others

[2]This process of stripping down, which is found everywhere in Kafka's work, brings to mind Marx's idea that in a sense the proletarian is the exemplary man because he is entirely dispossessed, exhibiting nakedly what is masked and perverted by property.

are stone masons or architects. He is *the Land-Surveyor,* meaning a man defined, summed up, bound by his title as Paris the Abductor or Achilles the Achaean are bound by theirs. His epithet does more than replace the name he doesn't have: it binds him to an epic plan of action from which he cannot escape and therefore assures him, if not of actual parity, at least of a sort of virtual equality with the Olympian gentlemen.

On their elevated plane, the gentlemen dutifully and strictly follow the rules of epic nomenclature. Exactly like their divine counterparts, their names are words carrying a specific meaning, rather like signs that announce not only their simple civic status but also their attributes, their areas of competence, and even the meaning of their acts. The most important of the "gentlemen" (at least for K., since officially he is only the head of the tenth department) is also the one whose name is the richest in meanings and certainly the most ambiguous (again, it resembles the Homeric names whose etymology is by definition ambiguous, even fantastical). The word *Klamm* is actually a substantive and an adjective. Used as a noun, it denotes a gorge, a ravine or gully, a strait; as an adjective, it signifies narrowness, constraint, penury, or the numbing effect of cold. In both cases, it expresses the idea of something confined, something that binds, separates, constrains, and chills. But it is still closely related to *Klammer,* which denotes a hook, a fastener, a bracket, and to the compound words that mean to include, to exclude, to fasten onto something. If we relate all of these associations to Klamm's principal function, which is to preside over conjugal union, it must be admitted that this modern Eros, who is responsible for the unhappiness of his subjects, could not be more aptly and truthfully named.

As are the other gentlemen with whom K. has contact,

though their names are more simply constructed than
Klamm's and therefore apparently less subtle. *Erlanger*—the
meeting with him is of primary importance for K. (who
misses it)—evokes the verb *erlangen,* to achieve honors, to
gain assurance, to attain a goal. Bürgel, who finds himself
confiding to K. the secret conditions of eventual success,
derives his name from the verb *bürgen,* to answer to, to
guarantee. *Friedrich* is obviously evocative of peace, as *Sordini* is of deafness (or of a damper on a musical instrument)
and *Sortini* of the fates he casts, unless it is of his own unhappy fate. *Momus* retains the mythological name that
marks him as the critic of Olympos (he is the one who reveals the faults of the gods and exposes them to mockery).
As for *Galater,* the gentleman who is nearly powerless because of his obesity, his graceful name must be connected to
milk. The names, of course, become less vivid and complex
as one descends the social hierarchy, so that the eminent
gentlemen have a much greater nominative value than the
secretaries of the second order. Indeed, an under-castellan is
called simply *Schwarzer* (the Black), and an ordinary worker
may be named, like everyone else in Germany, Fritz or
Oswald.

The law of significant denominations evidently has no
currency in the village where the people bear rather grim but
common names: the Lasemanns, Brunswick, Gerstäcker,
could pass unnoticed in any German province. The notables
of the place—the Mayor, the teacher, the two innkeepers—have no surnames at all, unless K. does not
know them and simply replaces the names with titles. On
the other hand, people who have personal dealings with him
are given epic names that are particularly striking: Arthur
evokes the legendary king, and Jeremiah the prophet of the

Old Testament; Barnabas is literally the Son of Promise[3] (like the apostle Paul's companion), and Frieda is the very incarnation of peace (there is another Frieda in the narrative who somewhat obscures the clarity of the case[4]). As for the other women K. encounters, they all bear typically Austrian first names (Mizzi, Pepi, Olga, Amalia), which were probably favored in the diverse countries of the old monarchy chiefly because they could be pronounced easily in all languages. Only the landlady of the Bridge Inn has an unusual first name (Gardena), whereas the patroness of the Herrenhof hasn't a name at all (K. doesn't give her a title and even addresses her with the personal pronoun).

A brief examination of this varied nomenclature is sufficient proof that Kafka did not abide by any strict rule of fictional anonymity, but on the contrary named his characters with a remarkably free hand. And we can see from this rich assortment of names that *The Castle* violates one of the basic tenets of epic law. In place of the strong ethnic and linguistic unity that marks the Olympian world of the epic, the Castle presents a cosmopolitan milieu where aboriginal names (those of the German gentlemen) comingle with foreign surnames, which perhaps become customary through long use, but still strike a discordant note. In the epic, names are in harmony with the material and spiritual order they support: the gods are all Greek, and though the

[3]The etymology proposed by N. Fürst, op. cit.

[4]This is the sister of little Hans, the child of the "girl from the Castle," the virgin mother, if she is to be believed. The sight of her plunges K. into a kind of reverie and the mystery surrounding her has provoked much discussion. Her virginity, her veil-like silken kerchief, the baby nursing at her breast, her suffering, and the role of intercessor that K. would like her to play make her appear to certain critics to be the incarnation of the Virgin. We will see below what her role really is.

Achaeans and the Trojans may be in conflict, Olympos
exists precisely to give them an example of national unity. In
The Castle, however, Olympos is at once highly centralized
and radically cosmopolitan (obviously an allusion to the old
Austro-Hungarian monarchy[5]), whereas the village consists of a perfectly homogeneous population that finds
mongrels and crossbreeds especially distasteful, as the general attitude toward K. indicates. The Castle governs the
village, then, but does not mirror it or really influence its
manners and ideas. The cosmopolitanism above does not
correspond to the exclusiveness below, and K., who is
persecuted from both sides, vacillates painfully between
the two orders of things. A resemblance between the realms
of the Castle and the village is continuously implied, but this
is quite obviously a lie, since they share no common principle.

A universal Castle where the gentlemen of various origins
work together without distinction of language or race and
collaborate with an ancient god who is the guarantor of their
beneficence—such a Castle ordinarily would require the
universality of the village and would favor, indeed demand,
K.'s easy admission. It does nothing of the kind. For the
Castle, the village, and K. himself, are moved by images
that have no common meaning, no contemporaneity, or
even any analogous substance. The Castle purports to be
universal, with a touch of Greek antiquity that ought to
remind us of its spiritual origins. The village, however,

[5]It is worth noting that the administration of the Castle (like the tribunal
in *The Trial*) gives a preferred place to the Italian gentlemen and does not
include any Hungarians or Czechs, for example. If we find it astonishing
that Kafka could, even ironically, elevate the Austrian bureaucracy to a
kind of Olympian dignity, we should remember the extraordinary dura-
tion and, even until its demise, the stability of the double monarchy that
must have seemed a permanent institution to its contemporaries.

remains bound to its archaic law and though it is touched by the ideas of the Castle, violently defends its almost tribal ways and narrow local patriotism. K., who is incapable of grasping these reciprocal relations and determining their origins, turns for help to the established canon of literature where the images surface pell-mell, regardless of their historical roots (Arthur, a creation of medieval literature, is entirely merged in spirit with the Biblical prophet, Jeremiah, and keeps company with Barnabas from the New Testament). In place of the two Homeric spheres whose opposition, resemblance, and interchange formerly underwrote the authority of the epic, *The Castle* contains three zones of experience that have no correspondence or avenues of mutual access, and the third consists of a single individual who is hopelessly estranged.

This linguistic irregularity weighs heavily on K.'s fate, but it is not the only consideration. In general, the Castle names that seem so suggestive and full of meaning turn out to be more deceptive than informative. In principle, they indicate precisely each official's sector of activity, but in reality they are neither precise nor comprehensive, nor are they confirmed by experience. Klamm, for example, not only presides over the joys and sorrows of love. He is also responsible for the organization, distribution, and security of work in the village (K.'s professional life, the accomplishment of his vocation, are entirely in Klamm's hands); certainly his ambiguous name, which evokes labor and effort, might also apply to this essential function. Nevertheless, Klamm's name does not properly correspond to the entire range of his jurisdiction, which is enormous and so diverse that no one altogether comprehends what it is. K.'s informants never tire of telling him that Klamm is everywhere, that he intervenes in all human affairs, that he determines all sorts of human relationships and influences every custom. Still, each person sees him differently according to the place, the time of day, the conditions of the meeting. The villagers' thoughts, feelings, and dreams affect Klamm's very appearance (though all agree that he wears a black jacket with long tails). Consequently, any notion is possible and the only certainty is his name. Yet this name is probably a mockery, a false label, and "the man who is called Klamm is perhaps not Klamm at all . . ."; he may well be one with Momus, for example (some think so). What characterizes him still better is the way he evades his petitioners, who link him, aptly, with Proteus[6] rather than with the god of love.

The name, function, and appearance of the gentlemen are nearly always deceptive, as if motivated by some hidden spite. The man K. spies on through the peephole looks nothing like Klamm the seducer or Klamm the tireless worker described in village legend. He is "a middle-sized, plump, and ponderous man. His face was still smooth, but his cheeks were already somewhat flabby with age" (3rd Ch.); he has a black mustache and wears a pince-nez. In his hand he holds not a pen but a Virginia cigar, and K. observes with astonishment that on his desk is a beer glass but no trace of papers. At the moment he observes Klamm, K. does not know that the gentleman is deeply asleep. He will learn later that this indefatigable worker has a prodigious need for sleep, and that, furthermore, he is chiefly celebrated for his somnolent manner, a dreamy and absent air that the Castle snobs try to imitate without success. All this scarcely con-

---

[6]Proteus had received the gift of prophecy from his father, Poseidon, but he often refused to speak, and to avoid his suppliants changed his shape at will. Odysseus, however, succeeded in extorting information from him by means of a ruse.

forms to the ideas of constraint and restraint associated with his name. From what K. sees of him, he evokes, rather, indolence (the inside of his carriage is entirely lined with furs), a taste for comfort, the cordial humor of a man-about-town. And the names of his colleagues are no less deceptive. Sordini is associated with silence, but at the same time he makes thunder (the enormous piles of paper heaped in his office continually fall to the floor, "and it's just those perpetual crashes, following fast on one another, that have come to distinguish Sordini's workroom" [5th Ch.]). Sortini has to do with fate or chance, yet he is chiefly known for his competence in fire fighting, though one doesn't know if his element is water or fire (during the village celebration that seals the fate of the Barnabas family, he is riding on the fire engine and there conceives his fatal passion for Amalia). Moreover, this area of expertise that seems to be erotic doesn't at all suit his appearance, for he is puny and retiring, and no one in the Castle is more awkward with women. Judging from his behavior towards Amalia, his realm seems to be neither water nor fire, but rather that intense intellectual activity that has probably deprived him of any natural life and has left his forehead indelibly wrinkled ("all the furrows—and there were plenty of them, though he's certainly not more than forty—were spread fanwise over his forehead, running toward the root of his nose . . ." ["Amalia's Secret"]). This intellectual who is cut off from the world and is obscene probably out of awkwardness and naïveté, is not in the least prepared for the high functions of chief of the Fire Brigade, which, in the minds of the villagers, are clearly related to love and life. Still, in part he justifies his name, for Amalia is certainly the victim of fate, brought to Sortini's attention by a borrowed garnet necklace that she is wearing strictly by chance. This is not however the case with Erlanger, Bürgel, Friedrich, and others, who, in their relations with K., quite baldly disavow the promises of their names. Erlanger does nothing to further the cause of his applicants. Bürgel says, "Who can vouch for everything?" [18th Ch.] *(Wer kann für alles Bürgen?)* If Friedrich is the bearer of peace, this is an additional mockery, for he is in disgrace and has scarcely any clients.

Not only the gentlemen, but all those who have any contact, intimate or distant, with the Castle bear what seem to be false signs. K.'s "assistants" are intrusive characters who present the most serious obstacles to his success. Frieda does not bring him the tranquility of love, but its pain. Barnabas does not deserve either the name "Son of Promise" or his title of "messenger." He is an abject and anxious child whom K. finally blames for his failure. Whether they are applied to gods or men, the labels that language fixes on people and things always lead to error. In the midst of these approximations and half-truths, only Momus shows any resolution; promising only criticism and negation, he at least can keep his word.

These falsifications are a serious matter, for if it could be established that Momus is the true master of the Castle, Klamm a caricature, and Bürgel a Greek god frozen in an absurd pose, K.'s investigations might be neatly and rapidly concluded. But there is no definitive proof, no certainty, and since K. wants to discover everything for himself, he cannot base his conclusions on the highly contradictory testimony of others. In this well-labeled world, names are indeed deceptive. But not all of them are, nor are they false in the same way or at the same moment. A thorough-going scepticism regarding these names, then, is no more intelligent than credulity, and can in some cases prove even more dangerous. The assistants behave as if they had sworn their master's ruin. Nevertheless, as K. learns too late, they are really very much his assistants, earnestly sent by the Castle to distract him, to help him cure himself of his excessive seriousness, which the Castle views as his worst sin. In the same way, Frieda and Barnabas could, in spite of everything, contribute to his happiness, though perhaps he doesn't know how to take advantage of their good will. Perhaps, too, he doesn't understand the facts very well. Still, he has no right to draw premature conclusions. Since he is unable to accept the equivocal verbal labels of the Castle or to reject them altogether, as the presence of Momus tempts him to do, he must continue his arduous task of confronting facts with words, without demanding a more definitive proof.

This entirely intellectual confrontation forms the basis of his Odyssean pilgrimage, a journey that is quite different from its model but very much in conformity with the tradition. K. can hope to understand the Castle only by talking about his concerns to all those who, rightly or wrongly, seem qualified to provide him with information. So he goes from house to house, runs back and forth between the Bridge Inn, the Herrenhof, and the Barnabas family, turning from one partner to the other (we see him with the two innkeepers, the mayor of the village, Olga, Momus, and Bürgel; and wherever he is he does almost nothing but talk). In a sense, his very presence generates a series of identical conversations, just as the person of the epic hero evokes certain tasks and ordeals. These conversations, which are substitutes for the action he is not capable of performing, have the predetermined outline, the obligatory character, the cyclical movement that unmistakably mark every true odyssey. As K., of course, does not act, in this respect he is

234 The Old and the NewThe Old and the New

clearly the antithesis of Odysseus. Yet he is bound to the repetition of his conversations—which each one of his interlocutors earnestly tries to change into a temptation and trial—with the regularity that the epic so highly values as a means of expressing the permanence of its order. Inspecting one by one all his possible avenues of knowledge, just as Odysseus toured the world, K. moves from Calypso to Circe (the two landladies possess a bit of magic too), from Scylla to Charybdis, from mystery to enigma, and so imbues what is essentially interminable gossip with the epic richness requisite to his enterprise. Once more, Kafka's hero draws his literary fortune precisely from his worst deficiencies. Constrained to do nothing but gossip and turn around in circles, he faces over and over again the same obstacles, the same dangers, the same enemies. And thanks to this continuous repetition, which prevents him from acting or achieving even a modicum of success, he makes his entrance with perfect legitimacy into legend.

Composed in the Homeric fashion with its pivotal feature a hero who is invulnerable to experience and incapable of development, *The Castle* appears to be a succession of episodes that are almost perfectly analogous but share few or no logical connections. Certainly this is why K.'s demands are always denied and he is continually prompted to take new measures. But each one of his encounters is independent of the others. What transpires in the first conversation has no observable repercussions, and with a single exception (his visit to the Barnabas home, which Frieda offers as the immediate cause of their breakup) the episodes of his story are juxtaposed without any buildup of tension and never approach an eventual dénouement. The incidents, therefore, constitute an open series that is susceptible to additions or deletions (the precise number of women K. knows or the steps he takes to further his aims has no bearing on the logic of the narrative). Indeed, one can imagine even a partial inversion of the facts—K. might see Momus after his meeting with Bürgel, visit the Mayor before speaking with the Gardena, meet Pepi before Olga, etc. *The Castle* is not so entirely composed of discrete episodes that it could be read in any order at all,[7] but given the episodic and relatively autonomous character of its parts, it would certainly neither gain nor lose much if it were read in a different arrangement. The fragments and deleted passages, moreover, suggest that Kafka had not definitively fixed the number of order of his chapters. What would he have interpolated or shifted around if he had been able or willing to finish the novel? We cannot say. Even though its development is more consistent than *Amerika* and *The Trial*,[8] which are both decidedly fragmentary, *The Castle* is not distin-

[7]Because Kafka left his three novels unfinished, we are able to gain a clear understanding of his method. In general (and this holds true even for the long stories like "The Great Wall of China") he didn't compose his narratives by following a continuous thread but by connecting discrete episodes that shared only certain points of contact and often displayed enormous gaps (evoking the construction of the wall itself, on principle fragmentary and full of gaps). We should also note the presence, in the posthumous texts, of numerous variants and analogues that indicate how important the principle of repetition was for Kafka.

[8]The "episodic" composition that transforms Kafka's novels into pseudo epics even as it transcribes an actual contemporary situation, has also caused a great deal of critical furor. Generally, the order of the chapters seems to be so loosely established that other, if not better, possibilities could be conceived. The one that Brod adopted for *The Trial*, for example, has been violently attacked by a philologist who has pointed out a number of contradictions in the progression of events, which, he maintains, would be inconceivable for an artist as scrupulous as Kafka, who was so attentive to matters of verisimilitude (Cf. H. Uyttersprot, *Eine Neue Ordnung der Werke Kafkas?*, Antwerp, 1957). However well founded this criticism might be (and this could be determined only by an examination of the manuscripts), it is interesting because it underscores the exceptionally loose character of Kafka's composition. Nevertheless, as it is actually published, *The Trial* seems at first glance to be completely coherent and presents no particular anomalies.

guished by its continuity; it continually begins again at each
point where the tenuous thread of the novelistic action
seems about to snap. Whatever Kafka's ultimate conception
may have been, the novel remains bound to the principle of
eternal return, which opens it to the sweeping space of the
epic but also condemns it to remain unfinished.

Here, as on other points, Kafka's art makes a virtue of
necessity. Instead of mitigating the loneliness, destitution,
and helplessness of his hero—which would change the integrity of his character and transform him into an exemplary
type—Kafka exaggerates K.'s defects to such a degree that
they soon cease to be the accidental, relative inadequacies
common to all of humanity. K. becomes a kind of degree
zero of the human, an absolute starting point from which
anything is possible. The epic character of *The Castle* results
entirely from this radical abstraction, by which Kafka so
uncompromisingly translated the spiritual situation of his
contemporaries and his own rootlessness. The Homeric
poem was the image of a world, an order of things and
assumptions that offered the poet a viable law for life and a
subject for poetic inspiration.[9] Kafka's novel reflects with
equal precision the chaos, the disarray, the isolation, which
in his time became the hidden norm of existence. The two
works, the epic and *The Castle,* articulate absolutely contrary facts, but they play the same revelatory role. One
reveals the *totality* of an order that individual experience can
grasp only in its details; the other the *totality*[10] of a disorder

[9]Friedrich Beissner's words on this subject are very much to the point:
"Homer, who set the norm for all of Western literature, created in a world
and created a world that was still solidly anchored in its order. The Muse, a
living, worshipped divinity, prompts the rhapsodist to sing the glory of
men . . ." (op. cit.).

[10]This enterprise has been authoritatively analyzed in the work of
Wilhelm Emrich: *Franz Kafka,* Bonn, 1958.

that life itself disguises and that the individual, in any case, cannot fathom. These works may be separated by an enormous gulf, but they have in common an all-encompassing vision that is the justification of ancient art and has by now become the most impossible of quixotic longings.

Nowhere has the complete deprivation that Kafka proposed had such remarkable consequences as in the realm of language. This is understandable, since language in *The Castle* is the object and tool of research, as well as the means by which truth is revealed or veiled, served or betrayed. This deprivation leads, in the first instance, to the exclusion of all modes of lyric expression that would falsify the actual situation of the artist. Kafka is not one of those ancient bards whose song responded to the needs and aspirations of a whole people. He is a modern writer, isolated in the midst of a world where literature long ago lost any definite function and consequently has no responsibility or mandate, free precisely because of its inutility. His lyricism would be as ridiculous, tiresome, and false as the pitiful piping of Josephine,[11] which is moving in its way but serves no purpose and is not even a talent beyond the capacities of the most humble mice. In Kafka's eyes, no shred of epic grandeur clings to the contemporary poet; he is not stronger but weaker than other men.[12] His work is probably dispensable, and in the final analysis it is of interest only to himself. Stripped of any social reality, he hovers in an empty space like those flying dogs who seem to be normal, but who,

[11]Cf. "Josephine the Singer, or the Mouse Folk," in *The Complete Stories,* Schocken Books, Inc., N.Y., 1946.

[12]Cf. *Kafka m'a dit,* by Gustav Janouch, Calmann-Lévy, 1952. "Truly, the poet is always smaller and weaker than the average person in society. That is why he feels more intensely, more deeply, than other men the weight of his presence in the world."

instead of living on the earth, float in the air and are generously paid for their efforts by the canine society ("They have no relation whatever to the general life of the community, they hover in the air, and that is all, and life goes on its usual way; someone now and then refers to art and artists, but there it ends. But why, my good dogs, why on earth do these dogs float in the air?" [13]). Suspended in an opaque heaven far from the labor and suffering of men, art has become an absurd phenomenon, and the artist himself an imposter and a parasite. Certainly Josephine is in good faith when she imagines she can save her people with her song. But the mouse folk find laughable her pretension that in exchange for her services she should be excused from all labor. Far from being saved by their national singer, they in fact protect *her* and minister to her needs. The mouse folk love Josephine very much and indulge her caprices, but they are inflexible on one point: the artist must bend to the common law and earn her living by honest work. If she refuses, they will be easily consoled for their loss.[14]

In addition to these general proscriptions against lyricism, Kafka had personal motives for cultivating a spare, clean prose that is reduced to the strictest economy of means. His own situation was so full of the contradictions, ambiguities, and falsehoods of the writer's condition that what was for others a source of uneasiness was for him a serious affliction that affected not only his work but his actual use of language as well. Every modern writer is an isolated person without any purpose or definite status;

[13]Cf. "Investigations of a Dog," *The Complete Stories,* Schocken Books Inc., N.Y., 1946.

[14]"The time will soon come when her last notes sound and die into silence. She is a small episode in the eternal history of our people, the people will get over the loss of her" ("Josephine the Singer, or the Mouse Folk").

nevertheless, he is usually part of a human group that is bound together by a native soil, a common language, and a shared past and future. Kafka was a foreigner in his own country and the language he spoke was imported, a gift from which he profited, so to speak, by fraud. If he loved the German language ("Language," he once said, "is an eternal beloved"), he did not use it with complete freedom but rather with a certain discomfort, doubt, and scruple. Historically, his German is not quite a living language. It is the artificial language, at once abstract and corrupted, of a small group of Prague Jews who had no native soil or social roots, and were as alien to the Jewish culture of Eastern Europe as they were to Germany and Bohemia. The chief virtues of this language, desiccated by such restricted use, were in a sense administrative. Moreover, Kafka did not feel that he was legitimate heir to this language but only a guest, a visitor tolerated by tacit agreement, and as such bound to a certain discretion. Although he had learned it in his childhood and had no other means of expression,[15] the German language did not do justice to his native gifts. It was a familiar yet inaccessible tool that translates his Jewish feeling in only a very approximate way and therefore falsifies the nuances of his thought. The uneasiness that Kafka experienced when he pronounced the basic words of his language—*Vater* and *Mutter,* for example, which rang almost shockingly false to his Jewish ear[16]—was so basic to his very existence that he could never forget or dispel it. He could, however, describe it accurately in a style appropriate

[15]He spoke Czech fluently but did not write it. During the last years of his life he devoted himself assiduously to the study of Hebrew.

[16]Cf. on the subject of these problems of language: Marthe Robert, Preface to the *Journal* and Kafka's numerous remarks in his various notebooks.

to an affidavit, which was indeed a discreet way of lodging a complaint.

With the inflexibility dictated by his need for precision, Kafka created his language through the force of renunciation and deprivation. So as not to be the usurper of German, he hedged himself in, as it were, on both sides. He not only renounced the verbal resources whose free exploitation is the poet's basic right; he deprived himself equally of the vivid prose that the novelist might naturally employ to render psychological nuances, geographical and social differences, and formal contrasts. Hence the unique qualities of his style, which is pure and neutral, without any rare vocables or neologisms, closed to those archaic verbal associations of which Germans are so fond, but also lacking in color and variety. (Kafka satirizes this monotony in the art of the painter Titorelli in *The Trial,* who always paints the same landscape with the same sky and the same gray tree.) It has often been remarked that all of Kafka's characters speak a homogeneous language in which nothing betrays their social origins, their habits, or their temperaments. None of them is greedy, timid, intense, cultivated, vulgar—all are flattened in such a way that the lovers speak as if they were indifferent; the lowest of the porters has the same tone, the same vocabulary, the same delivery as the most prestigious of the gentlemen; a barmaid, a little kitchen maid, even a child (little Hans, for example) express themselves with as much concision, grammatical correctness, and aptitude for abstraction as the intellectual of the novel, K. himself. Picturesque styles, affective tics, nuances of dialect or slang, the slips of everyday speech, have no part in that verbal universe where equality before the word comes to compensate, at least in principle, for the effects of the social hierarchy. In principle, however, not in fact, for it is a formal and abstract equality that operates at the margins of society, the very place where Kafka felt himself relegated by the inequities and anomalies of his condition.

In fact, Kafka's approach to language is doubly ascetic, marking his style with more and more stringency as it evolves. In his youthful writings, we still find a kind of poetic verve, abundant metaphors, and unexpected verbal constructions.[17] The major stories of his maturity and his three novels, however, preserve no vestige of those lyric tendencies that he fought in himself; only a few short texts, nearly prose poems, attest to their continuing existence.[18] In *The Castle* and the last stories ("The Burrow," "Josephine the Singer," etc.) the work of purification begun ten years earlier (we can date it at 1912, the period of "The Judgment") is pushed so far that except for very occasional metaphors that are bracketed by their isolation, there is scarcely anything left to be done. In the whole of *The Castle* there are barely two or three imagistic passages (among them the account of K. and Frieda's embrace), a few poetic comparisons (of Klamm and the eagle, in which K.'s fantasy delights), and several isolated figures of speech ("official decisions are as shy as young girls" [15th Ch.]) in which,

[17]Cf. "Description of a Struggle" *(The Collected Stories),* and on Kafka's early style: Klaus Wagenbach, *Franz Kafka, Eine Biographie seiner Jugend,* Berne, 1958.

[18]Cf. the fragments in *Wedding Preparations in the Country,* as well as the stories in *The Great Wall of China* ("The Vulture," "The Bridge," etc.). In many instances, a final long, musical sentence breaks the dryness of a neutral and impersonal text, but most often Kafka's lyricism is expressed in a syntactical fashion, sometimes, as in "A Country Doctor," by irregular, abrupt sentences following the rhythm of the doctor's escapade, sometimes, as in the story of the circus rider ("Up in the Gallery"), by an endlessly run-on sentence that makes up the entire sketch.

finally, the metaphor tends to mock itself.[19] Otherwise, the novel is written in a language that is neutralized, purified of all affect, beautiful only because of the richness and suppleness of the sentence, fascinating because of its implacable rigor—a language that is, in the end, graceful because it refuses to be decorative.

This exercise in purity bears the same significance as the experimental reduction by which Kafka shapes his characters. It is evidence, in the first instance, of a personally ambiguous situation that eludes direct expression. Indeed, the nature of such a situation is to suppress the possibilities of a frank explanation that in other cases remains a weapon against isolation. If Kafka could have made himself understood by frankly exposing his position and gained the sympathy of others through a moving account of his plight, his dilemma would have been half resolved. His original laments would then seem false and ridiculous. Therefore, he is silent about the real curse of his life and limits himself to invoking it through the vigorous constraints of language. In a sense, his style becomes the equivalent of a content that, if translated, might sound something like this: as a Jew who is culturally and linguistically German, living in an enclave foreign to my race and to my borrowed language, I have no mother tongue that I might enrich, renew, exploit or over-

[19]Kafka wrote spontaneously in the form of the *parable,* but he mistrusted this propensity to symbol and image. We have proof of this in the narrative entitled, precisely, *Parables,* as well as in many a passage in his *Diaries.* This one, for example: "'. . . It is at this fire that I warm myself during this sad winter . . . .' Metaphors are one of the things that make me despair of literature. Literary invention lacks independence, it depends on the maid who makes the fire, on the cat who warms itself near the stove . . . All this corresponds to autonomous functions having their own laws. Only literature cannot help itself, cannot accommodate itself, it is at once a game and an affliction."

turn at my whim, as anyone who possesses a legitimate heritage can do without giving it a second thought. Consequently, I shall create nothing, invent nothing, I shall pass through German literature with the discretion appropriate under the circumstances, hoping to leave no trace of my passage.[20] I write because I cannot do otherwise, but at least I have carefully mitigated my indiscretion by taking my inspiration from the only language open to me, as it is to anyone: the language of the official documents that establish my legal existence as an Austrian citizen and, though I have no right to complain, cripple my actual life. In all logic, I have no other muse than the all-powerful bureaucracy whose rules I must obey.

In fact, Kafka composed his work aided by the German of the chancellery, which created a superficial unity among the diverse minorities within the old Austrian Empire, a conventional and abstract bond that served to mitigate the confusion of languages. This bureaucratic language was imposed in all the provinces of the empire and was meant to insure a political domination as well as to normalize continuously disturbed human relationships. It soared above individual differences and, at least on paper, regulated national disputes, camouflaged conflicts, and finally made the empire seem indestructible. Kafka's unique genius was to clothe his bureaucratic vision of the world in the epic style that the anomalies of his personal situation and his own intransigence did not allow him to create.

More than any of his works, *The Castle* evolves directly from this epic transposition by which the idiom of gov-

---

[20]If this view does not completely explain Kafka's frequently expressed desire to destroy his work, we can nevertheless assume that it is intimately related to it.

ernmental offices comes to approximate the noble language
of Homer (which, we should note, also originated as the
specialized language of a caste). The Olympian gentlemen
impose on everyone the pseudo-universal speech that in-
sures their domination, propagates their vision, and seems
all the more absolute as it annihilates the nuances and vari-
ables of the human condition. Forming an elite beyond social class and history, the gentlemen reinforce their political
despotism with a verbal tyranny that transforms their pro-
nouncements into eternal truths and their words into ora-
cles. Kafka embodies this complicity between *power* and
words—a fact of daily life but one that is rarely recognized—by means of a singular semantics that creates a
shroud of mystery and ambiguity when it is applied to the
simplest situations. The words "castle" and "village," "assistants" and "gentlemen," are in themselves perfectly
transparent. But Kafka takes them in their absolute grammatical sense with no modifiers or predicates. Each of these
basic vocables then becomes the point of departure for an
enigma, since it raises questions such as *where? whose? when?
what for?*, which the text, faithful to the tyranny of the gentlemen, regularly leaves unanswered. These same words,
moreover, which describe beyond the shadow of a doubt an
actual situation (the Castle has a telephone), are insistently
employed in the powerful and noble sense that they originally had, and which, displaced, necessarily leads to error.

In the context of the novel, the key words (if one can call
them that) have double meanings—one modern and
exhausted, the other ancient and vigorous—which continually and simultaneously affirm and thwart each other. For
Kafka, the Castle is clearly the residence of the privileged,
but it is equally the place defined etymologically as an enclo-
sure *(Schloss-geschlossen)*. The "gentlemen" are gentlemen

in the bourgeois sense of the term, but they are also the lords and masters *(Herren)*. The "assistants" are both companions in the medieval sense and modern employees *(Gehilfen)*. As for Barnabas *(der Bote),* he can be taken equally for a messenger, an errand boy, or a vulgar apprentice, since carrying letters seems to be the essential point of his mission.[21] This mutation of meaning explains the extraordinary dignity that clothes characters, objects, and places, whatever their niche in the hierarchy or their particular value. The two village inns, for instance, are simple inns, nothing more, and K. is not at all mistaken about their precise functions. But Kafka treats everything about them with such respect and seriousness that from the first we invest them involuntarily with mysterious powers. Of course nothing in these establishments justifies such respect; not only are they quite plain and disorderly, they are positively filthy and disreputable. The Herrenhof is the village tavern and brothel, and the "landlady" of the Bridge Inn seems to play a rather suspect role. Yet there is the old meaning of the word "inn" *(Hof),* evoking the magnanimity of feudal lords, beauty, and courtesy.[22] It doesn't matter that the Herrenhof is a sordid place; it bears an aristocratic sign that raises not only its proprietors but also its barmaids and servants, and to a certain degree even its clients, high above their objective station. (The

---

[21]It is interesting that in translations the old and noble meaning is generally employed, even though the current meaning would do as well. No doubt this choice is dictated by aesthetic considerations ("assistant" and "messenger" are more elegant than "employee" and "postman"), but it also demonstrates the power of the illusion that Kafka created throughout his work to disabuse his reader.

[22]In German, the movement from the royal or princely meaning to the modern commercial one is still extremely noticeable. The same word means the court and the hotel (Hof), the page and the groom (Page), shield and sign (Schild), etc.

same is true of the Bridge Inn, though it is more proper and less prestigious.) Within this house that reeks of the stale smell of sour beer, the patroness is a lady, the barmaid is a person respected and envied by the villagers, the most menial tasks have the quality of important acts, and the servants obey a mysterious law that is almost priestly. K. can enter this banal and disturbing place but he hasn't the right to go beyond the public room. The rest of the house takes on a sacred aspect because it is forbidden to him, placed under an interdict of unknown origin (and strictly meant for him).

One might explain this magnification of persons and places by the presence of the gentlemen, but it is equally true at the Bridge Inn, where the gentlemen never go. Its patroness is also a venerable woman who might even possess formidable power, since it is she, finally, who determines K.'s fate. It is more likely that the inns take their quasi-sacred character directly from the Castle itself. The ceremonious tone in which the Castle is mentioned, the hierarchy that governs the inns, the prevailing etiquette—all this provokes the thought that between the two sorts of places there is, if not a perfect identity, at least a singular resemblance, and, as K. suspects when he observes the intimacy between the landlady of the Bridge Inn and Momus, perhaps even a disturbing complicity. The topographical puzzle of the novel would thus be explained: the Castle and the village are not opposed like heaven and earth, but rather, like the old and the new, they are strikingly similar, forever trying to disentangle themselves and remaining inextricably entwined. The inn below is sordid *and* sacred, for it is all that remains of the old Castle, whose memory survives vaguely in the roots of words. This survival lends the inn an aura of dignity, but at the same time—and this is the source of the novel's magic—deprives it of a portion of its reality.

We can see that the Land-Surveyor, by virtue of a word taken back to its earliest source, finds himself in a situation entirely comparable to Don Quixote's. Don Quixote takes all the inns he encounters for castles, while K. takes inns for what they are and invests them with the noble functions they once served in another world, light years away from their present commercialism. K. distinguishes perfectly well, even too well, between the Castle and the village. The source of his confusion is rather the elevation of the inn, such as it is, with its triviality, its tedious work, its filth and debauchery, to the rank of the aristocratic institution that once embodied not only luxury and power but the most exalted idea of hospitality. K.'s error seems superficially to have nothing in common with Don Quixote's extravagance, since everyone around him makes the same mistake; yet the result is the same. It does K. no good to be clear-minded and even gifted with an exceptional lucidity. He is nonetheless a victim of this displacement of respect and faith that Cervantes already perceived to be so important in his own time. In a period when there are no more castles, the aristocratic coats of arms become signs for inns, pages become grooms, subjects become customers; and meanwhile, the universal law that was symbolized by the castle crumbles into a profusion of rules (the prohibition that prevents K. from passing the night at the inn is simply a police ordinance). But on another side, the debasement of sacred institutions, the degradation of human "commerce" to profit making, the fragmentation or vulgarization of exalted objects, does not at all imply the disappearance of piety. Quite to the contrary, the force of piety and awe remains intact; but lacking its original object, it is grafted onto substitutes that are more or less debased or ridiculous, so the old systems of authority that are emptied of their original content continue to govern underground. Once nothing is sacred, anything can be. Kings are created from functionaries, heroes from bit players and adventurers, art from trash, the ideal from power or success—or from anything, provided that it nourishes faith, respect, and the need to worship. This is the meaning of K.'s unusual and yet distinctly modern conduct. By treating the most ordinary places like sacred shrines, the most idiotic characters like potentates, the most degraded women like queens, the most bourgeois gentlemen like gods, K. reveals one of the latent realities of his time.

It is not then the dearth, but rather the abundance and radical diffusion of the sacred that leads to K.'s failure. If there were a rigorous separation between the Castle and the village, communication between the two spheres might at least be possible. K. would be able to experience the village as it is and decide, quite objectively, whether to go or to stay. Yet the actual separation is not clear. The gentlemen frequent the village and in principle they exalt everything they touch: the inns where they sleep, the women they seduce, the beer they drink, and even their brutal domestics. In reality, however, this metamorphosis is only partial, a pseudo spiritualization that splits reality in two, destroying its contours and solidity. The ubiquitous presence of the gentlemen casts a charm over the life of the village: an inn is no longer simply an inn, it is an undefined place where beer becomes a magic potion, erotic consummation a rite, police ordinances taboos, and rooms sanctuaries where only the initiated may enter. Objects distorted and deflected from their original purpose in this way, however, are in fact trivialized even as they are apparently exalted. Half castle, half village tavern, Kafka's inn achieves neither the ideal of the first nor the veracity of the second; it is a caricature of human commerce, a chaotic world where spiritual confusion is the surest ally of terrorism.

K. is less equipped than anyone to disentangle the elements of this hybrid world in which reality is estranged
from itself. K. feels exiled; he understands concrete reality
only as an object of investigation and desire. Hence, he
cannot properly distinguish it from his own dreams. From
the moment he arrives in the village, he dreams of what the
others actually possess, he passionately desires what they do
out of necessity and habit, and, in a sense, he transforms the
world into a private carnival of images. He is incapable of
discerning the true systems of authority, for his extreme
solitude not only hinders his actions but also aggravates the
distortion of his perspective, since from his position at the
bottom, or even outside, of the social order everything
seems to him at once impressively superior and opaque.
Having no place in the world, K. envies and admires without distinction all those who do, though they may be subal-
terns and themselves oppressed. He is awed by titles, ranks,
and situations, provided they have an official sanction, the
significance of which otherwise escapes him. As he has no
sense of the nuances of power, the lowest-ranking porter in
uniform impresses him as much as a high-ranking dignitary;
the least of men, if he is an employee, seems to K. clothed in
a nearly sacred majesty. Finally, the whole of the society
with its functions, its ranks and titles, assumes for K. the
aspect of a fantasy world, normal in its appearance and yet
alien, more charged with temptations and dangers than the
fabulous lands of Odysseus. This is the source of the magic
that thwarts his ventures, a magic that is truly terrifying,
whose chief weapon is his own confusion and impotence
before the very thing that fascinates him.

Instead of inventing Dulcinea and battling windmills, K.
makes Klamm into a god and a little barmaid into the incarnation of the highest ideal. Doing this, of course, he does
not seem as mad as Don Quixote, for he does not become

incoherent. On the contrary, he keeps a clear head, and if reality deals him a few underhanded blows, it is reality itself that seems to make no sense. No doubt the difference between K.'s good sense and Don Quixote's madness is striking, but it is ultimately superficial, for K. confuses the two opposed spheres as absurdly as Don Quixote does. Yet this difference palpably changes the style of Kafka's epic transposition, which seems natural and serious, even realistic. K.'s adventures are novel without being wildly shocking, enigmatic without any resort to artifice or arbitrary marvels. This alteration of style corresponds precisely to a change of era. By Kafka's time, the violent collision between the real and the imaginary, the high and the low, the old and the new, from which Cervantes drew his unique comic power, had ceased to be possible. The folly of idealism was no longer a crisis; it consisted of an imperceptible shift of meaning that overturned the deepest values of life all the more drastically because it left their surface intact. The old and the new, the Castle and the village, still maintain a formal antithesis. But in point of fact they mesh and mutually exchange roles; one is perverted by the other. This abnormal alliance has the singular effect of bewildering the individual and terrorizing the collective population. The life of the village is under a spell, but no one perceives it; the sorcery is from moment to moment, hence it has become the norm, and although objects may be seriously affected, they nonetheless follow their course seemingly unchanged.

Kafka can therefore dispense with the anachronism that is the chief ploy of *Don Quixote*. K. does not struggle in another world but in a world become other by means of an incongruous transaction. Here there is no collision, no violent and comic clash of contraries, no explosion, but an apparently normal unfolding that is gradually and continuously deflected by magical mutations representing only the chaotic underpinnings of the real. Composed of banal material that Kafka never sought to modify, the epic of *The Castle* is quixotic without resort to archaism, and timely precisely in the way it takes the old strictly at its word. Instead of thrusting Amadis into some contemporary village, *The Castle* encloses both images, both conceptions of the world, both ideologies, within the same word which bears these double meanings according to the most sophisticated lexicons. Kafka's novel, then, passes in the most natural way from epic totality to modern totalitarianism, from Olympian order to bureaucratic tyranny, from aristocrat to scribbling official, from action to gossip—and from heroism to literature, which is, as we know, its first concern. This passage is navigated quite without effort or parody, since Kafka has at his command a modern and understated discourse in which *official authority* fills the empty place of nobility.

II. BOOK AND LIFE

> "There's a great deal of writing there," said
> K. . . . "Yes, a wretched bore," said
> . . . Momus.   The Ninth Chapter

The previous discussion helps us to see how the Land-Surveyor, with his unusually developed quixotic nature, can easily disguise the substance of his projects and seem, superficially at least, to be more a critic than a follower of Don Quixote. Madness allows the Don to know exactly what he has to do without a moment's hesitation; unflappable and self-assured, he forever answers questions that haven't been asked. K., who is uncertain of himself and hes-

itant, forever asks questions that no one answers. Don Quixote confidently follows the path marked out in advance by
Amadis and allows no misadventure to shake his resolution.
K. must carve out his way as he goes, with no book or
heroic figure as his guide, and so he lives in a chronic state of
error and spends all his time conjecturing on the possible
directions he might take. The two heroes seem worlds
apart, for Don Quixote "sallies forth" in order to escape
from life, while the Land-Surveyor sets out to enter it.

The two figures do meet, however, or rather they
coexist, within K. himself, who is none other than an
abashed and cautious Don Quixote trying hard to resist his
idealist tendencies. And this struggle offers us still another
version of K.'s adventures. As he approaches forty he is
living in the illusory world where Don Quixote, ten years
older, finds refuge. But K. breaks out of this wholly interior
existence, this "elsewhere" that is his true native land, and
comes to the village to plant his feet, finally, in the real
world. Of course, the sincere desire to change is not
sufficient in itself. K. may mistrust the ideal images associated with his solitude (the sound of the Castle bell or the
dazzling appearance of his messenger), yet he almost always
yields to their fascination. He hesitates between two pro-
grams, so to speak: the realistic plan to become a simple
village worker and disappear among the inhabitants, and the
purely quixotic one that impels him to go directly to the
Castle and discover the absolute law that will give meaning
to his life. Yet it is certainly the second plan that dominates
the novel. His intellect carries him toward the village, a
bitter cold place where he expects only a healthy disillusionment and the growth of his own humanity. His soul,
however, leads him in the opposite direction, toward a

problematic Castle where, in spite of everything, he hopes to find happiness.

K.'s dilemma consists of two quite unequal propositions, between which, in fact, there is no real choice. The village exists as a palpable reality, however desolate, and a reasonably sober person might well imagine settling there. But the Castle, at least as K. conceives it, has no reality except in his mind; it is an unfounded hypothesis, an illusion perhaps, certainly a gamble. K., however, stubbornly clings to the second alternative: he will become a worker, marry, and make a humble place for himself in the village, and one day, when the time is right, he will learn the secret of the Castle. Or perhaps the hidden order of things will simply be revealed to him all at once. These calculations are his downfall. His thoughts about the Castle distract him from his work and his human task, while his preoccupation with the village estranges him from his spiritual goal; he remains hovering between the two worlds in a no man's land where he may perish alone.

K. hopes to resolve this dilemma by carrying out his two plans simultaneously—that is, by exploiting the life of the village in order to wrest from the silence of the Castle some rule of conduct, some legal authorization of his actions. But for an inexperienced outsider like himself, the human village is no less mysterious than its invisible government. Everything K. encounters there is deceptive, elusive, bound to incessant transformations that torment even the villagers themselves. He is betrayed by his senses at every turn, things change shape before his eyes, words and sounds come to him deformed, as if undermined or deflected by an unknown obstacle. He is the dupe of enchantments and the victim of apparitions (he does not have real meetings, people always materialize suddenly,[1] taking him by surprise). And so, going from mirage to mirage, he trusts in nothing, neither what he himself sees and feels, nor what he is told by others. Even his most immediate perceptions are misleading; he must go to great lengths to interpret them before taking a decisive step. Since he cannot experience the simple pleasure of being, he reads the palpable world as if it were a disturbing half-sealed book, spelling it out word by word in order to reconstruct its hypothetical text.

K.'s lack of talent for living compels him to perform this labor of Sisyphus by which he must continually interpret his own judgments and the evidence of his senses, and deduce from them hypotheses about the Castle that he then intends to verify one by one. He is undeniably gifted for this task— rectitude of judgment, a sense of proportion, and visual acuity are the requirements for his profession. But this obligation to interpret is also what prevents him from ever arriving at any conclusion, for he lacks the basic knowledge ordinarily transmitted through the experience, mores, and traditions of culture. Indeed, the eccentricity of this position makes all his hypotheses equally plausible and equally unfounded.[2] K. has no proven criteria to use as controls, no properly established external facts, because he has nothing in common with the surrounding world: he is a stranger in the absolute sense of the word, not only to this particular village but to all the villages of this world (this is why he chooses at random and is so oddly determined to remain

[1]This is the meaning of all magical "apparitions." Ghosts are ancestors who return and haunt the present; the occult is the old that surfaces once again. This fundamental law, so familiar to primitive peoples, Kafka applies in all his works, in which the mystery is always the result of an untimely intrusion of the past.

[2]Like all those interpretations of Kafka.

there). The native village to which he continually alludes, but of which he has no living memory, does not exist on the maps; it is an "elsewhere" without a name, an interior desert peopled by his dreams, an abode of death where he was sole master and inhabitant.[3] Hence his tardy arrival in the village from this land that still fascinates him is nothing less than a desperate attempt to be born[4] into the world and to seize in one moment the arrears of an entire life. When he comes to the village he is not born, yet he wants to survey the human ground, to modify the distribution of things, to impose new boundaries on the world—in other words, to revolutionize something he has never known. This is clearly madness, but for the villagers it is so scandalous and threatening that only the most indulgent will excuse K.'s inconceivable puerility.

Those villagers who are most inclined in his favor, or least hostile, earnestly try to make him understand his mistake. The Mayor tells him that the village is not concerned with changing its property relations and therefore has no need of a land-surveyor ("'There wouldn't be the least use for one here. The frontiers of our little state are marked out and all

---

[3]K. never talks about his past and no one questions him about his mysterious country. He remembers only a single episode from his former life, having to do with the cemetery in his native town; he once managed, as a child, to climb its wall: "He stuck the flag in, it flew in the wind, he looked down and round about him, over his shoulder, too, at the crosses moldering in the ground; nobody was greater than he at that place and that moment" (2nd Ch.). He comes from a land of death, and although he sincerely wants to live in the village, it is death that draws him to the Castle, the place where all the meanings of life find, relatively speaking, their final end.

[4]Cf. in the *Diaries* (January 28, 1922), the admirable passage where Kafka describes his situation as a long wandering between the "desert" and "Canaan" ("Forty years ago I wandered out of Canaan. . ."). Also the note dated January 24 of the same year: "Hesitation before birth. If there is a transmigration of souls, mine has still not reached the lowest degree. My life is a hesitation before birth."

officially recorded'" [5th Ch.]). K. can go ahead and survey
if he likes, but he must realize that officially he will never be
employed. And the Mayor adds: "'Nobody keeps you here,
but that surely doesn't amount to throwing you out.'" He
deliberately simplifies the truth that seems to K. so complex
and dramatic: the village will not help him to be born, but
neither will it make him die. Life will tolerate him indiffer-
ently, as it has tolerated even the most unwelcome of his
models; it will take only defensive measures against his
revolutionary zeal.

All the *adults* attempt to restrain the *child* in generally the
same language, but not being of their world he cannot hear
them. They never stop repeating to him that he is a stranger
and that this explains the disproportion between his efforts
and the meagerness of his results, as well as his perception of
mysteries and enigmas that for others are simply matters of
course.

The problematic issues that K. turns over in his mind,
then, are caused only by his condition as outsider and his
consequent estrangement. It would have been better for him
to stop thinking and instead to adapt himself. When Frieda
realizes that he will never respect the order of things, she
decides to leave him and explains clearly why:[5] "As a
stranger you have no rights to anything here. Perhaps here
we are particularly strict or unjust toward strangers, I don't
know, but there it is, you have no rights to anything. A local

---

[5]Deleted passage. One wonders whether Kafka deleted this passage because it authorized too specific a translation of the text as a whole. Here
Frieda interprets quite clearly the most ambiguous words in the novel:
right, assistants, authorities. But her conception is too biological, too vi-
talist, in a sense, to account for all the images that are sustained by the
Castle. In general, we can say that in *The Castle* (as in *The Trial*), the passages Kafka deleted are less ambiguous than those that come before or
after them.

person, for instance, when he needs assistants, takes such people on, and when he is grown up and wants to marry, he takes himself a wife. The authorities have a great deal of influence in these matters too, but in the main everyone is free to decide for himself. But you, as a stranger, have to make out with what you are given; if it pleases the authorities to do so, they give you assistants; if it pleases them to do so, they give you a wife . . ." (Appendix, p. 458). With the realism K. so much admires in her, Frieda reveals to him the alleged mysteries of the Castle: the average villager adapted to the realities of daily life takes what he needs; his existence is itself sufficient justification, and the authorities do not curtail his liberty. The local person doesn't need truth or rights, for if he is a native of the village he is at one with the truth.

There is no common ground for compromise between Frieda's realism and K.'s inflexibility. K. believes justification is possible and he pursues it to such lengths that his extreme individualism, his difficulty being born into the human community, his estrangement, makes him unfit to enjoy life in an immediate way. He insists upon going to the Castle and speaking personally with Klamm in order to ascertain that his place, his occupation, and his wife will be his by right, not as a favor or a gesture of tolerance. Frieda thinks this is simply unreasonable obstinacy, a kind of sickness of the mind that seems to destroy beforehand all their possibilities for a life together. And from her point of view, she is right. Only a presumptuous child or a dangerous dreamer could expect a formal mandate from the community specifying and confirming his duties and privileges in advance. Nevertheless, this illness is K.'s only escape from his futile effort to learn the basic rules of life: since reality conceals from him what everyone else seems to know from birth, he will go directly to the supreme tribunal on which reality itself depends.

No one in the novel doubts that such a tribunal exists, particularly because each of the villagers conceives the Castle according to his own interests or desires. Their belief in the Castle is essentially an admission that there is some place, above or beside them, in the midst of their daily struggles or at an unbridgeable distance, some force that mysteriously ties together the scattered elements of their history and for good or ill determines their collective fate. Some accept this force on which tradition has imposed the name of "Castle" with resignation (the peasants), others thoughtfully (chiefly the women), others through suffering (the Barnabas family) or even, paradoxically, by challenging its power (Amalia). Each one has had, or believes he has had, a personal experience on which his feelings and ideas are exclusively based. If there is a common notion of the Castle, it seems destined to remain unformulated.

Thus the Castle is known only through entirely subjective representations and a vague common belief that K. mistrusts because it contains no larger coherent idea. In his view, most of the images of the Castle that have any currency are simply received ideas, legends, or gossip, a blend of experience and prejudice that he regards with cautious scepticism and sometimes with contempt. Furthermore, K. wants to verify personally each of the diverse reports he has so painfully gathered, but his judgment and even his perceptions are warped by his own prejudice. So he is forced to conduct his struggle on two fronts, one outside, the other inside himself, thus becoming both the aggressor and the victim. Everything he sees and hears, all that he reads and learns immediately become part of this incessant and unequal struggle for life.

First let us turn to what he observes. The precision and

acuteness of his observations indicate that he has a quick and practical eye sensitive to the smallest details and sharpened by an unbounded curiosity. But he cannot trust his visual perceptions because things continually change their aspect, presenting by turns such various and contradictory faces that K. cannot deduce even a provisionally coherent notion of their essential reality. In this respect, the chief object of his curiosity is the most irritatingly elusive. According to his angle of vision, it is a "little town" or a "wretched huddle of village houses." Yet he discovers details that don't mesh with either of these hypotheses, and the more he studies the building the more he judges it utterly absurd. He compares the Castle tower to the church tower of his native town, and suddenly it appears to him "uniformly round, part of it graciously mantled with ivy, pierced by small windows that glittered in the sun—with a somewhat maniacal glitter—and topped by what looked like an attic, with battlements that were irregular, broken, fumbling, as if designed by the trembling or careless hand of a child, clearly outlined against the blue. It was as if a melancholy-mad tenant who ought to have been kept locked in the topmost chamber of his house had burst through the roof and lifted himself up to the gaze of the world" (1st Ch.). But what can K. conclude from these disordered impressions? Even with the sharp outline of its angles, the tower remains so vague that he has to complete it figuratively in his thoughts, unwittingly transforming his perceptions into a *vision*. He adds "a somewhat maniacal glitter," "the trembling or careless hand of a child," "a melancholy-mad tenant," which seem to explain the incoherence of the tower as a whole. Actually, these images swim up from the depths of his consciousness and express his own situation only too well to be merely an objective description.

In a general way, all of K.'s visual perceptions are confused, despite his flawless vision and a capacity for attention that is almost never relaxed (except at the end when he lets himself fall asleep). On the morning after his arrival, K. notices a portrait (on the wall of the Bridge Inn) that is so blackened that from his couch he thinks it is only a frame with a plain back. On closer inspection, he distinguishes a picture representing "the bust of a man about fifty," but the man's pose is so odd that K. has difficulty making it out: "His head was sunk so low upon his breast that his eyes were scarcely visible, and the weight of the high, heavy forehead and the strong hooked nose seemed to have borne the head down. Because of this pose the man's full beard was pressed in at the chin and spread out farther down. His left hand was buried in his luxuriant hair, but seemed incapable of supporting the head" (1st Ch.). In other words, the painter has caught the man pulling at his hair. The picture is not a painting but rather a snapshot, the photograph of a fragment of time fixed in the intensity of thought, confusion, or despair. K. finds this man handsome and at once identifies him with the Count, but he is insensible to the man's suffering, which is an image of his own.

All the images he encounters have the same quality of puzzling snapshots.[6] One example is the photograph of a messenger that the landlady of the Bridge Inn gives him to examine. At first, as usual, he sees nothing; then he makes out a young man lying on a board stretching himself and yawning. He is quite wrong, the landlady tells him, yet K. persists; he is certain that the young man is lying on the board. Finally he corrects his error: the young man isn't lying down, he is soaring, the board is a rope, the young

[6]Cf. also in *The Trial,* the portrait of the judge who seems about to jump out of his frame, fixed in the same way that Don Quixote is frozen in battle with the Biscayan.

man is actually leaping into the air—this time he has perceived it correctly. The young man is a messenger photographed at an official training session. At the end of this laborious analysis to which K. has applied himself with childish zeal, he has grasped the objective content of the image. But was it worth the effort? The photograph—the landlady's memento of her affair with Klamm—is "faded, cracked, crumpled and dirty" (6th Ch.). K. studies it attentively but it communicates to him only a blurred reality, a life congealed and soiled by time, a caricature of eternity. It is the vague memory of an old messenger, of a myth that seduces him but doesn't tell him anything about his own messenger.

The world is full of these *copies* of life. Whether they are obscure, like the portrait of the would-be count, or malevolent, like the illustration of K.'s love affairs, they are never anything but the crudest ocular tricks. In fact, they are spawned by life itself, which also deals in images, arranging its motifs, grouping its figures, composing its faces, deploying its lights and reflections with art or treacherous artifice. This, at least, is K.'s experience. As an outsider, he never sees the world as it should be in its nakedness, but rather he sees finished tableaux, a book of images where he is only too happy to lose himself. Since he perceives nothing accurately, everything K. sees is the occasion for endless daydreams that cause him to retreat into solitude; from his own point of view, this retreat is his worst sin.

The deepest meaning of these daydreams is best illustrated by the story of the "girl" from the Castle,[7] that mysterious figure who has provoked so many premature if uninspired interpretations. K. meets this woman at the home

7The text says *Mädchen*.

of peasants where he barges in, uninvited, to rest for a moment after his strenuous walk through the snow. Once more he sees nothing because the room is filled with smoke. Then his attention is attracted to a scene in one corner that seems to astonish him though he cannot explain why: "From a large opening, the only one in the back wall, a pale snowy light came in, apparently from the courtyard, and gave a gleam as of silk to the dress of a woman who was almost reclining in a high armchair. She was suckling an infant at her breast . . ." (1st Ch.). K. observes attentively that this woman seems to be of another class but must be a peasant, to judge from the look of her children. Suddenly his perception changes: ". . . the woman in the armchair lay as if lifeless, staring at the roof without even a glance toward the child at her bosom" (1st Ch.). And this immobility, this deathlike indifference, bears him into a world of vague dreams that for a moment engulfs him entirely. Absorbed by his contemplation of this "beautiful, sad, fixed picture," K. falls into a state of vacancy, ecstasy, or sleep, he isn't sure which, and is only roused by a "loud voice," the brutal call of reality. Come to himself, he seems to forget this strange trance, but just as he is about to leave—he is literally thrown out—he makes an adroit turn and suddenly stands before the woman: "Out of weary blue eyes she looked at him. A transparent silk kerchief hung down to the middle of her forehead. The infant was asleep on her bosom . . . ." And before this tableau that irresistibly evokes—not only for him—the painting of some sorrowful Madonna, he cannot refrain from asking: "Who are you?" The laconic answer he receives: "A girl from the Castle," is clearly not of the kind to raise his spirits.

This brief scene is crucial to K.'s fate. He imagines he has forgotten it, but it helps to draw him toward those irrational hopes of salvation that so seriously jeopardize his realistic plans. The woman in the armchair has no corporeal existence for K., she is an apparition, an envoy from the Castle whose support he hopes to gain. She is silent, however, and despite the interrogation he imposes on her son, K. never learns anything more about her. Therefore, she is easily idealized, like the angelic messenger who later turns out to be an ordinary servant (the silken reflection of their clothes lends them both a "celestial" air). And Frieda is right to take K.'s passionate interest in this woman as proof that he is hopelessly lost.

The vision of the woman in the high armchair deceives not only K. but also certain commentators on the novel, who blithely identify her with the Virgin and then feel they can place K.'s entire story within an essentially religious framework. The supernatural light emanating from this figure of the virgin-mother to whom K. clings as a last hope of salvation is sufficient proof that Kafka meant the Castle to be the mysterious seat of grace. The "girl from the Castle" is a stranger to the administrative and juridical realm of the gentlemen—at least it is not clearly stated that she takes part in these activities—which is supposedly another reason for seeing her as the granter of mercies. It is not difficult to understand the basis for this misconception of the text. K.'s faith in the image is taken literally when the actual context indicates that it is an illusion—the very illusion that most contributes to his downfall. Because he is incapable of finding within himself the strength to act and think according to the concrete terms of his own life, K. forfeits the individual, unprecedented choices that would make him a free man for readymade solutions weighted with the temptation of an enormous cultural past. Instead of objectively evaluating a situation that is by definition new and unique, he continually relates the unknown to the known, the new to the old, his own present to the ethical and religious ideas of an accomplished past. This proof of K.'s radical estrangement is Kafka's way of expressing, through quixotic exaggeration, the basic human need for precedents and models.

Indeed, K. is not so mistaken about the meaning of these "visions" as we might think; in numerous moments of lucidity, he treats Barnabas and the "girl from the Castle" as will-o'-the-wisps who simply distract him from his goal. This is what makes his conflict so insoluble: although his keen eye ruthlessly exposes all preconceived ideas, and collective and anachronistic dreams, he remains torn between the demands of a mind rebellious to myths and the yearning of a childlike soul in search of the absolute. These extreme tendencies are both so powerful that neither can triumph over the other, but can only cast over everything a malignant spell that prevents K. from perceiving and embracing things as they are. Even Frieda changes shape before his eyes. He sees her as she is, "an unobtrusive little girl with fair hair, sad eyes, and hollow cheeks" (3rd Ch.); but at the same time he finds her beautiful. Moreover, he is not astonished by this contradiction, which he explains in his usual way as the hidden influence of the Castle (". . . it was the proximity to Klamm that had made her so unbelievably beautiful . . . ."). He compliments Frieda on her delicate hands, yet he isn't sure whether he is only flattering her or is compelled by something actually there: "Her hands were certainly small and delicate, but they could quite as well have been called weak and characterless" (3rd Ch.). Perhaps it is K. who sees meaning where there is none, corrupting the honesty of his vision by the poisonous effect of words. Whatever there is of this problematic beauty, it yields to the cold speculations it provokes. At the end of several days of living together, K. remarks that Frieda's beauty has abruptly vanished.

His perspective is entirely warped by these illusions and requires tireless attention to correct, with no definitive results. K. sees things that escape the others, though they may not exist at all or be particularly noteworthy. On the other hand, he does not see what everyone else takes for granted. His assistants look alike to him, so much so that he fuses them into a single person ("you resemble each other," K. says, "like two snakes"), indicating that his perceptual impairment rests entirely upon a value judgment. The villagers, of course, distinguish between the two companions quite easily and find nothing insubstantial about them. Furthermore, these false twins whom K. despises and mistreats seem to bear a family likeness to Barnabas, the messenger whose seductive appearance feeds his hopes of deliverance. K. doesn't want to believe that the angelic Barnabas and the vile assistants have anything in common. Yet with his large eyes, his silken garments, his fascinating smile, Barnabas is not much more than a well-built boy, a kind of powerful and slovenly laborer. Indeed, K.'s malady is the same sort of illness every foreigner suffers when he plunges into the life of an exotic country. The inhabitants of life are, for K., the natives, people of another race whose specific similarities are stronger than their individual differences. He sees the peasants as a European traveler of the nineteenth century might have seen Negroes or Chinese. And K. is aware of this perceptual distortion. For him to see clearly, however, not only means to see correctly but to be capable of living, or, at the very least, of making a start.

Because he has no certain knowledge of the inner reality of things, he clings desperately to their exteriors, assuming that between the two at least some instructive analogies might exist. Since he is not initiated into life, he attempts to extract its secrets by examining its external aspect, its gestures, signs, costumes, and ornaments—in other words, its theater. The "young man dressed like a townsman . . . with the face of an actor, his eyes narrow and his eyebrows strongly marked," who welcomes him so rudely the evening of his arrival, is only the announcer of this drama mounted in his honor that he fears may dissolve into a farce.

K. is ignorant of the subject, the protagonists, and the dénouement of the drama. Furthermore, he has no idea of the number and distribution of the roles, not to mention the author and the actors whose identity will remain hidden from him until the end. To play his own part, therefore, he must instantly seize the words, gestures, and signs that the others address to him, and reconstitute from their performance the meaning that otherwise escapes him. This is not an easy task, for the actors' words and gestures do not necessarily correspond to their roles and almost always contradict each other. People tell him disagreeable things in a rather friendly tone, yet they accompany quite neutral statements with various gestures expressing mockery or menace. Smiles contradict words, the tone of voice doesn't match the contents of the discourse, expressions do not support the dialogue but fly off along their own track. Although he never leaves the stage (he cannot disappear since the novel exists only through him), the other characters speak to him as if he were in the wings or repeat his words as if once they had left his mouth they were unintelligible without an interpreter. Even so, this discordance that puts K.'s attention and intelligence to such a harsh test is probably just another ruse, for everyone but K. finds these apparently disjunct signs perfectly coherent.

Where theater replaces life, costumes replace bodies. Therefore, K. assigns extraordinary importance to questions of attire. In the novel, where such serious things are played out, a surprisingly prominent place is reserved for fashion. For K., whose sight always comes up against the impenetrable surface of things, fashion is a crucial business, almost a means of knowledge; for the garment not only covers the body, it also veils and reveals the whole person. It is not a utilitarian or purely aesthetic convenience but the nexus of a mass of meanings that together constitute a system of values. Clothing, then, is a language that must be interpreted conjointly with the language of words, with as much if not more precision.

K. attaches a symbolic value to the garment out of a stubborn certainty that there is a close correspondence between manifest and latent meaning, and that the outer layers of things, deceptive as they may be, necessarily contain a fragment of truth. Clothing, as man's most external and yet most intimate possession, seems to K. a spiritual envelope, a sign of the union of body and spirit, the infallible index of a total truth of the personality. A language that is half secret, but eloquent in its way, the human costume has a grammatical logic, a syntax, a semantic whose rules can be objectively studied. This, at least, is K.'s hope.

For once, this notion is to some extent in harmony with the conception current in the village—and actually works against him since, as we have noted, K. himself is dressed in rags. In the social life of the villagers, apparel in fact plays a quite remarkable role, the more surprising if we think of the extreme poverty that is the general lot of this small community. Everything connected with the manufacture of clothing is held in the highest esteem. Barnabas' father seems to have owed the enviable position he enjoyed before his disgrace chiefly to his profession of shoemaker. Perhaps the misfortunes of the family were simply the result of the dark machinations of their competitor, Brunswick, who has since become the important man, the political schemer of the village (there are two shoemakers in this impoverished place). Amalia clearly drew her high reputation and uncontested power from her ability as a dressmaker. In moments of doubt, Olga wonders if her brother is not committing a serious error by neglecting his position as shoemaker for his hypothetical activities as messenger. In general, people appear extremely preoccupied with problems of dress, and they unburden themselves on this subject to K. in endless conversations. This is one of the ironies of the novel: this hero in pursuit of the ideal spends a good part of his time seriously discussing clothes and finery. One of Olga's greatest torments is owing to her brother's costume, which looks like the official messenger's suit (K. has been taken in by it, to his misfortune) but was actually put together by his sister some time before the family tragedy. Pepi attributes Frieda's success to the unusual fact that she wears boots and spends extravagant amounts of money on her underwear. Pepi herself has concocted a special outfit that she thinks is appropriate to her activities as barmaid, but she doesn't have the right shoes and this is why she loses her post. The landlady of the Bridge Inn can endure her life only because she once purloined from Klamm a wrap and nightcap that seem to have some magical virtue—her sufferings vanish the moment she puts them on (the nightcap has become too small and K. finds it grotesque). Finally, the landlady of the Herrenhof has an almost maniacal passion for dresses; she possesses an enormous number and continually acquires new ones. These refined costumes, which are much too luxurious for her position, arouse a sense of mystery in K., as if in the depths of their crammed wardrobes they concealed the key to his life or a sign heralding his end. What he has not found in the course of his wanderings he suddenly encounters in these worn, old-fashioned dresses whose obsolete splendor seems to promise him some ultimate truth.[8]

The Castle, interestingly, does not impose any sort of uniform on its subjects and agents. The servants are not liveried, the secretaries, as far as we know, are clothed like bourgeois gentlemen, and Klamm always wears his black jacket with long flaps (a reference to his funereal functions, which are less popular than his erotic ones[9]). The assistants and Barnabas wear some sort of tight-fitting hose, and one of the patrons of the inn wears a black frock coat done up to the chin. Indeed, the village fashion is astonishingly diverse, if not anomalous, since side by side we find town and peasant dress, period costumes (the hose of the assistants has a certain medieval flavor), ecclesiastical garments, city clothes, *fin de siècle* finery, and the black jacket, the inevitable ornament of bourgeois rites and ceremonies. Disparate in period and style, these clothes are always worn out of season, in the face of common sense and custom—summer dress is worn in winter, evening jackets during the day, ceremonial dress in the public room of an inn. Yet for this very reason these costumes gain a kind of immutability (except for the landlady of the Herrenhof, no one changes

[8]The last chapter of the novel concludes with the landlady's words to K.: "I am getting a new dress tomorrow, perhaps I shall send for you . . . ." These words, like other aspects of this woman, suggest the dark figure of Fate (Moire) and surely herald K.'s approaching death.

[9]Klamm's black jacket, his single definite attribute, is ranked alongside the dark dresses of the landlady of the Herrenhof, the deathlike silence that envelops the Castle, the flag planted in the graveyard, and the bell whose sound announces the anguished fulfillment of the deepest desire. All of these images reveal the ultimate meaning of the Castle, where everything leads inexorably toward death.

clothes). Moreover, the clothes adhere to the wearer as if they were one with him, the palpable form of his soul.

The lack of standard uniforms indicates the Castle's propensity to spawn disorder rather than impose any binding unity. Nevertheless, the Castle seems to have some concept of "official" costumes and legislates an etiquette of dress to which everyone attempts to conform, although, of course, its precise terms are not known. One must be dressed in a certain way, for instance, to be a barmaid, though no one knows exactly how. And even those concerned do not know in what manner the "official" messenger's costume differs from the one worn by Barnabas. Since these details are matters of conjecture, one must have a special instinct to discern them; whoever lacks this instinct violates the unspoken etiquette and is automatically punished[10] (namely by being demoted or not promoted). The Castle intervenes in all this, in its mysterious way, by simply sanctioning what has been established by usage. The villagers and Castle functionaries are never well or badly dressed; they are either in violation of or in conformity with the prevailing powers, unseemly and subordinate or proper and powerful.

The innumerable problems of dress that are posed by the novel with such seriousness[11] reveal a satiric intention not only with regard to fashion but to everything that relates to propriety, good form, and convention. Just as Kafka transforms simple costumes into a set of taboos in order to ex-

[10] We will see in the following chapter that the law of the Castle is generally characterized by the purely mechanical nature of its sanctions.

[11] Kafka had a predilection for clothes. Very elegant himself, he passed for a dandy among the young people of Prague. By chance, perhaps, the women closest to him often had to do with fashion. His first fiancée, Felice B., whose name is nearly synonymous with Frieda's, was the manager of a large dressmaking establishment. Milena was a fashion writer, Kafka read her articles and in his letters "comments on" her dresses.

pose their irrational and constricting character, so he gives the mysterious decrees by which a society decides what is "done" and "worn" the rigid form of court etiquette. But the satire cuts two ways, for it is also turned against K. who wants to adapt to and finally make his way in the official ranks. As a pariah with the ambitions of a parvenu, he does what is "not done," draws false conclusions from what he sees, perceives everything from a distorted angle, and behaves like a boor. Conformist out of an absolute nonconformity that threatens the very foundations of his existence, K. seeks to be initiated into the secrets of proper comportment just as he tries to enter the Castle, driven by a combination of despair and childish hope. Seen with an impartial eye, his efforts to "arrive" are at once shocking and ridiculous, and increasingly expose the personal flaws that are hidden by his isolation.

The habits and customs of a people are always unintelligible to those who do not know them from the inside, who haven't received them from birth. This is a law that K. underestimates and moreover wants to disprove by his example, since he intends to settle in the village and become like its inhabitants (". . . once they could no longer distinguish him from Gerstäcker or Lasemann—and this should be done quickly, it was the key to the entire situation—every door would be open to him . . ."). This "assimilation" is only one of his aims, but to fulfill it he must adapt himself to the life of his future fellow citizens. His most urgent task, then, is to decipher their etiquette of dress; yet while he clearly observes the effects of this code, its motives and precise rules always elude him. Once more, the lack of good breeding and savoir-faire drive him to a desperate solution: not being fashionable himself, he "reads" the fashion of those who are in order to determine the meaning, the norm, even a fleeting suggestion of this elusive order. Again, he turns to the commentary on the original text that life denies to strangers like himself.

With no comprehensible external norm, K. refers for this exegetical reading to the internal scale on which he reckons his problematic accounts. In his inner world, fabrics, colors, styles and accessories are meaningful elements, something like the letters of a text or the signs of an alphabet. Labelled according to an immutable and ideal system of value, each one of these elements contributes to the meaning of the whole. In this way, a color that is associated with a particular fabric and style instantly becomes as rich in significance as a long sentence. Thus, white is pure, silk noble, gray abject—colors represent the shimmering diversity of life (there aren't many in the village, the prevailing tones are gray and dull), whereas black usually heralds death. This system inspires him with such confidence because he has no better way to classify what surrounds him.

But the method doesn't serve him very well, for if his own system and the etiquette of the Castle coincide at certain points, they are hardly in perfect harmony. And K., despite his efforts, never succeeds in learning on which details they agree and on which they diverge. Barnabas' white garment, with its purity and its silken gleam, seduces K. in spite of himself and stirs him to extravagant hopes. This costume, however, is not an official uniform and only conceals torn and soiled underwear. Is this a trick played on him by the Castle? A mockery? Is he the victim of some sorcery or is he led into error by the falseness of his own system? When his eyes are finally opened—yet nothing indicates that this is the moment of true clarity—the young man radiant with light who appeared to be a savior inspires him only with anger and disgust. But it is too late. By overestimating Barnabas, K. has underestimated his assistants, whose appearance seemed base and repellent for the same suspect reasons; he has lost Frieda, too, and ruined all his plans for the sake of a simple silken sheen.

K. is not only continually deluded by his flawless vision, he is equally betrayed by his other senses. Over the telephone line to the Castle, K. hears a noise he has never heard before on a telephone: "It was like the hum of countless children's voices—but yet not a hum, the echo rather of voices singing at an infinite distance—blended by sheer impossibility into one high but resonant sound that vibrated on the ear as if it were trying to penetrate beyond mere hearing. K. listened without attempting to telephone, leaning his left arm on the telephone shelf" (2nd Ch.). Once again, a purely sensory phenomenon plunges him into a kind of reverie from which he must be brutally torn. And though he says nothing about it, the reader can easily divine K.'s thoughts and imagine him instantly ravished by the harmony of some celestial sphere or the delights of an angelic choir. All wrong, of course, if we are to believe the Mayor's subsequent explanation: "'In the Castle the telephone works beautifully of course; I've been told it's being used there all the time; that naturally speeds up the work a great deal. We can hear this continual telephoning in our telephone as a humming and singing, you must have heard it too. Now, this humming and singing transmitted by our telephone is the only real and reliable thing you'll hear, everything else is deceptive. There's no fixed connection with the Castle, no central exchange that transmits our calls farther . . .'" (5th Ch.). So K. is disabused of his initial perception only to fall again into error, for he concludes that the telephone is useless. According to the Mayor, however, all the answers coming from the Castle are significant, even those of a subordinate or overworked official. As usual, K. cannot imagine any middle ground between absolute meaning (the thousands of voices merged in eternal harmony) and utter absurdity (the gentlemen answering any call at random merely for the sake of a little diversion). As always, received images and habitual patterns of thought prevent him from correctly perceiving and appreciating the value of what is only, in the end, the enormous clamor of life.

K. is too sober-minded to seek an explanation for his experience in the malice of quixotic enchanters. Yet he is no less bewitched than Don Quixote and hasn't even the consolation of knowing his enemies. His presence alone seems to abolish, or at least pervert, the function of natural law: what seems to lie within his reach abruptly shifts to a great distance, and what seems to be far away is actually near. He does not perceive real distinctions but only nonexistent ones. He may be speaking with someone when all at once the other person looks at him blankly, as though he were mute. And he doesn't even have the right to complain that beings and things elude him, for perhaps it is he who deprives them of their flavor and substance. Witness the bottle K. finds in Klamm's carriage whose odor makes him fall into one of his habitual reveries: ". . . involuntarily he smiled, the perfume was so sweet, so caressing, like praise and good words from someone whom one likes very much, yet one does not know clearly what they are for and has no desire to know and is simply happy in the knowledge that it is one's friend who is saying them. 'Can this be brandy?' K. asked himself doubtfully, and took a taste out of curiosity. Yes, strangely enough it was brandy, and burned and warmed him. How wonderfully it was transformed, in drinking, out of something that seemed hardly more than a sweet perfume into a drink fit for a coachman! 'Can it be?'

K. asked himself as if self-reproachfully . . ." (8th Ch.).[12]
As usual—but here he is conscious of it and reproaches
himself—K. does not succeed in savoring the real taste of
Klamm's cognac because he begins by idealizing it, imagin-
ing that it is an aphrodisiac or a magic potion whose consumption brings union with a loved one, absolution from
sin, and immediate justification. K. is so attuned to these
idealistic summonings that endlessly confuse the language
of reality that he will have nothing to do with any simple,
life-sustaining drinks.

The singular charm of Kafka's art is usually explained by
the utterly original way that he unites fantasy with the
meticulous and nearly pedantic observation of ordinary
things. Actually there is no fantasy in his work. The magic,
the marvelous elements, the continual irruption of irrational
forces, are only what emerge from the rigorous transcription of real facts, however veiled, whose multiple effects
everyone can observe for himself. Kafka declares—and this
declaration, we should note, replaces the epic articulation of
order—that the individual is not in a position to understand
or even perceive the novelty, the unique actuality, of his
own life. Needing a rationale for his life, he can only retrieve
from the past the ethical, religious, and esthetic justifica-
tions that because they are traditionally transmitted by edu-

[12]Klamm, with his portly bearing, his pince-nez, his cigar, redolent with
the stale smell of beer, clearly evokes a paternal figure. He is the "ruler of
women," the domestic despot whose terrible and capricious decrees fall
like a thunderclap on his children's heads. Clearly, Kafka borrowed
Klamm's features from his own father, as he is described in the famous
letter (cf. *Letter to My Father*). Many details in the novel confirm this,
particularly the extraordinary role given to the beer and the stronger
drinks K. tries to sample. Kafka, we know, was a vegetarian and abstinent.
It is as if in this book that retraces a pathetic and ironic effort to adapt to
conventional norms and to accept reality, he were trying to conquer his
repugnance through the mediation of his protagonist.

cation and culture, have more reality in his mind than the demands of a situation that is new and therefore problematic. Whatever his pretensions to make objective judgments calculated according to the actual events of his own life, man allows himself to be ruled by traditional representations, age-old collective images that ultimately become confused with his own truth. The spell of the old transforms laws, ideals, and the spiritual and pragmatic goals of the past into a legitimate order, while the problems of the present are thought to follow these known models and so to be solved in advance. This explains the extraordinary reversal of Chinese chronology ("The Great Wall of China") by which the people adore and fear the emperors many centuries dead but refuse to believe in the actual existence of the reigning emperor. Throughout Kafka's work, the latent power of the old, the survival of archaic, hidden laws (the *occult* here is nothing more than the *accomplished past*), intervenes to distort life in the present and drive the individual to despair, unleashing anarchy and terror, just as the old commandant of the penal colony does after his death. This commandant, who is as inexorable and despotic as the archaic law he embodies (he is soldier, judge, mechanic, chemist, and draughtsman), has died long ago and is buried beneath the flagstones of the teahouse. Yet he continues to terrorize the colony through the mediation of the officer and his diabolical machine—both are worn and defective—whereas the new commandant is liberal, frivolous, irresponsible, and possesses little actual power. The explorer, invited to a spectacular execution ordered in the name of the old law, witnesses with horror the murder of the officer and the destruction of the machine. Is the past annihilated? No, for according to a popular belief, the old commandant will return one day to restore his special brand of order and justice.

Terrified by this notion, the explorer, who is less courageous than the Land-Surveyor of *The Castle,* takes flight at once.

These archaic survivals have such fatal consequences only because they are not perceived—in this respect the sadistic fury of the penal colony represents a moment of crisis[13]— by the individual or by the society as a whole, both equally incapable of perceiving the unprecedented novelty of the *moment.* In this regard, the villagers are even more obtuse than K. He may not always be able to discover the untimely encroachments of the past, but he is on his guard and never relaxes his critical stance. Whatever their intellectual or social level, the people of the village never judge the Castle in terms of the present; all of their muddled but authoritarian ideas derive from the past, which they accept uncritically and use as the basis for all judgments. K. needs objective information that is immediately relevant to his unprecedented and highly individual situation. But he receives only dated news (Barnabas' letters are old and dusty) and information based on "common talk" that really amounts to nothing more than gossip. All the women of the village,

[13]As a demystification of the old (the past), we can say that all of Kafka's work traces out a curative effort that is largely successful if we think of the enormous differences between the old commandant of *The Penal Colony* (1917, the year that Kafka became ill) and Klamm of *The Castle,* who is on the whole quite humanized (1920–1922). The old commandant, the image of a cruel and absolute superego, knows no other law than the law of talion and the blind repression of his machine. Klamm is neutral and benevolent; he refuses to speak—that is, to judge—and K., who suffers from this silence as if it were a cruelty designed especially for him, is still able to discern its supreme wisdom. K. is not savagely destroyed like the officer, and although he foolishly continues to wait for a judgment from the Castle, he is little by little led to a more flexible and larger understanding of the true nature of authority. In the end, as we will see in the following chapter, he is even capable of restoring to the gentlemen their value as elemental forces, and of linking them to the natural world: he hears one of them imitate the crowing of a cock to greet the coming day.

without exception, attempt to initiate him into this tradition, confiding to him the details of their own pasts (most often their love affairs) and of already accomplished events that they believe contain some useful instruction. Gardena wants to teach K. how to live by telling him the story of her love for Klamm and the failure of her marriage, Olga by recounting the family tragedy and Amalia's rebellion. Pepi sketches him a picture of his future based wholly on her brief experience as an embittered adolescent. Only Frieda is to a certain extent capable of confronting the present and making a future for herself—K. is right to see this as proof of her wisdom. But when she is deceived by K., she too falls under the spell of the past—in the guise of the assistants, who, as K. learns to his amazement, were her childhood companions. Courageous and determined to free themselves, the women of the village remain accomplices and victims of the looming archaic survivals that constitute collective law.

In spite of their apparent competence in the world of action, the men of the village are hardly more able to grasp the flux of the present. Their talk is different from the women's sentimental effusions, but nevertheless refers to the same span of time—the recent or distant past. From the Mayor to Bürgel, the authorities whom K. consults always refer to precedents having the force of law, which in their eyes, of course, is quite logical since the event has meaning only in the past; individual problems are never urgent or important, they are and have always been questions that are settled in advance. From the Mayor himself, K. is amazed to learn that the question of his appointment goes back many years ("For me it's an old story," says the Mayor). It was therefore determined well before K. came to the village to claim his post. The intricacy of K.'s current situation is explained by this reversal of the Castle's chronology in which past and present are constantly inverted. K. is summoned long after his appointment was decided, announced, then revoked and finally lost in the office files. By coming *now* to claim his right, he is behaving in a way that is anachronistic, chronologically and morally inappropriate. In the Castle's bureaucratic offices, there is no before and after: effects precede causes, and decisions follow their implementation, so that affairs that have been settled are nevertheless always in progress. The decision about K.'s appointment was made, as always, in advance, "but in any case it couldn't be discovered by us at least, by us here, or even by the head bureau, which clerk had decided in this case and on what grounds. The Control officials only discovered that much later, but we shall never learn it; besides, by this time it would scarcely interest anybody. Now, as I said, it's just these decisions that are generally excellent. The only annoying thing about them—it's usually the case with such things—is that one learns too late about them and so in the meantime keeps on still passionately canvassing things that were decided long ago" (5th Ch.). It is because these questions are always decided in advance that they remain forever pending. K. will not obtain his post, but "in the meanwhile Sordini would have been working away here all the time on the same case until he was exhausted," which puts K. outside of time, in a pseudo eternity where the real exigencies of his life, his personal demands, count for nothing. The Castle—which as we know is neither an "old stronghold nor a new mansion" but a hideously eclectic edifice (like the village school, "combining remarkably a look of great age with a provisional appearance" [1st Ch.])—robs the individual of the fulfillment of his time and dissipates his suffering.

This state of things, born of the disjointed chronology of the Castle, is a perfect justification of K.'s almost paranoid suspicion that he is being frustrated in his legitimate rights and persecuted by invisible enemies. To protect himself against aggression from the forces that hold sway over the village, he has no better weapon than interpretation, since the Castle's upending of time manifests itself most perniciously in the special realm of language. The messages and talk inspired by the authorities are never addressed to the present, but K. has no other source of information or law to orient his life. So he submits each word to an exegesis that is all the more rigorous as its results remain unconfirmed (he hasn't any sure *code* and is ignorant of the integral *text*). This accounts for K.'s suspicious manner in conversations, almost like that of a detective, and the aggressive way he goes about conducting his inquiry.

We can see now why K.'s activities are so futile. No man reduced to his own resources can sort out the old from the new, free himself from the tyranny of archetypes, and still found his individual existence on a solid collective base. K. wants to gain total comprehension of the world by a personal act and will not allow himself to be swept along by obscure collective currents—he wants to talk with Klamm face to face. He bears himself, from the first, as an entrenched individualist ruthlessly determined to expose the ideas, beliefs, aims, and consolations on which, in the final analysis, the whole society rests. But by taking this stance, he condemns himself to a terrible failure. Cut off from the world of the living, he can only find death, in which all the tensions of time, all contradictions, will effectively vanish, along with his quest and he himself. Toward the end of his odyssey,[14] K. wanders for a long time through the corridor

[14]The nineteenth chapter, *The Castle*.

of the Herrenhof where he surreptitiously witnesses the early morning distribution of the files. There, for the first time, he is permitted to feel the natural joy that is also part of the Castle and from which he has been excluded by his excessive efforts: "This babel of voices in the rooms had something extremely merry about it. Once it sounded like the jubilation of children getting ready for a picnic, another time like daybreak in a hen-roost, like the joy of being in complete accord with the awakening day. Somewhere, indeed, a gentleman imitated the crowing of a cock . . ." (18th Ch.). All around him K. hears the sounds of life (he even hears the pounding of a hammer, as the gentlemen sometimes do carpentry[15]), but he will not be distracted from his task and continues scrupulously observing the distribution of paperwork bearing the Castle's daily decrees. The distribution is carried out according to rules that, again, elude him. Yet he suspects that the scrap of paper as big as the page of a notebook, which the servant tears to pieces before his eyes, might well be the slim file that contains the story of his life. It is at this moment, when he is closest to conceiving the totality of existence, that he rushes to his doom.

In the corridor, where his presence alone is an unthinkable scandal—the landlady with the black dresses tells him afterward that for a time it prevented the sun from rising[16]— all he learns is the imminence of his own death. Yet, is death

[15]Like Kafka himself, who tried to compensate for his lack of contact with reality by some manual labor. For a long time he worked at gardening, and even when he was ill he did carpentry.

[16]K.'s enterprise is a challenge to life. We can compare this whole passage, where his presence is described as an obstacle to the progress of the world, to an aphorism in which Kafka says of himself: "Everything he did seemed to him extraordinarily new, of course, but also, through this impossible wealth of newness, extraordinarily marked by an almost intolerable dilettantism incapable of becoming historical, breaking the chain of

really proof of his failure? During the week that represents a life of effort and struggle, has K. actually gained nothing, learned nothing, seen nothing that at least in part justifies his strange sacrifice? Of course, he has not found access to the supreme authority and the village has mocked him. But he has forced the gentlemen to take notice of him—Klamm has not dared to confront his gaze—and nothing has been able to prevent him from pursuing his experience and disrupting the village with his importunate questions. In the end, he has exhausted all his hypotheses, pushed all interpretations to the limit, imagined all explanations, eliminated all errors, and criticized his own assumptions. In this sense, he has succeeded, for on the ground where he has gambled his fate, the exposure of illusions and tendentious representations is the only way to unmask the false Castle and do justice to the true.

----

generations and for the first time cutting off everywhere, even to the very depths, the music of the world, which, until then, could always be at least faintly heard. Sometimes, in his pride, he feared more for the world than for himself."

The True Castle

"They say that we are all from the Castle, and perhaps it's true . . ."

OLGA

THE CASTLE will never be revealed to K., despite his hopes, and hence there is no simple key to the novel. Yet we must still come to terms with what he has learned in the course of his odyssey, which is also, in many respects, a scientific investigation of considerable significance. In place of the revealed truth that K. expects to bring him personal gain, an image of the Castle emerges rather indirectly, through everything said, believed, and hoped for on its account—that is, through the statements made by the men and women of the village.

Individually, of course, the villagers are childishly naïve in their preposterous and mistaken notions of the Castle. Collectively, however, they express some part of the truth that is inherent in their culture and their time, and in this sense they have the privilege of erring within the boundaries of the truth—a privilege that K. will never share. As Kafka has said, "It is not in the individual but in the chorus that a certain truth can be found . . . ,"[1] a paradox that requires K. to consider seriously all the statements of the villagers bearing on the various aspects of the Castle, even the least

[1]Aphorisms in *Wedding Preparations in the Country*.

credible and most absurd. Like the ethnologist who decides to study some primitive people, not in order to discover a personal truth or new ideology but to disentangle from the chaos of appearance the deep structure of a given society, K. welcomes raw data that have no absolute value but are indispensable for a systematic and wholly relevant knowledge of the Castle.

K. then combines his odyssey with an investigation "of the terrain" (again, this is the meaning of his land-surveying), which he conducts with a method suitable for discovering the village customs and the principle of the singular social and spiritual organization that the natives attribute to a certain Castle. Applying this method to a civilized country of the twentieth century is a procedure surely not without a certain cruel irony,[2] but from K.'s point of view it is quite justified. The village is as alien to him as any obscure, exotic tribe, which, though contemporary in many ways, is riddled with archaic survivals that entangle it in a net of superstitions and apparently absurd taboos. This village is the contemporary witness of an ancient, fossilized civilization that to the chance observer seems entirely foolish, illogical, and cruel. Its singular customs, its secret practices, its primitive beliefs, and the complexity of its organization are at once repulsive and fascinating. But K. does not yield to his initial disgust. He is determined to observe this unfamiliar culture in a methodical, comprehensive way and to remain neutral, suppressing his urge to

[2]Kafka is not describing a "Persian" in Paris but a man without a country in Europe, the national of an interior (not imaginary) land in a real country that a fresh glance transforms into an exotic one. The satire is all the more merciless in that it has no need to exaggerate to show the illogic or injustice of certain facts of culture.

formulate a private judgment influenced by his upbringing "elsewhere," a judgment that would prompt him to revolt. Assisted by well-disposed native informants, K. is in the privileged but delicate situation of the specialist whose method he has adopted. Superior to the people of the village because of his abstract knowledge and his method, he remains, nevertheless, inferior to the meanest peasant who is part of the Castle, naturally sharing its wisdom.

K. does not succeed in completing his inquiry because he simply cannot wait to inspect and analyze what he has learned. It is always the same dilemma: he wants to settle in the village, to marry and work there, like the others. But this project can be realized only if he knows in advance the law of the Castle that gives the life of the community its meaning and cohesion. He cannot separate his research from his personal existence, but if he fuses them—and he does this in spite of himself, compelled by events that is, in the language of the novel, by the mechanism of the Castle that always confuses the "private" with the "administrative"—he necessarily compromises both his tasks. If only he were content to compile a thorough, significant dossier on the Castle; but he requires much more: he demands that the indigenous social organization and the occult powers that govern it sanction his "technique." K. is mad, of course, to expect Klamm to ratify his appointment as land-surveyor, to anticipate this foreign god's blessing on his work and his marriage; after all, he has come to the village to *study* Klamm, not to *believe* in him and make him the arbiter of his fate. This confusion between faith and knowledge, however, is not only a result of his own weakness; it is prompted by the Castle itself and so seems quite normal to everyone in the village. That it does more harm, all things considered, to K.'s personal happiness than to the validity and depth of his inquiry is abundantly demonstrated by an examination of his data.

K. collects his observations day by day. He doesn't have time to complete them and certainly has no chance to classify or take an inventory of the data. But even if these data affect K.'s precarious situation (like the situation of the writer who can never embrace the totality of things), they are not so incoherent that he cannot draw from them some generalizations. K. has indeed many sources of information about the Castle: his conversations with the men and women of the village, his personal relations with the secretaries (Momus and Bürgel), the deductions he can make from his own experience, and, finally, the two letters from Klamm that deal directly with his affairs. His data fall naturally under a certain number of rubrics (corresponding to the chapters of the novel) whose order is dictated by the nature of the information—direct or indirect—as well as by the social standing, the sex, and the intellectual level of his various informants.

A quick glance at this dossier instantly reveals some particular features that help us to understand the whole. First, the classification of various kinds of information indicates that what K. learns from experience occupies infinitely less space than what is transmitted to him by hearsay, and that among his informers—men, women, secretaries, messengers, and peasants—it is the women who play by far the most important role (the peasants are insignificant, being half mute most of the time). The women of the village do seem to know much more about the Castle than the men, who are generally taciturn, either because they don't like to talk or because they simply haven't anything to say. The secretaries, on the other hand, are extremely loquacious, though Klamm is always silent (from time to time he makes some inarticulate groans), aside from his small quantity of writing. In a general way, the bulk, contents, and style of the information gleaned in this way correspond to the diverse categories of village life that K. automatically orders according to laws of his own (by which he tangibly falsifies his principle of impartiality). But it is evident in retrospect that where the problems of the Castle are concerned, the most interested and most informed persons are the women and those officials who can be ranked among the intellectuals.

The variety and inconsistency of this data should cure K. of his illusion that there is a unique and universal Castle, for clearly there is not one Castle but as many Castles as there are human, sexual, intellectual, and social groupings. No doubt everyone is talking about the same phenomenon, yet there is little resemblance between the women's version of the Castle and the men's, between the gentlemen's concept of the administration and the Mayor's. And then there is the divergence of opinions within the different categories, which further complicates the classification of data and prevents any coherent generalization. Instead of the unity he expects to find, K. discovers only multiplicity and instability, heterogeneous truths that have value—at least this is his final hope—only in the sum of their divergent meanings.[3] The Castle is not *the* whole that might be grasped in a sudden illumination, it is *a* whole, of which the individual, who is unable to integrate its various fragments, can know only a part.

The women in the novel form a relatively united group

[3]This explains why all the interpretations of *The Castle* are true: K. conceives of all of them and tries to understand the village by summing them all together.

sharing a few rather simple ideas (though K. often finds them perplexing). For them, the Castle exists chiefly through the gentlemen, the supreme agents of love whose caprice determines their happiness or misery. An affair with Klamm passes among them as a unique, almost ecstatic experience that yields memories to be savored for the rest of a hard, bitter life. The gentlemen's love—a love at once physical and spiritual, and therefore ideal—is the religion and the magic that allows them to bear the shabbiness of their ordinary lives (and their rather pitiful husbands), to work hard, and to realize certain ambitions (it is thanks to Klamm's love that Frieda, who used to groom the animals in the stable, has become a barmaid). Like all religions, this love has its impenetrable mysteries. It is not subject to objective proof and its initiates bear no special mark of election. Each of the villagers believes in it in proportion to his own faith. Therefore, Frieda's relations with Klamm, which K. readily accepts, are not so firmly established. These relations are confirmed by the landlady of the Bridge Inn, yet she herself has largely forgotten the amorous adventure of her youth even as she insists that Klamm is unforgettable. Klamm's unreality, as K. notes each time he tries to approach him, is tied in great part to this mixture of fantasy and vague sentiment that he inspires in the women. Was Frieda actually Klamm's mistress? Is this a rumor she began herself in order to assure the realization of her social ambitions? We will never know. Yet K. makes no mystery of the fact that it was solely her relations with the Eros and Don Juan of the Castle that made his future wife so seductive.

The village women's worship of the gentlemen hardly develops their capacities for real love. On the contrary, it seems that their worship of love stifles any real feeling for their comrades and husbands. The landlady of the Bridge

Inn treats her husband with impatience and contempt, and this man she married after the breakup of her affair with Klamm, this man with "his delicate features and almost beardless chin," gives K. the impression of being an adolescent, sometimes a child. Even Frieda, who is able to conceive of ideals other than Klamm and in this respect is perhaps the most mature woman in the village, is incapable of fully confronting the problems of domestic life in a realistic way. She loves K., does not hesitate to leave Klamm for the freedom of her private affair, and puts herself to work courageously accepting the trials and deprivations that are the consequence of her actions. But at the first conflict in their life together, she is repossessed by the Castle and goes off with the assistants, who represent its most grossly carnal aspect. In thrall to the Castle, bowed before all the powers of life, the women can only vacillate between Klamm, who embodies romantic idealism and all the insipid dreams of a vague sentimentality, and the brutal desire of his servants, who are images of the blind force of instinct. We can imagine that the desolation of the village, its sadness and eternal winter, are in large part due to this religion of love that corrupts intimate relations between beings and prevents them from joining together freely as people. The fact is that there is not one happy couple in the entire domain of the Castle. Everywhere the women are dissatisfied and despotic, the men suppressed and inadequate, domestic life dreary and sour. Instead of promoting love among his subjects as legend would have him do, Klamm, it seems, has cruelly banished it.

Yet it is from their experience and competence in these affairs of the heart that the women draw their surprising authority. For in spite of their emotional disabilities, they have solid ties to the most elemental aspect of the Castle and an intuitive knowledge that the men particularly need, condemned as they are to haunt the administrative—cerebral—spheres of the Castle. The women may be weak and submissive in the face of the Castle, but they reign despotically over the village, imposing a kind of matriarchal regime that is not institutionalized but is tacitly accepted by everyone and therefore given legitimate sanction. It is not the Mayor who manages public affairs but his wife Mizzi, a droll and bumbling person whom K. hadn't even noticed (although ordinarily anyone in skirts attracts his attention). The two inns are run by women. The Brunswick family owe its status to a woman. The Barnabas family subsist thanks to the efforts of Olga and Amalia who care for their old parents and entirely dominate their brother. Schwarzer has left the Castle (he is the only "official" who lives in the village) to live at the feet of the sadistic teacher Gisa, who has reduced him to slavery. And K., who shares the general prejudice, cannot see a woman without thinking she must have secret relations with the Castle and therefore possess some formidable power. All the men bow before this superiority, which does not, however, assure the women of the village happiness or freedom. It is a collective superiority, an aspect of their sex rather than their personal worth (K. admits to himself that he might have loved Pepi as well as Frieda), so that they too feel it as a kind of oppression and pray for deliverance. Hence, this comically reciprocal hope of salvation: K. wants the women to save him, but they on their side regard him as *their* savior.

The Castle's specialization in the area of love, which is fostered by the women and accepted by most of the men as a means of recovering the authenticity and spontaneity of their lives, has disastrous consequences for the whole village. The best example of this is the fate of the Barnabas family, once respected and prosperous but then shunned and persecuted as pariahs. The Barnabas story is the pivotal episode of the novel and a stumbling block for even the most astute commentary. As we have seen, *The Castle* can be read as a serial novel, as a text with serious theological motifs, as a satire of Judaism, or a protest against racial segregation. But none of these readings is confirmed by the text, whose contents, even after so many years of explication, remain elusive. These are the facts, then, of the Barnabas case which precede K.'s arrival and yet exert a decisive influence on the course of his own case, since Barnabas is thought to be his official messenger and his relations with Olga and Amalia are the immediate cause of his failure.

This drama occurred three years earlier at the annual festival of the village fire brigade, a celebration both popular and ritualistic whose orgiastic significance everyone still feels in some muddled way. On this occasion, all the villagers thought that Amalia, who was beautifully dressed and radiant with a mysterious inner light, would surely find a husband. Her sister Olga was so struck by her beauty that she impulsively hung her own necklace around Amalia's neck (a string of Bohemian garnets lent to her by the landlady of the Bridge Inn) to crown her triumph. During the celebration, chance thrusts Amalia into the presence of Sortini, the god of fate and fire who sits astride the fire engine shaft all day, apart from the crowd, until suddenly he notices Amalia. The Barnabas family and their friends observe this intrigue. Everyone is a little drunk (the sweet wine of the Castle has a magical effect) and Amalia's parents rejoice, believing that she has fallen hopelessly in love with Sortini (which is surely the case, her sister will say later, since no girl can resist an "official"). The next morning, however, the family are roused from their heavy (bacchic) sleep by a terrible scream. Olga rushes over to find her sister agitated with a letter in her hand which she tears to shreds and throws in the face of the messenger who brought it. The letter comes from Sortini, it is addressed to the "girl with the garnet necklace" and is couched in such despicable terms that Olga cannot repeat them. Amalia has kept silent from that time on, but by offending Sortini's messenger she has sealed her own fate and her family's doom. From the point of view of conventional morality, Amalia's gesture is perfectly justified and she would have been dishonored to behave otherwise. But the village is of precisely the opposite opinion: Amalia dishonored herself and shamed her family because she rejected the very essence of the Castle, that mixture of exalted, idealized representations and an eroticism all the more violent because it is not bound to any other aspect of the personality. The Castle is constructed in such a way that everyone takes for granted the obscenity of Sortini's message, since he doesn't belong to the department administrated by Klamm, who is the only official competent in the matter of love affairs. Sortini is an intellectual marked by sleepless nights of difficult thought. Love is not his province, and surely he cannot be expected to know how to write to a young girl. Klamm would have drafted the letter differently—not that he would be less brutal or obscene, but the message would be promptly idealized and its grossness would go unnoticed. Because of his incompetence, Sortini is unable to love Amalia as a distinct person (he addresses his letter to "the girl with the garnet necklace," meaning any woman, since the necklace belongs to Olga). He loves sex, but in this he is simply following the law of the Castle, whose excessive specialization leads precisely to a radical collectivization of life. The desire to be loved for oneself, in absolute purity and total respect for one's person, is a dangerous folly for the women of the village, an outrageous pride that threatens the very equilibrium of the community, an insult to the Castle and to the obscure powers of life whose accomplices and victims are the women.

Amalia's act is an absolute negation, a destruction of the very basis of existence, a challenge to the forces of nature. Her punishment is inevitable. The Barnabas family is wrong to impute its disgrace to a sentence passed by the Castle. The Castle has not intervened; the girl's quixotic decision (which might be comic, but the village has no sense of humor) has itself been sufficient to exhaust the family's vital resources for success.

Amalia has actually violated a taboo, and that is why she is struck dumb. She has flushed out the jealously guarded secret: everyone talks about the Castle and thinks about sex. The speculations that take place in the "departments" function only to mask purely erotic interests, which is why Amalia has such contempt for the mysteries of the Castle and refuses the proffered "initiation." She has discovered that its "affairs" are nothing but sordid sexual gossip: "I heard once of a young man who thought of nothing but the Castle day and night, he neglected everything else, and people feared for his reason, his mind was so wholly absorbed by the Castle. It turned out at length, however, that it wasn't really the Castle he was thinking of, but the daughter of a charwoman in the offices up there, so he got the girl and was all right again . . ." ("Amalia's Punishment"). K. declares that he would like that man, and Amalia replies, "As for your liking the man, I doubt it . . . it's probably his wife you would like." Indeed, this is rather unfair—K. does have other interests—but the remark puts an instructive emphasis on one of the profound realities of the novel.

The men are also implicated in this excessive overestimation of love that causes such bizarre incidents and conflicts in the village. But the higher they rise on the social and intellectual scale, the more complicated and elaborate their vision of the Castle, with the qualification that no one, high or low, can break the law of silence that protects the Castle itself. The civilized men, or those who hold official posts (this is the same in the terminology of the novel), are all inclined to identify the Castle with its offices—in contrast to the women, who view the supreme authority as an immense boudoir. In any case, the offices and their machinery are the only part of the Castle accessible to the personal experience of the villagers. K. himself has contacts only with the administration—if we can call his uninterrupted series of misadventures contacts—and so he, too, is inclined to believe that the bureaucracy exhausts the entire meaning of the Castle.

If the women could go to the Castle, they would certainly be forced to revise their deep-seated beliefs. Love, in fact, is the last concern of the gentlemen who devote their lives to incessant, vigorous work and take women when they need them, simply for relaxation (much the way they do carpentry). Indeed, from the male point of view, Klamm's department is not love but work.[4] This distinction is sufficient to mark the boundaries between the two Castles, which share only their exclusively masculine population (the women see men there, the men see only themselves; there are no goddesses, no "lady" officials). The gentlemen's prodigious capacity for work is proverbial, one of those rare

[4]We can see here an exact picture of bourgeois society at the end of the century, in which discontented women dreamed of an ideal love removed from the reality of their lives, while the men buried themselves in their offices.

points on which everyone agrees; no one knows what purpose this work serves, but the very fact that it exists is reassuring. The gentlemen work all the time, day and night, standing up, lying down, even sleeping (Bürgel receives K. in his bed, though of course he complains of insomnia). They have no leisure time or private lives, their existence and vocation are inseparable. In this respect, the gentlemen are all very much alike: Klamm, Sordini, Sortini, and Bürgel are all tireless workers, whatever the extent and nature of their respective areas of competence. This is why they are so easily mistaken for one another when they are observed at work amidst the incessant buzz and heaps of paperwork in their offices.

Confronted with this omnivorous activity, K. is too abashed to question the nature of the work itself. Yet he would very much like to know *how* this organization functions, for in its apparently bungling way it seems to determine the course of his life. The explanations he is given by the Mayor and Bürgel regarding the vicissitudes of his "appointment" are strictly private, and therefore K. is rather skeptical of them. Momus' explanations are official, but they are also enigmatic and possibly malicious, so they are not much better.

The Mayor's statements deal chiefly with the matter of bureaucratic infallibility. The official departments are infallible, which is not to say that they never make mistakes—no, they do make mistakes, as in the case of K.'s appointment, which is received by mistake after years of being shuffled around the various bureaus. But given the perfection of the whole, any possibility of error is dismissed on principle: "It is a working principle of the head bureau that the very possibility of error must be ruled out of account. This ground principle is justified by the consummate organization of the whole authority, and it is necessary if the maximum speed in transacting business is to be attained" (5th Ch.). K. asks if there isn't a control authority, and the Mayor replies that "Only a total stranger could ask a question like yours. Is there a Control Authority? There are only Control authorities. Frankly, it isn't their function to hunt out errors in the vulgar sense, for errors don't happen, and even when once in a while an error does happen, as in your case, who can say finally that it's an error?" K. is brought up short: he has been appointed, summoned after numerous discussions; his affair dragged on for years in the various offices, then his file was lost, and now the Mayor pronounces that the Castle will oppose his appointment with all the force of its authority. Nevertheless, the Castle remains infallible.

The Mayor's explanation also deals with the relative importance of various matters. K.'s case, it seems, is quite trivial: "'No,' said the Superintendent, 'it's not at all a great affair, in that respect you've no ground for complaint—it's one of the least important among the least important. The importance of a case is not determined by the amount of work it involves . . . But even if it's a question of the amount of work, your case would remain one of the slightest; ordinary cases—those without any so-called errors, I mean—provide far more work and far more profitable work as well . . .'" (5th Ch.). The Mayor explains the basic cause of K.'s difficulties: his singularity is irregular and perfectly insignificant in the eyes of the Castle, which values only *ordinary* cases, that is, the affairs of individuals who play out their role within the context of the great collective affairs. K. is alone and participates in nothing, he has no social significance. Although he likes to imagine his case prompting an enormous amount of work, the file he sees in the corridor of the Herrenhof has nothing in it comparable to those that document fully lived lives: it is no more than a thin sheet of paper.

K.'s fortuitous interview with Bürgel seems in part to contradict this pessimistic but not entirely grim picture, if we conclude that Bürgel explains how the individual can, not merely how he *might,* easily fulfill his desires. At the very end of his peregrinations, K. is summoned to meet with Erlanger at the Herrenhof. Once there, however, drunk with fatigue (he hasn't slept for a long time and we have almost never seen him eat), he enters the wrong door and hasn't the courage to leave. Bürgel immediately engages him in conversation, chiefly, he tells K., to lull himself to sleep. Astonished that K. has nothing to survey although he has the title Land-Surveyor, Bürgel goes into a lengthy explanation of the special circumstances—very special, indeed—in which a petitioner with a request to present might see his pleas instantly granted. Naturally, such circumstances are not conceivable, no such case has been documented, but theoretically this is how it could happen. Night interrogations exist that the secretaries particularly dread because during the night it is more difficult to preserve the strictly official character of the negotiations. These interrogations are quite customary, hence there would be nothing to prevent individuals from profiting from these occasions if only they knew how (though for some reason they never do). It would suffice for a "client" to come unannounced to a competent secretary in the middle of the night, without having received a summons; or, as this is impossible—the summons often arrives before the matter has been entirely thought through—to a secretary who has, strictly speaking, no competence in the case at hand. The secretaries are terrified of such an eventuality (though, of course, no applicant would conceive of being interviewed by a noncompetent secretary), because then they would be absolutely obliged to grant the individual's most personal demands. This is what makes the officials suffer: they can yield to individual desires only by violating their official task, which is by definition collective; at the same time it would make them extremely happy to encounter and satisfy a real individual, strong and free enough to go beyond the specializations that confine their thought. A person who would go in the night—the time of absolute subjectivity—to a secretary without official competence is capable of breaking the narrow mold of particular doctrines and ideologies (the departments) and annihilating all hierarchies in one fell swoop. Fearfully, joyously, the world awaits the man who might conquer it this way, in the depths of its silent night, thanks to the irresistible novelty of his "noncompetence" and an all-encompassing thought that defies classification.[5] K. sleeps and perceives Bürgel's words only through a fog of semiconsciousness. He understands this "revelation" quite well, but cannot take advantage of it, for he is plunged into a dream where he is in the midst of a struggle with a Greek god (or rather his *statue*) who squeaks like a young girl being tickled and doesn't seem to be a very serious adversary. In fact, the struggle has already taken place, or rather the outcome is known in advance (all news is out of date); before he has begun, K. witnesses the festivities that celebrate his triumph. Upon waking, he recognizes

[5]K. doesn't take Bürgel seriously and treats him as a "dilettante." The radical individualism that he proposes is, in effect, a quixotic solution, modern man being less capable than any other of motivating his own life in general, without reference to the particular compartments—intellectual, moral, religious, social, professional, etc.—into which his thought is divided.

Bürgel as his Greek god ("Here you have your Greek god! Go on, haul him out of bed!") and no longer pays much attention to his discourse. His dream, composed as always of ancient and static fixed images, prevents him from grasping the unique opportunity offered by his present situation, which is identical to the one Bürgel has described. It is true that he is in a weakened physical state, but this isn't an excuse, "'One's physical energies last only to a certain limit. Who can help the fact that precisely this limit is significant in other ways too? No, nobody can help it. That is how the world itself corrects the deviations in its course and maintains the balance'" (18th Ch.).

In contrast to the Mayor's common sense and Bürgel's high intellectual level, Momus' sarcasm seems vulgar. K. does not take this god of criticism and mockery too seriously, given his particular specialty, although he judges him essentially hostile. Momus is Klamm's secretary, but in reality he serves two masters, Klamm and Vallabene, whose prophetic name might offer K. encouragement if he knew how to interpret it.[6] The function of this "gentleman"— Momus—who is young, "very good-looking, pink and white, but very serious" (8th Ch.), consists of overseeing Klamm's writings that pertain to the village. He has written a report on K. and asks him to answer some questions to complete his file. K. refuses, although the landlady of the Bridge Inn, who is present at the exchange, affirms that his

[6]According to Herbert Tauber, *Vallabene* could be an abbreviation for *Vala bene la pena;* it would be, then, "that which is worth the effort." K.'s attitude makes this etymology seem plausible: he thinks that it is not worth the effort to respond to Momus' interrogation, but the secretary indicates the contrary by telling K. the name of his second master. The Trinity embodied by Klamm would thus have the following meaning: love, work, anguish that are *worth the effort,* in spite of the critical spirit and mockery that see them as negative.

only way of reaching Klamm is to figure in the secretary's protocol. K. is still skeptical; he is ready to submit to the interrogation only if Momus himself confirms that he will thereby gain admission to Klamm. " 'No,' replied Momus, 'that doesn't follow at all. It's simply a matter of keeping an adequate record of this afternoon's happenings for Klamm's village register. The record is already complete, there are only two or three omissions that you must fill in for the sake of order; there's no other object in view and no other object can be achieved.'" Will Klamm read the protocol then? No, Klamm never reads any protocol, it bores him. Under these conditions, of course, K. persists in his refusal; nevertheless, he is wrong. A bit later he perceives his error and becomes interested in this protocol, which, in fact, concerns him in a personal way. This time it is Momus who refuses to reply (in a passage which constitutes nearly a whole chapter that Kafka subsequently deleted), but K., seized by unusual courage, brutally pulls the secretary's briefcase away from him. " 'Why only now?' the secretary asked. 'You could have taken it by force at once'"[7] (Appendix, p. 452). K. sets about reading his protocol, which contains the account of his relations with Frieda mentioned above, a trivial insinuating account decorated with a drawing illustrating his ignominious conduct. K. judges this pitiful specimen of Momus' *writings* rather harshly: " '. . . it is merely gossip, trumped-up, empty, sad, womanish gossip; indeed, the writer must have had a woman to help him . . .'" (Appendix, p. 455). Momus has simply copied down the landlady's tattle, and K. suddenly perceives that the two gossips form a couple (of parents, as the context clearly indicates) who have

[7]It is one of the trivial lessons of the Castle: life belongs to those who possess it through violence. K., however, doesn't want to triumph over life by violence, but by the clarity of his vision.

a perfect understanding for the purpose of abusing him ("How they stood there together, those two collaborators, each helping the other with their miserable secrets!" [Appendix, p. 457]). His delusion is so great that for a moment he thinks of destroying his protocol (which would amount to suicide, since the protocol follows the course of his life) and finally unmasking, in the only way he can, the mocking, malicious gossip that fills the archives of the Castle.[8]

K. cannot do anything with the informed theoretical explanations everyone offers him so willingly (they all want to teach him how to live), not because he lacks knowledge of the Castle but because he has no practical rule, no definitive norm that would allow him to satisfy collective demands as well as his own. ". . . Perhaps he has a better theoretical understanding of the officials and official workings than we have, in this he's admirable; but when it comes to applying his knowledge, he somehow gets moving in a wrong way . . . he can't apply it, it mocks him."[9] The Mayor, Bürgel, and Momus actually do instruct him, yet their instruction is a kind of mockery because, not being from "here," he has no way to apply their truths. His incapacity to live, however, does not constitute a proof against the Castle and in no way detracts from the utility of the theory.

The statements of these experienced persons (responsible parties from every class) allow K. to construct a general theory of the Castle, but he continually tries to modify this conception, which doesn't suit his quixotic taste. From the various accounts he collects at random, it indeed appears that the Castle is not at all transcendent, as he persists in believing. It is an immanent power, ubiquitous and om-

[8]Gossip that might be called "oedipal" in Freudian terminology and that forms the inexhaustible mine of our literature.
[9]Cf. unpublished fragment. See German edition.

nipotent, which is the origin and goal of everything. And although his relations with the "offices" seem absurd and precarious, K. himself plays a part in this earthly Castle (therefore, properly speaking, he cannot "enter" it). The most degraded and exalted phenomena, instinct (the assistants) and art (Barnabas), all belong without distinction to that body whose function is chiefly to record what *is*. Neither transendent nor creative—in the whole of the novel, no one mentions a single *new* fact engendered by the Castle—the Castle limits itself to recording accomplished facts, and not only the facts but the judgments that precede and follow them, the desires, the unconscious thoughts, and the dreams that distort and influence their consequences. And all this is recorded in the very disorder of life itself, with a passivity and neutrality that the individual feels, rather bizarrely, as a burden and an injustice. Such a conception of the Castle seriously overturns K.'s personal beliefs. [10]

The Castle is, in fact, neutral; it ratifies individual initiative, records what happens and what is achieved, but contrary to general belief and superstition it does not intervene in the course of events. This is nicely illustrated by the two letters from Klamm that K. takes such pains to decipher and judges, in the last analysis, to be worthless banter. K. receives the first of these letters soon after his arrival at the Bridge Inn, following a significant incident. He has presented himself as the Count's land-surveyor, and Schwarzer

[10] We can measure the distance traveled from *The Trial* to *The Castle:* in *The Trial,* the world is shown as a tribunal whose justice is more than immanent, since the punishment precedes the sentence and even the completion of the trial. In *The Castle,* K. still wants to be judged, but the world is described as neutral, impassive, and therefore deceptive, even for the man who awaits a judgment. K. is not cured, but he recognizes his desire for justification as an illness.

has telephoned to the Castle to verify K.'s statement. The Castle has replied: no, the Count has no land-surveyor. K. insists, however, that they phone again, and the situation is abruptly reversed: the Castle confirms his status and even presents him with its apologies. After which Klamm sends him a letter that he takes to be an official document (though this is not the case), which reads " '*As you know,* [11] you have been engaged for the Count's service . . . . Barnabas, the bearer of this letter, will report to you from time to time to learn your wishes and communicate them to me . . . . I desire my workers to be contented . . .'" (2nd Ch.). Klamm follows precisely the direction of K.'s desires, acting on what K. himself has already decided ("As you know"). But Klamm does not confirm K.'s vocation of land-surveyor and gives him no tools with which to practice his craft. This would transcend the official's areas of competence, which are limited to things already accomplished and have no bearing on purely speculative projects. It is a matter of complete indifference whether K. is a practicing land-surveyor or something else; Klamm will record equally his success or failure, and neither will substantially influence the machinery of the Castle. [12]

Nothing is more painful to K. than this indifference, this neutral good will that Klamm displays toward his affairs. For K. wants a judgment, a hearing that will either justify the superiority of his acts, condemn him, if necessary, or grant him pardon. Klamm's second letter adds even more fuel to his indignation, since it warmly congratulates him

[11]My italics.

[12]Throughout the novel, there is certainly a harsh critique of the morality of success and competence. But Kafka also expressed some irony with regard to his own overestimation of pure vitality. The Castle does nothing but sanction vitality, it promotes the strong and crushes the weak, that's all.

for his work at a moment when he is in despair precisely
because he has achieved nothing. On this point, however,
Klamm is sincere and just, and if he were not so mute could
defend his position quite well. The Castle records K.'s "inquiry," the intellectual, erotic, social and other experiences
he has in the village, and which, to the indifferent community, have as much value as his land-surveying. Whoever calls
himself Land-Surveyor instantly becomes one; whoever
proves it by his actions, is promptly named as such; whoever takes on a particular job has immediate dignity. The
Castle's business is not to intervene in these contingencies.
Its secretaries are not supposed to discuss them, but simply
note them down in their books.

The Castle, to be sure, exerts its influence by the very fact
of its archival activities. Still, it does not act. It manifests
itself only by a certain passive resistance to individual decisions that are too contrary to its nature. This illuminates the
enigma of the assistants, in which K.'s blindness only hastens his fall. Who are these half-childish, half-demonic
characters called assistants, whose name alone seems to K.
an intolerable mockery? The truth is difficult to unravel.
Deep down, K. knows who they are, yet he is so inconsis-
tent on the subject, and there is such an abyss between his
judgment and the Castle's, that the assistants do indeed
seem to be the major cause of his chronic misperceptions. At
first, K. pretends that they are his "old" assistants who are
bringing his "equipment." When they appear suddenly
around a bend, however, he doesn't recognize them and
asks who they are. Immediately, the Castle records this fact
and qualifies the assistants as "new," a designation that K.
bitterly disputes, though he continues to treat them as unwelcome, uninvited strangers. This contradiction clarifies

another aspect of the latent conflict between the new and the old. The assistants are really part of K., they are his and have always shared his life: as such they are "old." But he has expelled them from his personality because he considers them an evil (he compares them to snakes); in this sense, then, they are "new," and it is understandable that he doesn't recognize them, in both senses of the word. Yet this doesn't prevent him from needing their help, for they represent a basic and inseparable part of him (his relations with Frieda illustrate this). He has sent for them, then, but treats them abominably and so contributes to his own destruction, for his life depends on the health and dignity he accords them. After beating them unmercifully and throwing them out once and for all, he finds Jeremiah again, alone, aged, sallow, like "a patient who had escaped from the hospital" (18th Ch.). K. doesn't yet realize that this illness heralds the end of his own life.

These two bizarre characters, who are so lascivious, lying, lazy, mischievous, and mocking, represent the virility that K. rejects but nevertheless cannot do without (we must remember that he wants to marry). This is evident when we consider the exact place they occupy in his life space. They are outside but attached to him; they surround him, engulf him, jostle him day and night, and though they are chased away they always ask to come back inside (of him, surely). They force K. into a repugnant promiscuity—he discovers that they have witnessed his first night of love with Frieda; he cannot leave his bed for a minute without finding the two assistants lying in his place when he returns. During the entire novel, their insistent—and literally displaced— presence is an obstacle to his complete happiness, but once he has chased them away for good, his life with Frieda becomes impossible and she leaves him[13] (to live with Jeremiah and care for him).

K. has no grounds for complaint. He chose Frieda for her realism and her deep sympathy with the nature of the Castle. It is natural that she should demand the presence of the assistants, protect them, caress them, coax them and value their aid, just as she is right, though perhaps lacking in generosity, to persecute Barnabas as much as K. admires and overvalues him. Barnabas, the messenger of art, the muse of infallible memory (he learns all his messages by heart and never makes a mistake), is also an integral part of K. that he has externalized and now regards as alien to himself. His relations with the messenger reveal this origin, which makes Barnabas a kind of brother to the assistants (this is why the three young men look alike), and which K. partly disavows, this time through an opposite error of judgment. As much as he scorns the assistants, he extols the virtues of Barnabas (at least when he sees him alone; all this changes when he meets him at home with his family).[14] But K.'s two erroneous judgments only aggravate each other

[13]The relations between K., Frieda, and the assistants are transpositions of the strange situation in which Kafka found himself precisely at the time he was writing *The Castle,* caught between Milena and her husband, whom she didn't love but who kept an irresistible sexual hold on her. The young woman, terrified by the ascetic life Kafka proposed to her, could not resolve to leave her husband to join him. After Kafka's death, she explained her actions in a letter to Max Brod, in terms that recall Frieda's decision in the novel. Cf. *Lettres à Milena,* Gallimard, 1956.

[14]The Barnabas family is actually K.'s own family, the fact that he doesn't recognize them as such proves only that he disowns them. The three children clearly represent the three solutions envisaged by Kafka to overcome his situation as a "stranger" to life: asceticism and silence (but he condemns these in the person of Amalia), art (but Barnabas is a "messenger of the lie"), a humbly accepted compromise with the sexuality and uglier realities of the Castle (but Olga, the most intelligent and courageous of the three, prostitutes herself in vain).

and precipitate his ruin. Frieda understands quite well that it is because he places such extravagant hopes in Barnabas that K. so sadistically berates his assistants and is even prepared to sacrifice her. After the final expulsion of Arthur and Jeremiah, which happens to coincide with K.'s visit to the beleaguered Barnabas family, Frieda sees that she, too, has nothing more to gain by staying with him.

K.'s sincere efforts to be admitted to the family of the Castle, his real love for Frieda, are irreparably compromised by the rigidity of his private system of values, which he believes conforms to that of the Castle. This misapprehension is entirely plausible, but it is as disastrous for others as it is for himself. Art is not his salvation, it is one *assistant* among all the others that the Castle puts at man's disposal. Klamm himself makes no distinction between the supposedly malevolent assistants and the radiant messenger, or, if he does, it is rather in favor of the former. In fact, he compliments the assistants on their zeal and only mentions Barnabas in passing. Barnabas, at any event, is the unwitting instrument of an enormous deception, K. learns from his sister Olga—as usual, too late.

Barnabas is not an official messenger. His tunic is an imitation; and though he has carried two letters from Klamm to K., they were obsolete and no one knows if they really came from Klamm himself. In any case, Barnabas has lied. He never carried messages before K.'s arrival and does not even know if he has been officially recognized. In its customary way, the Castle does nothing to disprove his *belief*. It lets him prowl as he likes through the "offices," waiting for the gentlemen at their desks who are positively interchangeable and dictate endless texts in feverish excitement. But the Castle has nothing to "reveal" to him that he might transmit to K. In reality, Barnabas is in precisely the same

situation as his master: he desperately seeks *official* sanction
for his position, which is superfluous; meanwhile, he simply
exists on the periphery of life. Olga, who has supported her
brother's projects, nonetheless asks K., "'. . . isn't it time
for him to marry and set up a house for himself? And instead
of that he is frittering his powers away between his handi-
craft and being a messenger, standing in front of the desk
up there, on the lookout for a glance from the official who
looks like Klamm, and in the end getting an old dusty letter
that is no good to anyone and only causes confusion in the
world . . . .'"[15]

K. has been horribly misled by Barnabas' gleaming tunic,
his huge eyes, his graceful bearing, and his prodigious
memory. The man from whom he expected aid is needy
himself, a timid and childish creature whose whole life
is only an illusion, for as Olga says, "'The messages are
worthless, there is no strength to be gained from them directly, you are too shrewd to let yourself be deceived in this
respect, and even if we could deceive you, Barnabas would
be only a false messenger, and from falsehoods no salvation
could come . . . .'"[16]

Aesthetic disputes are indeed the province of the Barnabas
family, for it may be that art is the only cause of their misfortune. K. visits these people, who as a family inspire him
with a violent repulsion ("The parents in their corner, the
little oil lamp, the room itself—it was not easy to endure this
calmly . . . ."[17]), only to talk about art and about his mes-

[15]Deleted passage, Appendix, p. 462. Kafka describes here his own situation. As a bachelor, torn between his legal work and his writing, he felt at
the end of his life that he had made a bad bargain and that his work would
suffer for it.
[16]Deleted passage, Appendix, p. 467.
[17]Deleted passage, Appendix, p. 463.

sages, while with the other villagers he discusses the most realistic features of Klamm that relate to his own marriage and settlement in the village. The members of the Barnabas family no longer have anything to lose, so they can turn to questions that do not immediately concern the Castle and that, for this reason, seem to be the object of a mysterious taboo. Excluded, stigmatized, outlawed, the Barnabas brother and sisters have the leisure to reflect: the very thing that led them unwittingly to their doom is what "distinguishes" them. This was precisely the predicament of Kafka, who distinguished himself in the villages of Bohemia where he tried to find a cure by writing *The Castle,* an attempt to discover whether literature was not, finally, a symptom of his illness.

K.'s ideas, taken with those of the three Barnabas children, represent Kafka's last meditation on art, illuminating his highly paradoxical attitude toward his work and at the same time revealing the true meaning of his impossible odyssey. For Amalia, art simply serves the fallacy of the Castle by which the trivialities of life are hypocritically "sublimated." She has insulted Sortini's messenger because of this hypocrisy that prevents the emergence of pure feeling. She repudiates the Castle because it allows man to disguise his lust with high intellectual preoccupations, and sanctions the ensuing confusion. At once rejecting the baser aspects of existence and the very idea of sublimation, she has nothing but contempt for her brother's service as messenger and confronts him with the truth of her silence. Olga sees things quite differently. Her family has offended the Castle and this offense cannot be effaced without making reparations, since no human being is really prepared to live *against* life. For her part, she tries to redress the wrong by conducting herself with utter humility before the obscure forces—

Klamm's domestics—that in spite of everything give the Castle its value and its incomparable authority. But this prostitution—K. admires her intelligence and courage—is not sufficient; it offers nothing "new" to the offended messenger. Therefore, Olga decides to endorse her brother's vocation, indeed to direct her efforts at reparation and reconciliation both below, in the domestics' tavern, and above, toward the high offices, where, in spite of everything and however awkwardly, Barnabas has gained entry. In contrast to her sister, whose ascetic heroism inspires Olga's deepest devotion, she affirms literature and life without being certain that these are not merely delusions (the messages are worthless and the domestics disgusting brutes). Art is perhaps only the artist's attempt to compensate life for his violations of its law and himself for his incapacity to live. It is a compensation that cannot be measured by success, for it never achieves its ends, yet it may achieve something else whose worth the artist himself cannot estimate.

Barnabas' personal viewpoint is not directly stated, for this representative of the Muse has almost nothing to say, and the few words he does pronounce are rather foolish. He has a memory but apparently no ideas. His position can, however, be pieced together through certain indications that, taken as a whole, are quite eloquent: his radiant appearance, his refined features, his status as a bachelor, the influence he has on his sister despite his youth and inexperience, his apostle's name—all reveal the meaning of his vocation better than his words could do. Humble, submissive, capable of absolute piety regarding the messages he learns to the letter by heart, Barnabas is a devotee of the writings composed in the Castle's bustling offices, a believer who has chosen the wrong object and made art his religion. Like all believers, he lives in fear and trembling, wracked by terrible doubts. He is assigned to Klamm's service, but Klamm does not deliver his letters personally, a clerk hands Barnabas the letters after an interminable wait, ". . . apparently without any instructions from Klamm, who merely goes on reading his book. True, sometimes Klamm is polishing his glasses when Barnabas comes up, but he often does that anyhow; however, he may take a look at Barnabas then, supposing, that is, that he can see anything without his glasses . . ." (15th Ch.). Klamm does not see or say anything; furthermore, is this gentleman really Klamm? And precisely what is one of his messages worth? ". . . It's not a letter newly written; indeed, by the look of the envelope, it's usually a very old letter, which has been lying there a long time . . . ." In the face of this miserable conclusion to his anxious vigil in the offices, which are perhaps only anterooms and where he never learns anything that is current and verified, Barnabas is plunged into despair, and instead of fulfilling his assignment, he throws the letter away.[18]

The religion of art is indeed what secretly undermines literature and prevents it from fulfilling its ends. K., by coming to the village, has sided with a truthful and realistic literature, since his land-surveying is both a craft and an exact science. He analyzes with a great deal of penetration—but we know he is very strong in theory—the reasons for this false situation, a situation that leads Barnabas astray in the hopes of saving his family, whereas in reality he is responsible for their ruin. This is confirmed by the peculiar fact that the entire family bears his name as a patronym. (The Barnabas family, in which we may see an image of Kafka's family, is "distinguished" and dishonored by this "son of promise" who might have been able, spiritu-

[18]Just as Kafka continually tried to destroy his books, and sometimes succeeded.

ally and socially speaking, to soften the pain of their "exile.") K. needs nearly the whole week of his stay, that is, a good part of his life, to realize finally the enormity of his error. Barnabas is too young, he lacks experience, he even trembles with fear. Fear prevents him from observing things correctly, so that he misses the necessary qualities of authentic literature; his reports from the offices are only "garbled tales," anxious and dated dreams that have no general significance and are, as he perceives, simply trash. Nevertheless, Barnabas is not solely responsible for this aberration. He draws his fallacious ideas from his surroundings, from his education, from everything that an imposing moral and social system and an authoritarian culture have permanently instilled in him. "Fear of the authorities," K. says to Olga, "is born in you here, and is further suggested to you all your lives in the most various ways and from every side, and you yourselves help to strengthen it as much as possible" (15th Ch.).

This is not to be condemned in itself, but "'. . . it's a mistaken reverence,' said K., 'a reverence in the wrong place, the kind of reverence that dishonors its object. Do you call it reverence that leads Barnabas to abuse the privilege of admission to that room by spending his time there doing nothing, or makes him, when he comes down again, belittle and despise the men before whom he has just been trembling, or allows him because he's depressed or weary to put off delivering letters and fail in executing commissions entrusted to him? That's far from being reverence'" (15th Ch.). K. glimpses here the truth he ought to have grasped much sooner. Barnabas has chosen the position of messenger because he is afraid of life, but this fear is exactly what renders his art worthless, for it prevents him from observing and keeps him locked into a passive dream apart from human work and its incessant creative activity (the letters that the gentlemen endlessly dictate). Dreaming of receiving from God himself a unique, awesome message, Barnabas spends his time waiting for inspiration, despairs at not obtaining it, does not even write, and destroys the little he has created. And in revenge for this tortuous wait, he meditates on life and casts suspicion and discredit on reality. In so doing, he picks a quarrel not only with the actual living world but with art itself, whose greatest value lies in work, scrupulous observation, a precise survey of the truth. Just as the idealization of love perverted the intimate relations between couples, so the cult of art, the lingering romanticism that elevates the artist to the rank of messenger of the gods—that is, quixotism—inexcusably corrupts the very thing for which Barnabas pretends to sacrifice himself. Don Quixote is the enemy of life and finally of the literature that he has so unwisely loved, bringing nothing but confusion to the world and only despair to himself. He is utterly condemned.

The Castle is an impartial and passive force that takes no part in the conflict that sets K. against his assistants and Frieda, that estranges him from his deepest impulses as well as from all creative strength, leaving him exhausted in a solitude very close to death. It is said that the Castle has punished the Barnabas family as it was said that Poseidon had chastised Odysseus, whereas in both instances the gods are only the revealers of accomplished fact. The Barnabas family is excluded by the village only through its own fear of life, Odysseus is condemned to wander only because he is afraid of the sea and cannot master it during his long years of trial. The supernatural neither suspends nor modifies the course of things, it merely illuminates the ultimate issue of causes and consequences whose connections always remain hidden.

The resemblance stops here, however. Of course, Olympos is only a metaphrastic dream that moves human action after the fact, but it is the collective dream of a whole group and so allows the individual to feel supported, guided, confirmed in his struggles and desires. Olympos links each moment of daily life (not only moments of ecstasy and communion) to the exemplary experiences that are regarded as divine in proportion to their general value, but are situated, in fact, at a human level that is perfectly accessible to everyone (the gods cry, laugh, become angry, lie, as do all men . . .). From this pantheon, which is distant enough to be perceived in all its details yet close enough to be imitated, men draw not only instruction but, as the Homeric poet delighted in demonstrating, an extraordinary enlargement of their powers and a reasonable faith in the resources of their condition. Through this unique achievement, the ideal was able to serve life without shaming it or crushing it beneath its law.

It seems clear that Kafka was attracted by this achievement at a critical moment in his life, when, converted to Zionism and ready to leave for Palestine, he tried once again to understand and classify the monstrous archives of Count West-West (the archives of occidental culture from which his own books could not completely be excluded). Proof of this can be found in a letter he wrote to Max Brod in 1920 regarding a work of Brod's that treated just this problem.[19]

[19]Max Brod: *Heidentum Christentum, Judentum,* 1920. Letter to Max Brod, 7.VIII. 1920, in *Briefe,* S. Fischer Verlag, Frankfurt, 1966.

I don't believe, frankly, in any "paganism" in your sense. The Greeks, for example, were well acquainted with a certain dualism. Otherwise what meaning would Fate and many other things have? Only they were especially humble people, from a religious point of view—a sort of Lutheran sect. They could not imagine the godhead too far removed from themselves. The entire world of the gods was only a means to keep the Absolute separate from the earthly body, to make a space for human breath. A formidable means of national education that bound the images of men, less profound than Jewish law but perhaps more democratic (there were scarcely any leaders or founders of religions [among the Greeks]), perhaps freer (it bound them, but I don't know how), perhaps more humble (because the view of the divine world only makes us conscious that we have never been gods, and were we gods, what would we be?) . . . .

Kafka seems to be weighing the reasonable, comforting norm of the Greeks against the profound and terrible aspects of Jewish law that he simply could not disown and that slip into the composite edifice of his Western Castle, as it were, through a hidden door. In any case, the two laws are not comparable. The first persists only in the mocking form of Momus and a grotesquely animated statue, the other in the features of an aged prophet quite ready to bemoan his fate.

Like Don Quixote, Kafka was tempted toward the end of his life by the Homeric model and dedicated his last novel to the task of assessing its vitality. In the disarray that had engulfed modern consciousness, and modern literature as well, it was perhaps more fruitful to imitate Odysseus, who restored a modest human order, than to reenact the grandiose sacrifice of Abraham at the risk of becoming a disillusioned Don Quixote.[20] Kafka honestly made an effort in

---

[20]Cf. letter of June, 1921, to Robert Klopstock *(Briefe):* "If mankind had been present at the sacrifice, it would have been horrified by the Abraham of former times; this Abraham believes that seeing him, mankind will die laughing . . ."

this direction, only to confirm that even this ideal, so well tailored to human reality, had become bankrupt.

The bold clear lines, the legible message, of the Greek ideal had in fact been muddied by centuries during which other laws had been promulgated (Jewish and Christian), other truths revealed, other models imposed by persuasion, education, sermonizing, and, when necessary, force. And nothing in external reality corresponded to this hideous modern conglomeration of ideas, philosophies, and doctrines. There was no longer an external place, imaginary but convincing, where individual and collective conflicts could be played out and resolved according to the assumptions of a common belief. The *Iliad* and the *Odyssey* now fought their battles within the closed field of inner life, a life that didn't coincide with the actual world but was rather archaic, abandoned to the sirens and cyclopses, impossibly contained within an invisible space. It follows from this that the epic author could no longer be witness to a mythic war that was fertile ground for instruction, but had become instead the vanquished party of a Trojan war where he was both the battlefield and the sole combatant. "Sometimes," says Kafka, trying as he so often did to make Brod understand the deepest source of his suffering,[21]

I imagine to myself an anonymous Greek who arrives in Troy without having intended to go there. He hasn't even looked around, yet he finds himself in the midst of the turmoil. The gods themselves don't even know what it's all about; he, however, is already being dragged through the city by a Trojan chariot. Homer will not sing for a long time to come, yet this fellow lies with glazed eyes, if not in the Trojan dust at least on the cushions of a chaise lounge. And why? Hecuba, of course means nothing to him;

[21]Letter to Max Brod, April, 1921 *(Briefe)*. During this period, Kafka was being cared for in a sanatorium, hence the allusion to the chaise lounge.

even Helen isn't important. Whereas the other Greeks have gone off to war, summoned and protected by the gods, he has gone off as the result of a paternal kick and fought under a paternal curse; what luck that there were other Greeks, otherwise the history of the world would have been limited to two rooms of the parental residence and the threshhold between them.

Entirely internalized, wracked by personal conflicts for which collective reality no longer offers any normative solution, K.'s enterprise lies within the realm of pure subjectivity. His goal is not, as it first seemed, to resolve in some harmonious way the opposition between a real village and an ideal Castle, but to find some part, even a shred, of reality capable of providing him with a point of departure and a few landmarks along the way. The high drama of K.'s quest is that life, in which he wants to assume his place, is only a product of his imagination, where his conscious thoughts (the officials in the midst of their work) live side by side with his unconscious representations and desires (the somnolent officials). All this is ordered according to the hierarchy of his beliefs and judgments, the source of what in the novel passes for the bureaucracy. So there is no opposition, and consequently no cooperation possible, between K. and the Castle. The administrative organism is only a dream in which the dreamer might try to embrace at a single glance a total reality already imaged, classified, and judged by himself. Everything that happens inside K. also happens in the Castle. The officials dream, write prodigiously, suffer from the least noise, dread surprises, leave their correspondence in abeyance, write their letters at the wrong time, live in seclusion, suffer from insomnia, and become positively ill at the prospect of changing their offices; and above all they love nothing so much as books—evidently like Kafka himself, who endowed them with all his writer's obsessions. The officials are the issue of perpetual intellectual activity, the agents of a compulsive mental chronicle that is pursued even in dreams, the witnesses of self-observation carried on for its own sake, at the expense of the integrity and health of the personality (the secretaries are concerned only with isolated sectors of psychic life, hence their highly restricted areas of competence). This does not prevent them from consuming enormous quantities of beer, from smoking cigars or from seducing women, for they also represent that powerful father, loved and hated, whose image Kafka tried all his life to capture in his work. In this world of perpetual movement, thought is continuous, simultaneously fixed as though by a magic charm, by unconscious images and cultural archetypes. Why, then, should it be astonishing that time is inverted, past and present fused, the new inextricably bound to the archaic? This Castle where time rolls backward is peopled by phantoms. To expect it to yield a clear norm that would instantly establish relations between the particular and the general, K. and Klamm, Kafka and the society whose meaning and entrance he sought in vain— this would be as unreasonable or as futile as the handsome man in the portrait who childishly tries to raise his head by seizing himself by the hair.

Kafka clearly must have condemned his last novel, for, as we know, he asked his friend to collect his posthumous work and destroy it.[22] On the deepest level, the contents of *The Castle* reveal the reasons for this peculiar resolution, which was not only the result of an unhealthy perfectionism, as we are so often inclined to believe, but of an extremely keen understanding of the precarious situation of

[22]Kafka had confided the manuscript to Milena Jesenska, no doubt to make her understand the complex reasons for their separation.

art and of the inextricable contradictions that beset the modern writer if he wants to be true without accepting the provisional nature of things.

Now, as then, art in fact is only justified by the relations it is able to establish between the particular writer, who is prisoner of his dreams and his subjective desires, and the "choir" of humanity that authenticates every individual life. Lacking this vital correspondence, literature never achieves anything but the muddled dreams of Barnabas or the rumors Momus collects—"stories" that deal either with domestic dramas, with the gossip of the "bureaus," the infantile desires or ostensibly practical decisions of the "officials"—and these are passed off as the history of the world, indeed, as the history of the human spirit. Turned toward the dream, such a literature is subtly deceptive, for its "messages" do not come from above but from the past; it is a collection of clichés that only perpetuate the old romantic lie. But it is just as worthless when it is entirely taken up with its "protocols," which are both quite useless despite their pretense at realism and specious because of their unavowed subjectivity. In either case this literature is gratuitous and fragile; nothing decisive can issue from it.

The only way open to a truly contemporary literature, therefore, is the investigation of the order that long ago replaced the articulation of the epic ideal. Is this investigation still possible in a time when everything proliferates and is propelled in a multitude of contrary directions, where the different orders—public, social, intellectual, affective—no longer converge except through the lens of ignorance or general deceit, while the enormous weight of collective humanity—the pitiful *substitute* for a real community— leads paradoxically to an unchecked interiorization of life? To this question, which becomes more and more pressing in the works of his maturity, Kafka, like Cervantes, answered both no and yes. No, if we expect the Odyssean inquiry to end with the recovery of Ithaca, the reinstatement of the Golden Age, the instant annihilation of centuries of intellectual creations and ideological battles that have changed not only the course of the world but the thought and even the endowment of the writer. Yes, if literature, renouncing the pretenses of order and ephemeral connections, has the courage and the humility to accept itself as it is—subjective, singular, irresponsible, and so powerless that it can misconceive its own strength. Positive or not, the answer does not depend on the world, but on a special spiritual discipline of the artist.

Is this to say that the grandeur of literature can no longer consist of anything but a grandiose statement of its failure? No doubt the events of *The Castle* carry this implication, but they also illustrate that the investigation needn't be completed to achieve an essential reality. The Land-Surveyor may be defeated in the course of his Odyssey; he has nevertheless discovered the paradoxical truths in which art can still find its vindication and perhaps even a last source of authentic inspiration. This vindication is simply that the writer remains bound to the truth, though it can never be verified. There is no longer either vocation, inspiration, or security through a higher tribunal, divine or collective. Art is the domain of contingency, it is terribly free, with a freedom all the more ambiguous as it is only the obverse of rootlessness. To accept this contingency without giving up the belief in a truth: this paradoxical and scarcely conceivable task is the one obligation that a self-conscious literature cannot shirk.

K. honestly attempts to fulfill the responsibility by defending his post as land-surveyor, the image of a precise and modest art that is related simultaneously to business, to the dream, and to exact science. True, he immediately redirects his energy away from his craft and toward a new ideal that is either a conception of an absolute or the sudden resurgence of Don Quixote's pride and madness. Yet K. himself refutes his own errors and in the process exposes two stubborn illusions: the "realism" of Momus, a trumped-up, self-satisfied art that has perhaps some administrative value but no longer any authority and no more meaning than a web of malicious gossip; and the religion of art, the old romantic religion that misdirects its piety and degrades its object without "saving" the artist. After K., who so powerfully absorbed the negativity of his time, illusions no doubt persist. But something within literature—even its very name—has imperceptibly changed.

It is clear that Kafka, in writing *The Castle,* wanted to discover whether it was still possible to express his own distinctive existence, and through that to cast on the obscurity of the present some true and lasting light, however small. He must have believed that he had to renounce this hope since the novel is left unfinished and in his last great stories the question is not even posed. In these ultimate fictions he resigns himself to a dehumanized art, so divorced from the world and men that it finds inspiration only in the spectacle of its own demise, in the depths of some mad beast's burrow, or in the corner of a circus cage. The paradox resolves itself, then, in the simplest fashion: Don Quixote has starved himself to death, his corpse is removed from the cage where he was exhibited; and immediately, to the great delight of the public, his place is taken by a panther, bounding with life, the embodiment of an irrefutable truth . . . .

Unfinished and consigned to the fire, *The Castle* seems to illuminate one of the possible versions of a literary legacy that is still badly understood. But if Kafka condemned the novel, he did not destroy it with his own hands. And he died correcting the proofs of his last stories, as though to leave forever in suspense the impossible quarrel of art and life.